LOST CANALS OF
ENGLAND AND WALES

LOST CANALS
of
ENGLAND and WALES

by

RONALD RUSSELL

DAVID & CHARLES
NEWTON ABBOT   DEVON

ISBN 0 7153 5417 5

Set in Garamond
and printed in Great Britain
by Latimer Trend & Company Limited Plymouth
for David & Charles (Publishers) Limited
South Devon House   Newton Abbot   Devon

Contents

List of Illustrations

Plates

Maps

Drawings

Introduction

By 'Lost Canals' I mean canals lost to navigation—the purpose for which they were constructed. Nearly all of them have been legally abandoned. Some, like the Rochdale and the Tennant, serve a useful purpose still by supplying water to towns and industries. Some, like the Croydon Canal and the Uttoxeter Branch of the Caldon, have been largely built on by railways; some —the North Wilts and the Glamorganshire—have been used for the widening of roads. Others, like the Wilts & Berks and the Wey & Arun, moulder quietly away in the countryside; while yet others—the Newcastle-under-Lyme canals, for instance—have almost entirely disappeared. For a small number there are hopes of restoration; among these are the Pocklington, the Montgomeryshire and the two Droitwich canals. Three major waterways in this last group I have purposely omitted: the Kennet & Avon, the Basingstoke and the Ashton. Of the first two of these, full accounts have recently been published;[1] the Kennet & Avon Trust and the Surrey & Hampshire Canal Society are actively concerned with restoration work. The Ashton is not legally abandoned; the Inland Waterways Association is leading attempts to restore the canal, and several local authorities support its return to full navigability. I have also omitted a number of small canals and branches, listed in the Appendix, whose interest is mainly for the specialist historian or industrial archaeologist.

Over eighty canals and branches are described in the following pages. There is a brief historical background account of each and a description of the present condition of the canal and of its more interesting surviving features. These include examples of the work of the great canal engineers, Brindley, Jessop, Telford and Rennie; bridges and aqueducts of different materials and design; locks and tunnels; terminal basins, warehouses and cottages of varying architectural style. But Time overtakes our exploits, and some of these features may well have disappeared before this book is in print. In the last few months Ilminster tunnel on the Chard Canal has been demolished and the Nantgarw treble locks on the

Glamorganshire have been filled in for a new road. Holmes
aqueduct on the Derby Canal, the first cast-iron aqueduct made,
has been removed, and much of the Shropshire tub-boat network
has vanished in the development of the new town of Telford.
More is threatened, but perhaps the new interest in industrial
archaeology may lead to the preservation of relics that might
otherwise be destroyed.

Why did these canals perish while others survive? And why
did the canal system altogether succumb in the way it did to
competition from road and rail? To these questions there is no
simple answer. Some canals were just commercial disasters, the
products of over-optimism during the period of 'canal mania'
towards the end of the eighteenth century; among these were the
agricultural canals of the South West. Others, because they occupied the most convenient route between towns, were particularly
attractive to expanding railway companies. When alternative
methods of transport became available, the heavy lockage on
certain canals (the Rochdale had 92 locks in 33 miles) quickly
made them unpopular with traders. Poor maintenance made some
canals difficult to use, and lack of uniformity in lock dimensions
led to tiresome delays. Parliament made some attempt to protect
the waterways; railway companies which took over canals were
usually under legal obligation to keep them trading and in good
repair. But the Parliamentary Act of 1873, which imposed this
obligation, was not enforced because of the public expense and
legal complications which would have been involved. So the
railways took advantage of the weaknesses in the canals' position
to draw the traffic on to their own lines. There were many weaknesses: excessive tolls for transferring goods from one waterway
to another; frequent stoppages owing to weather conditions and
locks under repair; the unbusinesslike way in which many canal
carriers conducted their affairs. It is true that on occasion a railway
company did something to observe its obligations; hence the
Newcastle-under-Lyme Canal survived into this century, long
after the other two Newcastle canals had been abandoned. But
this was exceptional; railway policy was 'to drive the traffic from
the water to the rails'—logically enough, since the railway companies were profit-making, not altruistic, bodies.

There were other weaknesses. The canals were unable to carry
passengers in any number. Timetables were seldom adhered to;

time was often wasted on the journey, and pillaging of cargoes was frequently reported. There was also what the transport historian W. T. Jackman[2] describes as 'a psychological reason'. As he says: 'The canal traffic was carried on comparatively quietly and unseen, there was nothing fast about it. The sight of an occasional horse passing through the country, mounted or driven by a boy, and hauling an insignificant looking barge which was managed by one or two persons, excited no surprise on the part of anyone. . . . On the other hand, the railway had an appearance of grandeur and ostentation that charmed the public. It seemed the embodiment of enterprise and boundless capabilities. . . .' Jackman contrasts the pessimistic attitude of the canal proprietors with the enterprise of the 'younger men, usually of the trading and industrial classes, who were actively pushing the construction of railways. The former often gave up the battle with the railway companies in despair, and perhaps at too early a period, before they had learned what strength they really had and how largely the traffic of the country would increase'. To this one can add, in regard to more recent closures, that had the value of canals for recreational purposes been appreciated earlier, fewer might have been abandoned after World War I.

After the setting up of British Waterways Board in 1962, a change of attitude became apparent. The result was the cruising network established by the Transport Act of 1968. Voluntary organisations, including the Inland Waterways Association and the many canal protection or restoration societies, have campaigned for improved standards of maintenance, against closures, and for the reopening of certain lines. As a result, the Southern Stratford has been restored and reopened, the sixteen locks on the Stourbridge have been repaired, and there are hopes for the resumption of navigation through Dudley tunnel. In some areas, local authorities have gone into action; the Brecon & Abergavenny has been revitalised with the financial help of Brecon and Monmouthshire County Councils, and Birmingham Corporation's enlightened planning is bringing new life to sections of the Birmingham Canal Navigations. Although it is true that British Waterways Board, now the statutory authority, lack the funds to maintain the total present length of some 1,400 miles in satisfactory condition, it does at least seem as if the days of the abandonment Acts are over.

The canals, it has been said, represented not merely a transport system but a way of life. On this topic, nostalgia is an easy mood to fall into. It is worth noting that infant mortality on canal boats in the Birmingham area in 1905 at 30 per cent was double the rate for Birmingham as a whole. Overcrowding in the very restricted accommodation on the boats was frequently reported; privacy was virtually unobtainable and there were no sanitary facilities on the boats at all. It was difficult, if not impossible, for the children to obtain any education, or to be kept even moderately clean.[3] That the conditions produced a tough and independent breed is not denied; but whether the passing of the conditions is regrettable is a different matter.

The canal boatman's 'way of life' came in later years to express itself in decoration; the tiny cabin with its ribbon plates, polished brass and Measham teapot, the roses and castles, painted tillers and tinware, the intricate ropework and the medallioned horse with crocheted warmers for its ears in winter. But there were two reasons, both ominous for the future of the waterways, why the boatman's family joined him to live on board. One was the necessity for speedier traffic to compete with the railways; longer hours could be worked when there was no need for overnight stops. The other was the reduction in real wages that compelled this step for reasons of economy. It seems to have been the second generation of boat families that felt the strong need to brighten and take a pride in their homes.

Yet life on the cut must have had its compensations. At least relative freedom, a degree of independence denied to the factory worker, and the feeling of belonging to a close-knit community—these are not mere clichés, as a few minutes talk with an old boatman will prove. Moreover, those who led the horses, worked the locks and steered the boats made their own contribution to the country's prosperity. For the canals and their people, the promoters, the engineers, the boatmen, vitalised the economy and changed the appearance of the country. G. M. Trevelyan writes[4] that through the canals 'the whole character and scope of British commerce began to assume its modern form of supplying necessaries for all, instead of merely luxuries for the rich'. He quotes Thomas Pennant, writing in 1782:

'The cottage, instead of being half covered with miserable thatch, is now covered with a substantial covering of tiles or

slates, brought from the distant hills of Wales or Cumberland.
The fields, which before were barren, are now drained, and
by the assistance of manure, conveyed on the canal toll-free,
are clothed with a beautiful verdure. Places which rarely
knew the use of coal are plentifully supplied with that essential
article upon reasonable terms; and, what is of still greater
public utility, the monopolizers of corn are prevented from
exercising their infamous trade. . . .'
The abandoned canals include many which contributed greatly
towards these changes, those of the East Midlands coalfields and
the South Wales valleys in particular.

The secret of successful derelict canal exploration is to brief
oneself beforehand on what used to be there. In a town, look at
the 6in or, even better, the first edition of the 25in or 50in plan at
the public library or Borough Engineer's office, and if possible get
a photostat of it. It is surprising how much can still be found if one
knows exactly where the canal ran and what buildings and struc-
tures it had. The plan will enable you to follow the Glamorganshire Canal through the car-parks of Cardiff, or the Wilts & Berks
into and through the new shopping centre of Swindon. Parts of
the Croydon Canal became streets, with houses built on either
side. Given the plan, the reason for the curving streets becomes
clear, and one can follow much of the route.

A hump across a street may be a clue, or a continuous line of
wall or hedge, or a piece of isolated walling. Realisation that the
continuous hedge at the bottom of a line of gardens was that of
the towpath makes the tracing of the line of Sir Nigel Gresley's
canal into Newcastle much easier. A concrete wall at the foot of
a cottage garden in Taunton runs on to what looks like a substantial stone buttress; this was part of the Taunton lift on the
Grand Western Canal, and helps to establish the line of the canal
through the present goods yard.

In the country, the 6in sheets are most helpful—although to buy
them all for a canal as long as the Wilts & Berks might prove
prohibitively expensive. For really comprehensive study, the 25in
is ideal. But one can still do well with the 1in OS map, confirming
one's discoveries by later consultation with the other plans in
public libraries. With this map, the best scheme is to mark every
road and river crossing of the canal, and make for those; they may
well yield a bridge or aqueduct. Changes in contour will suggest

the sites of locks, and the easiest road from the canal into a town the probable site of the former wharf.

Spring and autumn are the best seasons for exploring in the country. In summer the greenery may be too dense to be penetrated and the brambles and nettles become powerful deterrents. Overgrown by creepers, a lock chamber becomes an elephant pit for the unwary. Dry winter days are excellent. After rain, derelict canals may fill with water; so also may their environs, and one's boots may be waterlogged before the target is reached. Boots or gumboots are generally advisable; woolly pullovers that may catch on brambles or barbed wire are not. A walking stick is useful to sweep aside the nettles or test the liquidity of the ground ahead.

The proprieties should be observed. Many canals run through private property. Few farmers or householders will refuse a request to enter their land, and sometimes they may have interesting information to impart. An abandoned waterway does not automatically become public property.

I have divided the Lost Canals into eight geographical groups, each group corresponding with one of the volumes, published or in hand, of the 'Canals of the British Isles' series, edited by Charles Hadfield. The South and South East group includes the cross-country routes of the Thames & Severn and the Wilts & Berks, and the links in the London–Portsmouth line made up by the Wey & Arun and the Portsmouth & Arundel. There are also the vestigial Salisbury & Southampton and the almost completely vanished Croydon Canal. The South West has the largest number; among these mainly agricultural waterways are the tub-boat canals of Bude and Chard, the Grand Western with its lifts, the Torrington and the Tavistock in Devon. In this region only the Exeter Ship Canal and the Bridgwater & Taunton have not been closed. The Border Counties and Wales have two archetypal lost canals, the Leominster and the Herefordshire & Gloucestershire; the Montgomeryshire penetrates mid-Wales and the valley canals once served the industrial south. The Shropshire tub-boat canals form a large part of the West Midlands group, which also includes the complex navigations of Birmingham. The East Midland canals helped to develop the Nottingham and Derby coalfields; the inclined plane at Foxton also comes into this section. In the North West are the canals of the Manchester area, including two of the three great trans-Pennine routes, the Rochdale and the Huddersfield Narrow, the lost northern stretch of the Lancaster and the remote Ulverston. The seven North Eastern waterways range from the industrial Barnsley to the beautiful Pocklington and the Driffield Navigation. The East of England relied more on rivers for commercial transport but there are five canals of interest which can be followed, each of which served a pleasant town of distinctive character. The total mileage of the canals described is rather over one thousand.

All references are to the 1in Ordnance Survey maps; the usefulness of other maps has been referred to earlier. Maps prior to the Ordnance Survey, it should be noted, sometimes give the proposed line of a canal rather than what was actually made. One can spend a lot of time looking for the non-existent Alford Canal,[5] or the main line of the Dorset & Somerset.

I have not tried to describe everything that may be found on every abandoned waterway—this would be a labour of love but enduring to eternity. Those who want to know more should consult the volumes in the 'Inland Waterways Histories' series, as they are published, and the specialised articles referred to in the bibliographies. For the history of the canals, the books of Charles Hadfield are indispensable.[6] No historian is more devoted to his subject, more knowledgeable about it, or more lucid. Whatever is accurate in my brief historical accounts is due to his researches; whatever mistakes there are, are my own.

Notes

1 *The Kennet & Avon Canal*, by Kenneth R. Clew, and *London's Lost Route to the Sea*, by P. A. L. Vine.
2 *The Development of Transportation in Modern England* (1916, reprinted 1966).
3 Article 'Living Conditions on Midland Canal Boats', by S. R. Broadbridge: *Transport History*, March 1970.
4 *Illustrated English Social History* (1942).
5 See article 'The Alford Canal', by P. R. White: *Journal* of the Railway & Canal Historical Society, April 1970.
6 The volumes yet to be published are *Canals of Yorkshire and the North East*, by Charles Hadfield, and *The Canals of Eastern England*, by J. H. Boyes. The historical accounts in Chapter 8 are the results of my own researches.

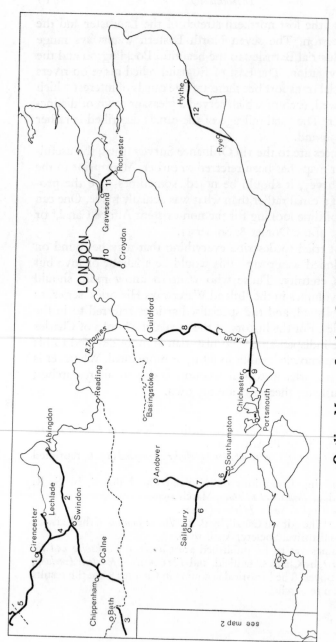

Outline Map 1   South & South East England

1   The Thames & Severn Canal
2   The Wilts & Berks Canal
3   The Somersetshire Coal Canal
4   The North Wilts Canal
5   The Stroudwater Navigation
6   The Salisbury & Southampton Canal
7   The Andover Canal
8   The Wey & Arun Junction Canal
9   The Portsmouth & Arundel Canal
10 The Croydon Canal
11 The Thames & Medway Canal
12 The Royal Military Canal

Chapter 1: *The South and South East*

THE THAMES & SEVERN CANAL

The first of the three southern cross-country routes to be completed, in 1789, the Thames & Severn Canal was finally abandoned in 1933, outliving the Wilts & Berks but without the prospect of restoration that keeps alive the Kennet & Avon: 28¾ miles long, the T & S was cut from a junction with the Stroudwater Navigation, which linked it to the Severn, at Stroud, pierced the Cotswold escarpment by the Sapperton tunnel, and met the Thames at Inglesham, half a mile upstream from Lechlade. A wide canal with 44 locks, it could take Severn trows on its western section and Thames barges and narrow boats throughout. As well as passing through some of the most beautiful country in southern England, it had four features of particular interest; the tunnel, the round houses, the pumping station at Thames Head, and the great inland port at Brimscombe. It also leaked.

The T & S took six years to construct and cost some £220,000. The promoters, who included several London merchants and representatives of the Stroudwater and various Midland canal companies, employed Robert Whitworth to make a preliminary survey of the route. However, the men who were mainly responsible for the line as built were Josiah Clowes, the engineer, and James Perry, a merchant with canal interests in the Midlands, who acted as superintendent. But the canal carried within it the seeds of its own destruction. Shortage of water at the summit level necessitated the construction of a pumping engine at Thames Head, completed four years after the canal opened; but poor workmanship in parts of the tunnel and fissures in the rock through which the summit was cut led to constant wastage. Added to this, several of the locks east of Sapperton were built with unequal falls. Only vigilant maintenance and speedy repair work could keep the traffic passing; that the T & S lasted as long as it did was a credit to the diligence and devotion of some, though not all, of its staff. Coal, much of it from the Forest of Dean, was the principal cargo, and for some years the company was able to pay modest dividends. But trade was affected by three factors. Competition from the Wilts & Berks and the Kennet & Avon was damaging; the poor state of the navigation of the upper Thames was a chronic hindrance; and the onset of the Great Western Railway cut the profits to vanishing point. At no time did traffic come up to expectations; indeed if it had it might have made matters worse because of the recurrent difficulties over water supply and the increased wastage owing to extra working of the locks. Yet so valuable an asset did the canal appear that remarkable efforts to keep it trading were made even when all seemed lost.

The T & S–Stroudwater junction is at Wallbridge, on A 46, south of the centre of Stroud. Here are the chambers of the two Wallbridge locks, and the toll house now on the premises of the W Glos Water Board. The basin has been filled in, but the towpath can be followed from Stroud, with a few short interruptions, to the west portal of the tunnel. For the first few miles it is a sad and rather dreary walk, the water full of weed and backed on to by garages and factories. The climb to the summit begins gradually, with five locks in the 3 miles between Stroud and Brimscombe. At the approach to Brimscombe the canal has recently been filled in, and almost every trace of the port itself has gone. Brimscombe was an interchange port, where goods from the Severn trows were transhipped into the barges and narrow boats, and vice versa. There was a basin 700ft long, with a coal store on an island, to deter thieves. A large and elegant Georgian-styled warehouse, three storeys high, incorporating the port office with a fine bow-window for effective surveillance, dominated the scene. Beside it was a long, single-storey transit shed, with ten windows in its frontage. A forge, barge weighing machine, manager's house, wharfinger's cottage and salt store all stood here, but only the latter two survive. The basin was filled in and the other buildings demolished by 1966, to make way for Benson's factory. On the wall of one of the modern buildings is a plaque recording the site of Brimscombe Port, Headquarters of the Thames & Severn Canal Co—'an important transport centre for over a century'. A stone inscribed with the date 1801 is inset in the wall by the plaque. Brimscombe was by far the busiest of the twelve wharves on the canal, with six cranes and a permanent staff of about seventeen. Tolls taken here provided the principal source of income for the company.

Following a narrow road between Benson's and the River

Frome, you come to the canal again, with a row of elegant iron railings and a bridge. Bourne lock, the highest lock capable of taking the trows, has been filled in at the end of Benson's premises. The blue door in the wall here is mentioned by Temple Thurston in his description of a voyage along this canal in his book *The 'Flower of Gloster'*, in 1911. Chalford, at the head of the Golden Valley, is 1½ miles farther on. There are many old mills and factories in Chalford, one of the largest villages in England. Here is the first of the canal's five round houses, all built in 1790 for the 'watchmen' or lock-keepers. Like miniature lighthouses, each had three floors; the lowest a stable, above it a living-room and on the top a bedroom. They were serviceable for the views they afforded of approaching boats, and picturesque as can be seen today, but not popular with those who had to live and work in them, and the design was not repeated in subsequent years. Yet, though two are now derelict, they all survive. The Chalford round house is now a private museum containing many items of T & S interest.

The Cirencester road, A419, hitherto on the north side of the canal, crosses it at Chalford. The houses sprawl up the hillside; signs of industry recede, the hills grow higher. 'In the nearer distance,' Temple Thurston lyrically wrote, 'the dense woods spread over the rolling land and, like an army in glittering mail, with golden trappings and with coloured plumes, they march down the hillsides to the water's edge. This part of the country,' he added, 'must be the most luxuriant in the whole of England.'

The canal was fed from a reservoir above Chalford, and also from a number of springs, and it still has a healthy look hereabouts. For 3 miles it continues its gradual climb through, among others, Red Lion lock, where the bridge has an inscription recording the appointment of Clowes as engineer, and Bakers Mill lock, by the fine Cotswold mill. Ten more locks, completing the rise of 241ft to the summit, bring the canal to Daneway, where there was a basin and wharf. The car park of the Daneway Inn is built on the site of the top lock; the inn used to be called the Bricklayers' Arms and was originally a canal house. It has changed little externally since it was built in 1784. From the inn the canal, now much overgrown, swings westward; a few hundred yards along, by the tunnel-keeper's cottage, is the gothic-styled west portal of Sapperton tunnel.

Sapperton, the third longest canal tunnel in the country, took just over five years to complete. It was dug by a number of contractors of varying efficiency, each responsible for his own stretch. Wooden doors were inserted to seal off fissures in the rock, giving much trouble when later they decayed, and some of the workmanship was skimped. But the major problems arose from distortion of the walls and invert for geological reasons, particularly when water penetrated to the fuller's earth through which much of the tunnel was dug, and caused it to swell. Built

Thames & Severn Canal: Coates Portal, Sapperton tunnel

to a width of 14ft 4in, at certain times and places the bore was squeezed to under 12ft. Temple Thurston said it took four hours for him and his boatman, Eynsham Harry, to leg through Sapperton, but as he exaggerated its length by ½ mile he may have exaggerated the time also. In fiction, Horatio Hornblower helped to leg the passenger-boat *Queen Charlotte* through the tunnel; but a more intriguing passage is that described all too briefly in Thomas Love Peacock's *Crotchet Castle*, when 'four beautiful cabined pinnaces, one for the ladies, one for the gentlemen, one for kitchen and servants, one for a dining-room and band of

music', with Dr Folliott, Mr Chainmail, Mr Mac Quedy and Lady
Clarinda among the passengers, navigated the Thames & Severn
on their way to North Wales. Unfortunately all that we are told of
their conversation at Sapperton is that 'they agreed unanimously
that the greatest pleasure derivable from visiting a cavern of any
sort was that of getting out of it'. Recent attempts at exploration
have revealed that the tunnel is now blocked by roof falls.

The line of the tunnel can be followed over the hill by the beech
copses and mounds marking the spoil heaps and shafts. The east
portal, in classical style but lacking the inscription and the statues
(presumably of Father Thames and Sabrina) for which the niches
were intended, is in Hailey Wood, near the village of Coates; there
is a signpost pointing along the track which leads to it from the
Coates–Tarlton road. Near the portal is the Tunnel House, now an
inn, where the workers lodged when the tunnel was being made.
The house lost all but the walls in a fire, but has been well restored.
When the Gloucestershire County Council took over the canal in
1900, for what proved to be the last years of its life, their engineer
found the summit level of the canal near the tunnel in such bad
condition that he had a ¼ mile stretch concreted. But nothing
so thorough was done to the remaining leaky 3 miles of the
summit, which continued to give trouble. The cutting is the only
major earthwork on the canal, and the water remains clear.

To the east of the road, the towpath leads to the Coates round
house. This was altered late in the last century at the request of a
watchman whose fiancée refused to marry him and live there
unless something was done. The stable was made into a room for
the house, and a kitchen was added. Now the staircase from
ground floor to first has vanished, the floors are very shaky and
much of the roof has gone. As at two of the other houses, the roof
is inverted, the beams sloping down from a parapet towards the
centre. Piping led off from here, possibly to a rainwater cistern. By
comparison with the Golden Valley the country here seems bleak,
but there is plenty of water bubbling underground. A mile or so
away are the springs that provide the source of the Thames,
marked by a memorial to the old man himself, in somnolent mood.
The canal, now dry, runs along the hillside above the source; both
can be reached from Thames Head Bridge, on A433, 3 miles south
of Cirencester. The parapets of the bridge stand on what used to
be the main road but is now a slip road to some cottages. A plaque

is affixed to the eastern one, but the hump in the road has been flattened. What at first looks like a parapet on the east side of the main road is a piece of recent dry-stone walling.

Two hundred yards along the towpath east of the bridge is the site of Thames Head pumping station. At first a windmill pump was installed here, but this was soon replaced by a Boulton & Watt steam engine, tapping the underground springs of the head-waters of the Thames. This engine lasted until 1854, when a second-hand Cornish engine was bought, which could deliver three million gallons a day. The engine house has now gone but the well, over 63ft deep, gapes in the undergrowth that has covered the foundations of the structure, and you can crawl through the conduits between the canal and the top of the well. The dwelling house, occupied until recently, and outbuildings are in good repair, and excavations would reveal the galleries and adits that fed the water to the pump.

The canal winds on towards Siddington, south of Cirencester. The Smerril aqueduct, a single-arched masonry structure (which also leaked) that took the canal over the Cirencester–Kemble road, has been demolished, but its site is easily discernible. At Siddington, where there is a junction house, a short branch to Cirencester left the main line; of the branch and the wharf by Querns Hill in Cirencester only the wharf house remains. After the junction begins the descent to the Thames by the four Siddington locks, followed in about a mile by a converted lock house and the three locks on the north side of South Cerney, beside the Cirencester–S Cerney road. The canal course winds across the fields on the north side of the River Churn; at Cerney Wick there is a round house, neat and inhabited, by the lock chamber, and at Latton, behind the first cottages on the right entering the village from Cirencester, is the junction with the North Wilts Canal (qv). The site of Cricklade wharf, with the wharf house, is a mile along from Latton by the junction with the minor road to Kempsford. This road runs roughly parallel to the canal, which is on its southern side, with some stretches holding water from time to time, and others having been ploughed up. The dilapidated Marston Meysey round house stands by a bridge on a track south of the road just past the left turn to Marston Meysey village. The canal is crossed by the road near Kempsford church, soon after passing the wharf house, and then swings north east across the fields to Inglesham.

The last locks before Inglesham are the Dudgrove pair, out in the fields. At Inglesham by a picturesque group of buildings—a round house, a cottage, a bridge and a lock chamber—the canal enters the Thames. The wharf, boathouses and offices were built at Lechlade on the river, and some of the buildings remain on the west side of Halfpenny Bridge. The three wharf houses at Cirencester, Cricklade and Kempsford are of a unique design, incorporating wharfinger's house and warehouse in a single structure.

Before its demise, two attempts were made to revive the T & S. In 1882 the canal came under GWR control; in 1895 a group of canal companies known as the Allied Navigations and including the Sharpness and Staffs & Worcs formed a Trust, together with the local county and urban district councils, to take it over to prevent closure. But their estimates were inadequate, their funds insufficient and their engineers over-optimistic; despite repair work the water continued to drain away. When the Gloucestershire County Council took over from the Trust a stronger effort was made to put things in order, but despite the money spent the trade which had left the canal did not return. What traffic there was, was virtually confined to the Stroud–Chalford section. A few pleasure craft ventured on to the canal, but there was no trade to Lechlade after 1911. The canal between Whitehall Bridge, near Daneway, and Lechlade was abandoned in 1927, and the remainder in 1933. Occasionally a hopeful letter proposing restoration appears in the Press, but it would be a mighty undertaking and the outlook is not bright. Now the birds nest in the derelict round houses of Coates and Marston Meysey, and the leaks in the Thames & Severn have no effect on the nation's trade.

OS sheets 156 (Stroud–Chalford) & 157 (Chalford–Lechlade)
The Thames & Severn Canal, by Humphrey Household (a detailed illustrated history)
The Canals of South & South East England, by Charles Hadfield
The Thames & Severn Canal, by J. Graham Epsley & W. E. Duncan Young
The 'Flower of Gloster', by E. Temple Thurston

THE WILTS & BERKS CANAL

Pope's description of the Alexandrine might be equally well applied to the Wilts & Berks which 'Like a wounded snake, drags its slow length along' four sheets of the one-inch OS map, from Semington on the Kennet & Avon to Abingdon on the Thames; 51 miles long, with four short branches and one longer one—the North Wilts Canal from Swindon to Latton, opened 1819—the Wilts & Berks was completed in 1810, its purpose to convey coal from Somerset and agricultural produce along its route. The canal took about fifteen years to construct and was opened bit by bit, the company finding money hard to raise and hoping for income as they went along. Somewhere in the linear wilderness that is now the Wilts & Berks are the remains of 45 locks. Water came first from a well near Swindon, and later from two reservoirs, at Coate and Tockenham.

The company shared in various ambitious schemes to extend their line towards Bristol and towards London, by-passing the Thames, but only the North Wilts link with the Thames & Severn was made. For some years small profits accrued but trade, mainly in Somerset coal, was never very heavy and the boats travelling westward were often empty. Extra trade for a few years came with the construction of the Great Western Railway's line from Abingdon to Chippenham, but the completion of the line in 1841 caused an immediate drop in canal receipts and dividends decreased annually. The company had not opposed the railway and had not foreseen its threat; as receipts fell so there was less money available for maintenance. In the 1870s tonnage dropped to less than 30,000 and overall losses appeared on the balance-sheet. Having failed to sell to the railway, the company wanted to close the canal. A group of local traders bought it in 1875 for £13,466; they leased it to some Bristol merchants in 1882, who returned it five years later having met with little success. In 1891 a company grandiloquently named the United Commercial Syndicate took over; they too failed to profit and, with the support of the Swindon Traders Association, they sought abandonment. In that too they were unsuccessful, and it was not until 1914 that Swindon Corporation obtained an abandonment Act, though traffic had stopped on the canal in 1906 and much of it was unnavigable.

There were no major engineering works on the Wilts & Berks which, with its 7ft 6in wide locks and narrow channel, looks a meagre undertaking compared to its neighbours, the Thames & Severn and Kennet & Avon, despite its greater length. It leaves the K & A beside Semington bridge, between the bridge and lock 15. The lock cottage on the K & A is now empty and the entrance to the W & B, under a bridge, is filled in. There is a fine house beside the line of the W & B, and its garden has been made on the canal itself. The cut continues beside A350 north to Melksham for some 200yd, and is then filled. Traces in Melksham appear to have been obliterated, apart from the parapet of a red-brick bridge in front of a new bungalow at the corner of Forest Road.

The line can be discerned heading north east out of Melksham across the fields, roughly parallel to the Avon. It passes by the Bell Inn, ½ mile east of the beautifully preserved village of Lacock, and eases round the contours of Nocketts Hill to the junction with the Chippenham branch, near Forest Farm. There is nothing to see in Chippenham, except for what is probably a wharf building at Ameys factory.

The main line continues under A4 and under a minor road north west of Studley. Here on the north side of the road the canal is worth following. First there is a collapsed bridge which took the old railway from Calne to Chippenham over the canal; 200yd farther on is a two-arch brick aqueduct, over the Marden, a tributary of the Avon. One arch of the aqueduct is barely intact, but it is possible to crawl across it with care. A well-preserved brick lock chamber is next; then comes the junction with the Calne branch, with a bridge and another lock. The branch turns south east, soon crossed by a bridge in advanced decay. A few yards on is evidence that the canal burst its banks in its dying throes. The wharf in Calne is now a car park opposite Harris's factory. There is an empty canal house at the end of the car park; behind it is the canal, with a lock half hidden in the scrub, some bits of ironwork remaining.

The W & B is culverted under nearly all the roads it meets in its wanderings; from the roads it can be seen as a line of hedges and small trees, sometimes on a low embankment, dividing fields and keeping the cows apart from the corn. It passes near E Tytherton —where there is a Moravian Church in a fine seventeenth-century house—and ½ mile west of Charlcutt, where the site of a small basin is clear. There are two lock chambers ½ mile east of Foxham Church; the canal then curls round the outside of Melsome Wood and comes up parallel to the Swindon–Chippenham railway line. Dauntsey lock, where the A420 crosses the railway, is filled in, and second-hand cars are for sale on its site. The lock cottage and outbuildings are by the main road.

From here until the approach to Abingdon, canal and railway are never far apart. There is pleasant walking between the canal and lake at Tockenham, through woodland carpeted with blue-bells in the spring. The canal passes to the south of Wootton Bassett; part of the parapet of a bridge can be seen where it is crossed by Marlborough Road, but the cut itself has been absorbed into gardens. On a very minor road east of Wootton Bassett (SU 095815) there is a grey stone bridge, filled in with sand but with good stonework, and the remains of a lock, with a derelict cottage, ¼ mile west. One mile east, at Hay Lane Wharf, the canal has been filled in and the cottage has been pleasantly restored. For the next mile a minor road lies virtually on the canal; at Wharf Farm it turns northerly to run into Swindon. From Sunnyside Avenue, by traffic lights on A420 on the edge of the town, the canal can be followed, either back into the country as a watered stretch to West Leaze, or into the town.

Through Swindon the w & b is first a wide grassy path between the backs of two rows of houses, used as a playground or for walking the dog. This leads eventually to the site of the wharf; Wharf Road is still so named, as is Wharf House. Then it becomes a car park, off Cromwell Road; then the centre of The Parade, a pedestrian concourse in the new shopping centre either side of Regent Street (there is a milestone in the wall of the bank). The bus station, another car park, Fleming Way and the County Ground all lie on the course of the canal. On the far side of Swindon the cut emerges between a school and Shrivenham Road, with a stone bridge still used by cyclists and walkers. For nearly 5 miles to Shrivenham it lies on the south side of A420 until it curves eastward under Station Road, Shrivenham, by the generating station. The junction with the Longcot branch is in the fields a mile east of the Military College. The branch ends in the garden of a substantial house, not connected with the canal, in Majors Road. The wharf cottages are still there, one inhabited by an old gentleman who used to load corn on to the boats when a boy, in the canal's last years.

From here to the Challows the line of the w & b remains clear, but there is little of interest. The road bridges have been levelled; each side there is generally a small rubbish dump, head-high nettles and straggly growth. The junction with the short Wantage branch is north of the town, near the south-east corner of a disused airfield. In the brambles there is a lock chamber on the main line. The site of Wantage wharf is behind a caravan dealer's on A417 near the town centre.

From Wantage to Abingdon several stretches have been levelled. There is a tree plantation along the course east of Grove Park, and some canalside cottages ½ mile farther north. A footpath across Cow Common indicates the w & b. Approaching Abingdon it appears on the south side of the Ock; it rounds a new housing estate on A34, and forms a grassed walk along Caldecott Road. The junction with the Thames is by Wilsham Road. An old warehouse is now the Hygienic Laundry; next to it is Wharf House, though not likely to remain much longer as the site has been sold for development. Wharf Cottage, brightly modernised, is next door. Iron piling marks the one-time entrance of the canal, and there is some old stone in the river wall. The river is smart with motor cruisers and dinghies; one would have to dig deep to find the dust of the Somerset coal.

OS sheets 166 (Semington–Melksham)
    156 (Melksham–south of Chippenham)
    157 (Lacock–Longcot)
    158 (to Abingdon)
The Canals of South & South East England, by Charles Hadfield

THE SOMERSETSHIRE COAL CANAL

Rennie's Dundas aqueduct, at Limpley Stoke on the Kennet & Avon, is one of the best-known features on the canal system of the southern half of England. Its three arches carry the canal over river and railway; a convenient lay-by on A36 makes it easy of access to sightseers who come by car. There is a basin at the west end of the aqueduct; on the south side of this there is a cottage with a pleasant garden, now privately owned. Here was the junction of the Somersetshire Coal Canal with the K & A; the cottage was formerly the lock-cottage, and the stones of the top of the lock can be seen among the flower beds in the garden.

The SCC was opened throughout in 1805. It was sponsored by the owners of mines in the Somersetshire coalfield, concerned about competition from S Wales and the Forest of Dean, and seeking to reduce the heavy cost of carriage of their coal to Bath. The first survey was made by Rennie in 1793, and the Parliamentary Act was obtained in the following year. The canal committee decided to build a narrow canal to take the conventional narrow boats, and sent two of its members on a 900 mile tour to investigate the construction of canals and railroads in other parts of the country. William Smith, who became surveyor of the canal, accompanied the tour. Smith, later to become famous as 'the Father of English Geology' on account of his discoveries of rock stratification, worked for the SCC until 1799 when he was dismissed, apparently for buying some land for his own cottage while also buying land for the SCC.

The original plan provided for a canal with two lines. The main line was to run from Limpley Stoke to Paulton, $10\frac{1}{2}$ miles, and a branch was to leave the main line at Midford and run $7\frac{1}{4}$ miles to Radstock. There were two steep gradients to be overcome, one at Combe Hay and the other on the branch at Midford. The time taken to solve the problem at Combe Hay was the main reason for the delay between the obtaining of the Act and the opening of the canal throughout. The problem at Midford never had to be solved, as that portion of canal was not constructed. A short stretch was cut at Midford to the foot of Midford Hill; from there to Twinhoe a tramroad was laid. The branch was completed from Twinhoe to the terminal at Radstock but was used very little, possibly owing to difficulties over water supply. In 1815 a tramroad was laid along the towpath and through the tunnel at Wellow to connect at Twinhoe; it was sold to provide the route for the Somerset & Dorset Railway in 1871.

At Combe Hay three attempts were made to master the gradient. The first—and the most terrifying—was by Robert Weldon's caisson lock. This consisted of a cistern 88ft deep and full of water. In this was suspended a caisson, a watertight wooden box, big enough to contain a narrow boat and its crew. The boat was floated in through sliding doors at the top; the caisson was then lowered by racks and pinions, emerged through sliding doors at the bottom and floated out through a short tunnel. Weldon had exhibited a model of his 'hydrostatick lock', as he first called it, on the Shropshire Canal at Oakengates; this had been inspected by members of the K & A committee, who recommended it to the SCC. Weldon set to work at Combe Hay, and by 1798 the lock was completed and trials began. They were, however, not altogether successful, although when the Prince of Wales visited the site on a rainy day in April everything, fortunately for Weldon, went well. But it was not always so. Because of the weight of the water, the brick walls of the chamber began to bulge; the committee, while publicly justifying their expenditure on 'that machine', began to have second thoughts. Money was short and the delay in completing the line was proving expensive. Called in to advise, Benjamin Outram rejected the caisson lock as being too costly, particularly as more than one would be needed; he recommended instead an inclined plane up and down which the coal would travel in boxes. The committee accepted his advice; the unhappy Weldon disappeared and the caisson lock was demolished. Exactly where it was has not yet been ascertained, but it was somewhere close to the house now called Caisson House, possibly near locks 5 and 6 of the Combe Hay flight.

In 1800 a double-track counterbalanced inclined plane was constructed, generally to Outram's proposals. The head of this was on the south-west side of Caisson House; three locks were built near the foot to take the canal down to its lower level. But the incline, of 129ft vertical rise, was not successful either, the delays in loading and off-loading the coal in wooden boxes being considerable and the machinery not being faultless. Hence, only a few months after the opening of the incline in 1801, the committee had third thoughts and joined forces with the owners of the K & A and the Wilts & Berks Canal (then under construction) to set up a fund to raise money for the construction of conventional locks on the SCC.

Progress now accelerated. A three-arch aqueduct at Midford over the Cam brook was completed; a pumping engine was installed at Dunkerton to raise water from the brook, and another at Combe Hay, sited in a wood to be known as Engine wood about a mile from Caisson House, to re-circulate the water which flowed through the locks. The 22 locks, which included the three built at the foot of the inclined plane, were completed, and by the beginning of 1806 the main line was in full operation.

Coal was the SCC's only considerable traffic. With the completion of the K & A and the Wilts & Berks canals the openings for Somerset coal were greatly increased; in 1820 the tonnage carried topped 100,000 and the company was able to tidy up its finances and pay reasonable dividends. Pleasure trips took place on the canal from time to time, and an elegant weigh-house was built at Midford. This is now demolished, but its pillars and general Doric styling are reminiscent of the bridge-keepers' houses which can still be seen on the Gloucester & Berkeley Canal.

Despite the threat from railways, the SCC maintained its prosperity through the mid-Victorian years. It had a virtual monopoly of the traffic from the thirty or so collieries in the area it served; consequently it kept its tolls relatively high and continued to pay respectable dividends. The colliery owners in time became critical of its cost and the poor standard of maintenance; moreover, the GWR, which had bought the K & A in 1852, began to discourage trade on that canal. The Somerset coalfield began to decline and its product to lose out in face of competition from coal brought from the North and Midlands by the expanding railway network. The SCC carried over 150,000 tons a year in the early 1860s; twenty years later, with the Somerset & Dorset Railway now using the line of the Radstock tramroad and the Bristol & N Somerset Railway now running into Radstock, the figure had dropped to an average of 30,000; 1889 saw the payment of the last dividend, and four years later the company went into liquidation. While negotiations for purchase went on, a little trade continued; but in 1898 the pumping stations were stopped. After further negotiations the GWR bought the canal in 1904, obtained an abandonment Act and built their line from Camerton to Limpley Stoke (the line used in the film *The Titfield Thunderbolt*, made in 1952) along its course. This line was taken up in 1958.

A convenient minor road, which leaves A36 ¼ mile south of Dundas aqueduct and passes through Monkton Combe, Midford, Combe Hay, Dunkerton and Camerton, gives easy access to what is left of the SCC. A36 crosses the line of the canal at the Viaduct Hotel; by Monkton Combe, the canal has been obliterated by the

Page 33 (above) *Thames & Severn Canal: inverted roof beams of Marston Meysey Round House;* (left) *Thames & Severn Canal: 'Gothic' window, Marston Meysey Round House*

Page 34 (above) *Salisbury & Southampton Canal: mooring rings in Canal Walk, Southampton;* (below) *Croydon Canal: ornamental water at Betts Park, once the bed of the canal, drained for cleaning*

railway, but William Smith's cottage (with appropriate memorial plaque), which faced the canal, can be found on the right of the road about halfway between Monkton Combe and Midford. There are traces of the canal bed at Midford station, and the stone three-arched aqueduct, which took the Radstock branch over Cam brook, is south of the road intersections (ST 759605). A mile farther on, just past a junction with a minor road heading north to South Stoke, are the Combe Hay locks. Several of them lie round the edge of a field on the north side of the road—a railway bridge stands at the entrance to the field. The locks have a total rise of over 150ft; much of the stonework and some of the iron-work is intact, and the remains of the gates are slowly decomposing. They can be followed, though heavily overgrown, along the right of the drive leading up to Caisson House and through the field opposite the house—the site of the inclined plane and also, possibly, of the caisson lock—but this is private property and leave to enter must be requested. On the west side of Combe Hay village, between refuse tips, is the short tunnel on the old railway line, originally used by the canal.

Near Dunkerton the canal was crossed by A367; traces of the bridge are in the lay-by a few yards northwards along that road. The small aqueduct over the road at Dunkerton has been demolished but a larger one over the valley survives. The line continues south-westward, behind the Jolly Collier inn at Camerton and under the road at Radford. From here it is possible to walk along the course for about a mile to the basin at Paulton, with the remains of the house once used by the man in charge here.

Of the Radstock arm nearly everything has disappeared. The basin was to the south of the Waldegrave Arms in Radstock, near the s & d level crossing. There is an odd relic, however, at Wellow, 4 miles north east of Radstock. Here the canal, and later the tramroad, passed under the road through a tunnel, 405ft long. The south portal of the tunnel is in a farmyard on the opposite side of the road to the church. It now provides shelter for farm implements. The tunnel, once used for growing mushrooms, can be followed inwards for about half its length. The top of the north portal, bricked up, could, until recently anyway, be found in a field behind the church.

C

OS sheet 166
The Somersetshire Coal Canal & Railways, by Kenneth R. Clew (a full
   history, with details of the caisson lock, and an itinerary)
The Canals of South & South East England, by Charles Hadfield

THE NORTH WILTS CANAL

The old canal companies were jealous of their water, their
tolls and their independence in general. Had this not been so,
some of them might have survived longer, for their failure to
co-operate made them easy prey to the voracious railways. The
North Wilts Canal was therefore a rare example; the product of an
agreement between two canal companies, the Thames & Severn
and the Wilts & Berks, whose waters it linked. However, lest the
picture look too harmonious, it was opposed by the Kennet &
Avon and the Oxford Canal, and its life as an independent concern
was short.

The Wilts & Berks was the chief progenitor of the North Wilts.
The T & S put up £5,000 towards its construction; other supporters
included several from the Forest of Dean, as it was thought that
the canal would help to increase the sales of coal from that area.
It was opened in 1819; leaving the W & B at Swindon, it fell
through twelve locks to join the T & S at Latton, 9 miles away.
There were double stop-gates at Latton, one pair controlled by
the T & S to ensure that no water would be lost to the North Wilts
if there was a difference in levels.

In 1821 the North Wilts Company, unable to repay a government loan raised to help with the costs of construction, amalgamated with the W & B. Its fortunes hence were tied to those of that
none-too-flourishing concern. For a time it provided a section of
a fly-boat route from London to Gloucester; the trade in Forest of
Dean coal did not materialise, and the main cargo was coal from
Somerset. As supplies from this source fell away, profits declined
and turned into losses. Various optimists kept the W & B going
long after its final dividend payment, until all ceased in 1906.

Attempts had been made to promote pleasure cruising on the
North Wilts in the 1890s, and Mr Charles Hadfield reprints a page
from a guide to the canal, written in 1893 by Mr Julius Auerbach.
The toll for pleasure boats was 10s, for which you had the services

of one lock-keeper, although you had to work the other locks and several swing bridges, including one at Swindon, yourself. Above the five Swindon locks, says Mr Auerbach, 'for some distance the voyage is at times very disagreeable, owing to the foul stench of the mud stirred up by the oars'—an experience which might be shared by anyone rowing on the Coventry Canal near Nuneaton today.

There isn't much left of the North Wilts now, although a few years ago most of its course was easily visible. The junction with the T & S is at Latton, 1¾ miles north west of Cricklade on A419. There is a lane beside the last pair of cottages on the west side of the road through the village; this leads to the line of the T & S, on the far side of which the low stone wall outlining the basin of the North Wilts can be clearly seen. A cottage stands by the junction. The aqueducts by which the North Wilts crossed the Churn and the Thames have both been demolished. The canal turned south east to edge around Cricklade, through a short tunnel (the southern portal is visible) and past the wharf. There is a road junction on B4041, just under a mile south of the centre of Cricklade. Here the road crosses the canal; by the junction on the east side a small three-arched aqueduct hides in the shrubbery, taking the North Wilts over the Key, a tributary of the Thames. For some 3 miles the course of the canal is on the east side of the minor road; in places it has been used for road widening, but the parapets of some bridges can be seen. The canal leaves the minor road south of Pry Farm and crosses another three-arched aqueduct over the Ray to enter Swindon from the north west. It met the main line of the W & B on the south side of the present Swindon railway station, ½ mile west of the old Swindon Wharf.

OS sheet 157
The Canals of South & South East England, by Charles Hadfield
The Thames & Severn Canal, by Humphrey Household

THE STROUDWATER NAVIGATION

Various attempts were made in the eighteenth century to link the wool town of Stroud to the Severn by using the small river called the Stroudwater. The schemes, practical and impractical, produced fierce opposition from the millowners, jealous of their water supplies. An Act of 1730 authorised river improvement; no work was done under this Act until the early 1760s when some 5 miles of the river were made navigable by making cuts and building weirs. At the weirs, boxed cargo was transferred from one boat to another by cranes. But the river was too small and the procedure too expensive for this to be a success.

Interest revived in 1774 with the rapid growth of industries in the Stroud valley. A survey of the following year by Thomas Dadford jun and John Priddey, of the Droitwich Canal, shows a canal 8 miles long falling 102ft to the Severn, though the locks are not indicated. Eighteen mills are marked within a mile of the canal, which makes little use of the Stroudwater for its course. The line was more than 2 miles shorter than the turnpike road from Stroud to Framilode on the Severn. Minor alterations were proposed by Thomas Yeoman, and then work began under the old 1730 Act. The validity of the Act was questioned by hostile millowners but the demand for coal and corn was such that the necessity of a canal could not be denied, and in 1776 another Act was obtained confirming the legality of what was proposed, and work proceeded. The canal was completed three years later, with twelve broad locks (one double) although without a proper towpath until 1827, craft being man-hauled or sailed. The cost was a little over £40,000.

The canal proved prosperous and the company had a busy life. Coal came down the Severn from Staffordshire and across the river from the Forest of Dean. The opening of connecting canals improved the Stroudwater's trade. The Thames & Severn enabled trows to get to Brimscombe and narrow boats to London, the latter being facilitated by the opening of the North Wilts in 1819, providing an easier route. The Gloucester & Berkeley connected with the Stroudwater in 1820, giving better access from the upper Severn, and when completed to Sharpness seven years later eased the passage of boats from Bristol and South Wales. Tolls were high but tonnage carried steadily increased; dividends rose to 21 per cent in 1824.

The Stroudwater withstood railway competition much better than its neighbour, the Thames & Severn. Tonnage continued to rise even after the opening of the Great Western line from Swindon to Gloucester, which passed through Stroud, although tolls had to be reduced. The opening of the Stonehouse–Nailsworth railway past Stroud, affected trade, however, and the Stroudwater company, having opposed the T & S plan to convert that canal to a railway, began to harry the T & S company to put their canal in order. Most of the traffic on the T & S came off the Stroudwater; very little came back in return.

After 1880 dividends fell below 5 per cent, but the company struggled on. It contributed from its now meagre finances to try to keep the T & S open, and continued to trade, mainly in South Wales and Dean coal, well into the present century. But by the time the last length of the T & S was abandoned in 1933, the Stroudwater was in poor condition and the attempt a few years later of the Severn & Canal Carrying Company to run boats on it proved a failure. Trading ended in 1941, when the last load of coal reached the gasworks near Dudbridge, having taken two days to travel 7 miles. In the following years a little revenue accrued from water sales, property and renting of moorings off the Gloucester & Berkeley, but the company was losing money and could not afford to maintain the bridges. In 1954 an Act was sought to abandon navigation and hand over the bridges to the County Council. There was strong opposition in Parliament, and from the Inland Waterways Association and the Council for the Protection of Rural England, but sufficient evidence to show that enough money could be raised to restore the canal was not forthcoming. The Bill was passed and the navigation abandoned. The County Council took over the bridges, and water supply, drainage and fishing became the remaining purposes of the canal.

The Stroudwater makes an end-on junction with the Thames & Severn in Stroud, at Wallbridge. It is culverted under A46 and is shallow and reedy until Lodgemoor Mills, where the Painswick stream enters it. It takes up water from land drainage, becoming narrower but faster-flowing. For about 4 miles the canal is close to the southern side of A419/A4096. The upper gates of the locks have been converted to weirs; some lower gates have been removed, others rot away. There is an original brick bridge at Dudbridge. Some lengths are kept for fishing, but a stretch has been filled in near Greenways printing works.

At Bridgend, south of Stonehouse, the canal is culverted. However, Nutshell bridge, by the church, survives together with an octagonal bridge house. The parapets have been heightened for the safety of pedestrians. A few hundred yards west the railway crossing has been replaced by an embankment through which the canal is piped; a small tunnel takes the towpath. Farther on, a sunken barge rises out of the weedy water. There is another red brick bridge ½ mile west of the railway; then the canal and main road run side by side. There are two derelict locks and clear water for the anglers of Stroud.

The canal has recently been filled in where the main road swings south west to cross it a mile before Eastington. The water continues for another 100yd. Then from Chipmans Platt to A38, about a mile, the canal has been filled in for construction of the M5/A38 interchange. The waterway resumes west of A38, with one brick bridge and one of concrete, with the canal culverted beneath it. An earth barrier blocks the canal near where it is crossed by the River Frome on the level. The canal is used for fishing again near Wheatenhurst. The bridge on the Wheaten-hurst–Frampton road has been lowered, but from here to the crossing of the Gloucester & Berkeley the Stroudwater is in good condition and used for the mooring of pleasure craft. Water is pumped off in the summer to spray the nearby meadows.

Saul junction lock now forms a barrage across the canal; west of here the hulk of another barge lurks in the reeds. There is another fishing stretch before the next road bridge; after this point the canal is choked with reeds as far as Framilode village. The basin and the lock into the Severn have been filled in, and eventually will be grassed over.

OS sheet 156
  143 (Framilode only)
The Canals of South & South East England, by Charles Hadfield

THE SALISBURY & SOUTHAMPTON CANAL

In any competition for the greatest failure among canal undertakings, the Salisbury & Southampton must have strong claims to winning the prize. 'This work,' wrote Sir Henry Englefield, in *A Walk through Southampton*, published in 1805, 'after a vast expense, has long remained in an imperfect state.' The expense was vast enough; some £90,000 for 13 miles of canal which was never completed and had an effective working life of no more than three years—though it did succeed in drowning an old lady thirty-five years after its own commercial demise.

It was not that the scheme itself was absurd or impractical. The original proposition received strong support from Bristol, whose merchants had hopes for a direct link with Southampton, and there is little doubt that had it succeeded it would have given great impetus to Southampton's prosperity as a port. But it was to be the railways, not the waterways, that were to provide the essential communications with the hinterland.

The Act for the Salisbury & Southampton was obtained in 1795. Joseph Hill was appointed surveyor; he produced an estimate just short of £50,000 for the construction of two lines of canal: one from the Andover Canal at Redbridge, at the head of the Test estuary, to run alongside the river and then tunnel under the high ground north of the centre of the city and divide into two branches, to the Itchen and the Town Quay; the other to run westward from a junction with the Andover Canal, near Kimbridge, towards Salisbury. But from the beginning the company was short of money. Many of the shareholders proved reluctant to meet the calls made on them, and progress with the work was slow and unsatisfactory. The Southampton arm, including the tunnel, had been contracted to Thomas Jenkins, on the recommendation of the Leominster Canal company—whose own tunnels were a notorious series of disasters. Called in as consultant, John Rennie produced a damning report and, although matters afterwards improved, the shareholders' enthusiasm continued to wane. Hill and the committee were at odds, and shortly he withdrew. A second Bill, to raise more funds, was passed in 1800, but capital was slow to accumulate as the company had already acquired an impressive band of creditors. George Jones was appointed resident engineer, and the work began to make progress. Trade on the canal began in January 1803, from the western end of the tunnel to West Grimstead, 4 miles from Salisbury. Work stopped as the company battled to find cash and fight off its creditors, both of which it failed to do. Parts of the line were seized by sheriffs when judgement went against the company for failing to pay Jones' salary.

Tolls were still being collected at the end of 1804, and barges continued to use the canal for some months after, until damage and lack of maintenance ended navigation during 1806. The com-

mittee met for the last time in 1808. Part of the Salisbury arm ran
dry and part became a harmless stream; but Southampton found
itself with a stagnant ditch and a tunnel liable to subsidence. It was
not until after the drowning referred to earlier that the council
obtained powers to fill the ditch in. The Southampton & Dor-
chester Railway used the canal for part of their line and intended
also to use the tunnel but, finding it unsuitable, had to cut a new
one. Parts of the canal tunnel collapsed when the railway tunnel
was being built; and subsequently it has continued to make its
existence known from time to time, as builders laying foundations
have discovered.

Of the Southampton arm, very little visible evidence remains.
The junction with the Andover Canal, beside Test Lane ½ mile
north of the road bridge over the Test, was obliterated by the
railway built in 1864. The course then headed for the present
traffic roundabout at the top of Redbridge Road, blocks of flats
having been built over it in recent years. It turned towards Redbridge Station; the wilderness in the garden of the station house
is in fact the old canal. Towards Southampton Central Station the
railway was constructed on or parallel to its course; a few years
ago there used to be a length visible south of the line towards
Redbridge Point, but this has now been filled in. The tunnel
entrance was to the north of the railway tunnel; the length of the
tunnel as constructed was 580yd, and it ran beneath the present
Civic Centre and Above Bar Street, emerging in the green known
as the Hoglands. The canal divided after emerging into the light.
Of the branch that made eastward to Northam, the coal depot on
the Itchen, there seems to be no trace at all. The other branch ran
south, parallel to Above Bar St and High St, and its course is
denoted by Canal Walk and Lower Canal Walk. Two small mooring rings survive at the top of a flight of steps in Canal Walk, at
the rear of Lankester's works; one wonders whether they were
ever used, as it is not certain that the tunnel was at any time
navigable throughout. This arm entered the river by the Gaol
Tower. It used the ditch of the eastern wall of the old town for
part of its course.

Of the Salisbury arm there is much more to be found. It left the
Andover Canal 3½ miles north of Romsey; the junction is on the
east side of A3057, between the 'Bear & Ragged Staff' and
Mottisfont Station. The first few yards of the Salisbury arm are

now a potato field, but the line of scrub and trees can be discerned heading westward, while the Andover ditch continues north. The minor road to Lockerley keeps close to the canal; part of this stretch has been filled by a stream, as can be seen opposite School Farm, just before you reach the village.

Fourteen locks were built on the Salisbury arm, presumably able to take boats 65ft by 8ft 6in, the same size as those on the Andover; most of them, however, have disappeared, though the sites of some are shown on 2½in OS maps as fords. There is no complete lock chamber left, though the bricks doubtless are still existing in various farm buildings and walls in the surrounding countryside. The most substantial lock remains are on the road from Lockerley Green to Holbury Wood (SU 289269). On the west side of the first bridge you come to is a length of brick walling, about half of the south side of the lock. From here you can follow the bed of the canal to the site of the next lock, near the level-crossing on the road from Lockerley to East Dean.

The line of the canal continues through East and West Dean, being crossed and re-crossed by the railway to Salisbury. Some of the ninth lock can be found (SU 246272) under a footbridge on a farm track on the north side of the West Dean–East Grimstead road. The width between the two portions of brickwork is about 14ft; 1½ miles farther on, by the church at E Grimstead, is the only well-preserved canal bridge surviving. It is brick-built, with a stepped parapet, and carries a farm road over the dry bed of the canal. Some yards west of the bridge, a stream joins the Salisbury arm, which continues mainly wet for the rest of its course.

The summit level is at Whaddon Common. Here the canal enters a cutting, which lies between the embankments of the Salisbury–Romsey Railway and the disused Salisbury & Dorset Junction line. On the south side of the latter embankment (SU 195271) the cutting deepens and widens, so that from the high banks one gets the impression of a large, long lake formed by nature, with thickly-wooded banks. Here at least it would still be possible to put a boat on the Salisbury & Southampton Canal. But, as unfortunately only too often happens, the more accessible end of the cutting has been found a convenient dumping place for the disposal of old cars and other unwanted hardware, sinking slowly into the quagmire at the water's edge. The cutting can be reached from the track of the defunct Salisbury & Dorset line, or from one of the turnings on the north-east side of the A36, between Whaddon and Alderbury.

Whatever was built of the canal south of the main road has now been virtually obliterated; the line rounded Rectory Farm, but work must have been abandoned somewhere near Alderbury House. Tunnel Hill at Alderbury may have been where the tunnel on the descent to Salisbury was planned to be built. And in the woods north of W Grimstead is the summit reservoir of the canal.

OS sheets 180 (Southampton), 168 (Kimbridge–Lockerley Green), 167 (Salisbury)
'The Salisbury Canal—a Georgian Misadventure', by Hugh Braun, *Wilts Arch & Nat Hist Mag*, Vol 58, No 210
The Bankrupt Canal, by E. Welch (pub by City of Southampton)
The Canals of South & South East England, by Charles Hadfield

THE ANDOVER CANAL

Opened in 1794, the Andover Canal maintained an unprofitable existence for sixty-five years. Constructed at the instigation of the merchants and gentry of Andover, the line, surveyed by Robert Whitworth, followed the valley of the Anton and the Test south to Redbridge, on the outskirts of Southampton. There were 24 locks down from Andover, taking boats 65ft by 8ft 6in; the main cargoes were agricultural produce down and coal and building materials up, but trade was always below expectations and no dividend was ever paid. Between Redbridge and a point just north of Kimbridge the canal also formed the connecting link of the two sections of the Salisbury & Southampton for the three years of that waterway's inglorious career.

The Andover Canal cost about £48,000 to build, and sold itself to the Andover & Redbridge Railway for a little over half that amount in 1859. Much of the canal bed was used for the construction of the railway line; from Andover to Kimbridge this too has now gone, although the station buildings and bridges still remain.

The entrance lock to the Test was just above the medieval bridge at Redbridge, and has been obliterated by the railway. The fine old bridge, no longer used or accessible, stands to the north of the modern road bridge; by the Anchor Inn in Test Lane are the canal company's warehouses. A footpath follows the line of the canal to Nursling, whence it runs to the east of Broadlands House towards Romsey. There is no trace of it on the immediate approach to Romsey, as it has been built over; but it can be found, looking like a canal and still holding a little dirty water, by the car park of the Plaza cinema on the south-east side of the town. It can be followed by a footpath under the railway bridge and north out of the town and across fields for over 2 miles, when it swings to cross to the west of the A3057 Stockbridge road, edges round the back of Timsbury Manor, where there was a lock, and continues northward as a marshy ditch until it coincides with the line of the old railway near Mottisfont station, a few hundred yards after the junction with the Salisbury arm of the Salisbury & Southampton.

At Horsbridge, 3 miles farther north, the canal leaves the railway for a short stretch; there are some canal buildings and the site of a lock at the back of the Railway Hotel. It rejoins the railway to pass through Stockbridge, where the company used to have a wharf, and there is evidence of the cut to the left of the A3057 on the north side of the town. The turning to Longstock crosses the canal by a bridge which has undergone some reconstruction; from here to Fullerton, 2 miles on, the canal is actually maintained by the Leckford estates for fishing. North of Fullerton station the canal crossed to the west side of the Anton; thence it generally coincides again with the railway, through Goodworth Clatford, where there was a lock, and into Andover. The site of the wharf is now occupied by Henley's garage, in the yard of which there is what looks as if it may have been a wharfinger's house—but it may not be there much longer.

There is not really very much to see of the 22 miles of waterway that connected Andover to Redbridge and contributed, if not greatly, to the prosperity of Stockbridge and Romsey en route. But for the fishermen of Leckford and the children and courting couples of Romsey the remains of the old canal still have their uses.

OS sheets 168 (Romsey-Andover) & 180 (Romsey-Redbridge)
The Canals of South & South East England, by Charles Hadfield
Hampshire Field Club, *Newsletter* Vol 1 No 8

THE WEY & ARUN JUNCTION CANAL

Only one of many schemes to link London to the south coast ports by inland waterway ever came to fruition. This was the London–Portsmouth line, by way of the Thames, the Wey, the Wey & Arun Junction Canal, the Arun Navigation and the Portsmouth & Arundel Canal. Lord Egremont of Petworth, millionaire landowner, patron of the arts and the race-course, a man concerned with the general improvement of standards of everything with which he was connected, was the chief promoter of the scheme; and the Wey & Arun Canal was its essential central link. Work on the canal began in 1813 and was completed three years later; a comparatively short time, but there were no great engineering problems nor complicated lawsuits. The canal was 18½ miles long, able to take barges up to 13ft beam; there were 23 locks, no tunnels, 35 bridges, eight wharves, five lock houses and two small aqueducts. The works were designed by Josias Jessop, and the cost was a little over £100,000, not much over the original estimate.

But the procession of barges winding their way to and from London through the southern counties never materialised. With the end of the French war, coastal traffic revived, and there were too many impediments on the route, particularly on the Arun navigation, to make it attractive to merchants wanting to transport goods as quickly, easily and cheaply as possible. For many years, too, local trade was slow to develop; it was five years before the company was able to pay a dividend, and seven more years before it could pay a second. There was an increase in traffic on the opening of the Portsmouth & Arundel Canal in 1823, but the rapid failure of this waterway put things back much to where they were. In the 1830s, however, matters improved; local industries were developing along the route of the canal, and timber, coal, chalk, agricultural produce and seaweed for fertiliser were the principal cargoes. In 1837, Lord Egremont died; although his holdings in the Wey & Arun company showed a considerable loss, there is no doubt that the undertaking had been of great benefit to the countryside through which it passed, bringing employment, agricultural improvement and the establishment of local industries. Two years after his death, tolls on the Wey & Arun reached their highest figure, £2,524; but now the railways were beginning to penetrate the south (the Croydon Canal had succumbed in 1836), and the Wey & Arun, chronically short of water despite the construction of two windmills on George Rennie's recommendation, was in no state to provide stiff competition.

Yet, as for the time being no railway company wanted to use the line of the Wey & Arun, the canal survived until 1871. Indeed, it even gained revenue for transporting materials for railway construction at either end. But in 1865 the Horsham & Guildford branch became its direct competitor, running parallel to the canal for some 6 miles. The canal tolls were now so much reduced that little profit was made from carrying 3,000 tons of railway building materials. The works fell into disrepair and many shareholders lost hope; efforts were made by the Arun Navigation to keep the Wey & Arun open, for there was still something to gain from the little traffic it carried, but all efforts failed, the company went into liquidation and the canal was closed in 1871. William Stanton, the bargemaster of Bramley, continued to work the northern end of the canal for a few months more, but he died in the following year. Bits of the property were sold off, but some stretches today seem to have no legal owner at all.

The canal leaves the Wey, which is, of course, still a navigation, at Stonebridge Wharf, Shalford, 2 miles south of Guildford. The wharf is now a clutter of rather untidy moorings, backed by rows of summer caravans. It passes under the A281, and runs parallel with the road to Bramley. First left past Gosden School brings you to the site of a tannery and two bridges, one over the abandoned Horsham–Guildford railway, the other over the canal. Nothing remains of the Tanyard lock, but the Gosden aqueduct, carrying the canal over the Bramley stream, still stands—or rather one side of it does, the stonework of the other having been destroyed. The weed-filled dry bed continues southward past the site of another lock and the house where William Stanton used to live. It continues keeping company with the railway to Run Common, where it can be picked up from a minor road heading east from the A281. The road bridge over the canal has gone, but the cut on the south side now holds water, and the site of the Run Common wharf can be found about 50yd along. After another mile the railway leaves the canal, which continues south to Elmbridge Wharf, 1½ miles west of Cranleigh on B2130. Still watered, it winds southwards, crossing the A281: Compasses Bridge, ½ mile north west from Alfold Crossways, is by the gate of a very secret-looking airfield. The Three Compasses Inn, near the bridge, is where the Earl of Egremont, the municipal worthies of Guildford, and a company of friends and shareholders, drank and made speeches before embarking on a fleet of barges at the bridge for the inaugural voyage on the Wey & Arun. The bands that played then have long put away their instruments and the water under the bridge is weedy and stagnant.

The summit level of the canal is in Sidney Wood, which can be entered by a bridle path (TQ 026354). Having circled the grounds of a private house, it is easy to find the dry bed of the canal to your right, and to follow it through the wood. In the depths of the wood it is hard indeed to imagine that anyone could have visualised this as a main transport artery linking London with the south coast—hard enough to imagine a single rowing boat, let alone horse-drawn barges carrying timber and coal, even bullion from Portsmouth to the coffers of the Treasury in Westminster. Some of the lock sites can be discerned, but very little else remains except the cut itself curving its way through the closely planted trees. The lock house, now converted into an elegant private dwelling, is in the heart of the wood; this used to be the company's headquarters, and there are remains of the wharf, though not of the workshops which used to stand nearby. The course of the canal can be picked up the far side of the lock house, and followed until it leaves the wood 1½ miles west of Alfold and straightens out past Sidney Farm until it turns east near Loxwood.

A short distance along a public bridleway by the Onslow Arms at Loxwood, on B2133, is a well-preserved lock chamber with some fragments of the gates in the mud at the bottom; then the canal winds east through Brewhurst and rounds Drungewick Manor. The site of Drungewick aqueduct, demolished in 1957, can be seen from a minor road leading to the manor (TQ 061309). The remains of Drungewick lock are along the canal to the east of this point, but it may be a struggle to fight through to them.

Half a mile farther on, the canal picks up the course of the River Arun, which it follows on the western side southwards to the junction at Newbridge, on A272. The junction was actually on the south side of the road, but the canal bridge is now blocked.

More than most lost canals, the Wey & Arun leaves an abiding impression of improbability. Possibly the idea needed the ruthless engineering of a Telford to make it a success. Nevertheless, it was not the weakest link in the line from London to Portsmouth, and there are many worse ways of getting to London than by way of Sidney Wood.

OS sheet 182 (170 for the Shalford–Bramley section)
London's Lost Route to the Sea, by P. A. L. Vine (an excellent, fully detailed account of the London–Portsmouth line)
The Canals of South & South East England, by Charles Hadfield

THE PORTSMOUTH & ARUNDEL CANAL

The distance from Portsmouth to London by inland waterway would be 100 miles less than by coaster, and the Portsmouth & Arundel Canal was intended to complete the route of which the Thames, Wey, and Wey & Arun Canal were the other links. It was estimated to cost about £125,000; an Act was obtained in 1817, and the first section, the Chichester Canal branch, opened in 1822, the whole being completed one year later. The canal ran from Ford, on the Arun 2 miles south of Arundel, westward to Salterns on the Chichester Channel, with a short branch from Hunston to Southgate basin, Chichester. The course then became a dredged channel north of Thorney Island and Hayling Island; it entered Portsea Island at Milton locks and continued, as the Portsea Canal, for over 2 miles to the basins in Portsmouth. The total length was 27¾ miles. Apart from a feeder to the Chichester branch, water for the main section was supplied by a steam-powered pump at Ford; there were frequent complaints that salt water from the canal polluted domestic supplies and damaged crops. In 1831 the Portsea Canal, never a happy undertaking, was replaced by a cut at Cosham, north of the island, so that boats could navigate right into Portsmouth harbour. But no surgery could cure this ailing patient.

The trouble with the Portsmouth & Arundel was that traders did not want to use it. The complete London–Portsmouth journey took four days; there were 52 locks to pass and more than the usual inland waterway hazards of floods here and water shortage there. Moreover, although the controlling companies reduced their initial tolls, coastal shipping rates were lower still. In 1824 only 3,650 tons of freight travelled between the canal and London —less than one-twelfth of what had been hoped for. And most of the trade came down from London, there being little regular through traffic back except for a monthly load of bullion that continued until 1826. In the previous year the Portsmouth Barge Company, the largest traders on the canal, had sold out; then Lord Egremont, a major backer of this concern as of the Wey & Arun, gave up his shareholding. Trade dwindled to a few hundred tons a year. The efforts of the energetic manager of the company, George Palmer, brought about something of a revival between 1832 and 1836 (58 tons of soldiers' baggage and 1 ton of acorns were among the items carried to London in 1832), but receipts failed to cover even the cost of maintenance. Only the Chichester branch made a small profit. Then with the Victorian era improved coastal steam ships, better roads and extending railways made the Portsmouth & Arundel superfluous. The company met more infrequently; and then met not at all. Although not officially closed until 1896, the barge canal between Ford and Hunston had carried no traffic for about fifty years, and much of it was dry. The Chichester–Salterns length was transferred free to Chichester Corporation and continued to carry a little traffic until about 1906.

Now owned by West Sussex County Council, the Chichester Canal is still watered; the section by Salterns lock was reopened in 1932 as a base for yachts. The rest of this canal is preserved for fishing, and it is possible to walk the length of the towpath. The original bridges were iron swivel bridges, each named after one of the company's major shareholders; Poyntz Bridge, so inscribed, survives as a footbridge at Hunston, at the junction with the main line to Ford. Southgate basin in Chichester is at the end of Basin Road on the south side of the city, near the level crossing; a couple of the original buildings remain amongst later development and the dimensions of the basin appear to be unchanged.

Much of the bed of the canal to Ford can still be followed, but as there were no major engineering works and locks only at the ends there is little of any special interest. Anyone holidaying at Bognor Regis could take a few hours off from the crowded beach to inspect ½ mile of derelict waterway beside a minor road east of A29 at Lidsey; it ends at Lidsey Sewage Works. On the west of

Page 51   (above) *Chard Canal: the Tone aqueduct;* (below) *Torrington Canal: the Beam (or Rolle) aqueduct, over the Torridge*

Page 52   (above) *Grand Western Canal: aqueduct over the Tone near Nynehead;* (below) *Grand Western Canal: lift chamber, Nynehead*

Barnham, opposite the little church there is a farm track; this crosses the canal 150yd along. There are some fragments of a bridge; the canal can be clearly seen heading eastwards, but on the other side it has been completely obliterated.

At Yapton, on A2024, a rough road on the north side of 'The Shoulder of Mutton and Cucumbers' (an intriguing thought) leads to a well-preserved brick bridge over the canal, and you can walk alongside the bed to emerge in Canal Road. Between Yapton and Ford there is nothing to see. The canal joined the Arun just south of the railway, by the 'Ship & Anchor'. The bridge and locks were demolished some years ago and the entrance to the canal now belongs to the 'Ship & Anchor' marina and is used as a berth for yachts.

Much of the Portsea Canal was sold for railway development in the mid-nineteenth century, while Goldsmith Avenue has been built on the canal line. Portsea lock may still be found (SZ 678999). The upper courses of the brickwork of the wide lock are well preserved, but only three rotting stumps of timber are left of the outer gates. Some of the framework of the inner gates remains, and the canal extends for about 50yd, being used as a mooring for small boats, as far as the headquarters of the Langstone Harbour Fishermen's Association. Inland, Locksway Road leads to a caravan site, where there are traces of an embankment, and there is a hump in Ironbridge Lane where it crosses the course, though no other evidence of a bridge.

The Portsmouth & Arundel Canal cost a great deal of money—not far short of £200,000—and for its shareholders and employees it was a financial disaster. But, like the Wey & Arun, it was a work of imagination and good intent. For a few years boats did sail through Sussex to London, and for a few more years the canal brought sailing ships close to the spire of Chichester Cathedral. The canal's greatest legacy may well be Turner's splendid painting in the Tate Gallery. At current market prices, this might just about repay the original shareholders for their unfortunate investments.

OS sheet 181
London's Lost Route to the Sea, by P. A. L. Vine (see also Wey & Arun)
The Canals of South & South East England, by Charles Hadfield

THE CROYDON CANAL

'The union of the River Thames and the English Channel through the Croydon Canal' was a toast proposed at the shareholders' dinner on the opening of the Croydon Canal in 1809. That there was ever a Croydon Canal at all seems improbable enough to the present-day wanderer through the suburban monotony of Deptford, Lewisham and Penge; but there is a print of 1815 showing a white horse drawing a barge along the quiet waterway, with a lock to the left, fences and gates in the foreground, a hill rising above the village of Deptford in the distance and only the occasional cottage amongst the rural serenity of fields and trees. And Croydon, then a town of only 7,000 people, was linked with the Thames not only by the canal, but also by the double-track Surrey Iron Railway, the first public railway company in the world. Horse-drawn truck and horse-drawn barge kept pace with each other for some twenty-five years.

The Croydon Canal, 9¼ miles long, left the Grand Surrey Canal ¾ mile west of Deptford Dockyard, and climbed by 28 locks, taking boats 60ft by 9ft, to Croydon, being supplied by two specially constructed reservoirs and a pumping station at the Croydon summit. Coal and general goods were brought up to Croydon, and stone, lime, fuller's earth and timber taken down. Trade was below expectations, and the canal, which had cost £127,000 to construct, was expensive to run and never paid a dividend of more than 1 per cent. Unusually, there was a small revenue from pleasure boating; the waterway passed through pleasant villages and beautiful countryside, especially at Penge Forest. In 1834, the London & Croydon Railway began negotiating for the purchase of the canal for the route of its line; as the parties could not agree on a figure, the matter went to an independent jury, who valued the canal not merely as a property but as a navigation; their figure of £40,250 was much nearer what the canal shareholders had wanted than what the railway company had offered. The deal was completed and the canal closed in 1836; but before it was drained it overflowed and flooded 200 houses. West Croydon station was built on the canal wharf, and the railway used the bed of the canal for much of its line.

There is very little of the Croydon Canal left to see. There are some retaining walls at West Croydon, which can be seen from the car park beside the station, and 'Brick Bridge' incorporates a canal bridge. Near Anerley station is a small pleasure garden known as Betts Park, between Anerley Road and Weighton Road. Here about ¼ mile of the canal has been preserved as an ornamental water-garden; it has been lined with concrete and is cleaned out every winter. In 1840 the railway sold day tickets partly for the benefit of anglers visiting this stretch, which was then abounding in fish.

South Norwood Lake, a 7 acre sheet of water south of Penge, was one of the original reservoirs of the canal. Some of the railway retaining walls may also be canal works, but this is difficult to establish. The probable junction with the Grand Surrey remains as a short arm and basin off the main canal. But withal, in the words of F. Slous, writing in 1843:

'The magic steam whistle has sounded his knell,
And the spirit is lost of the Croydon Canal.'

OS sheet 'Greater London'
The Canals of South & South East England, by Charles Hadfield

THE THAMES & MEDWAY CANAL

The original estimate of the cost of a canal to join the Thames and the Medway was £24,576, made by Ralph Dodd in 1799. The Act was obtained in the following year, and work on the Thames end at Gravesend soon began; but other engineers who were consulted, including Rennie and Ralph Walker, criticised Dodd's original line and recommended tunnelling instead of cutting through the chalk hills between Higham and Strood, the town on the Medway opposite to Rochester. As the years passed the work was delayed and the estimates grew. In the event, the time taken to complete the canal was three years longer than its duration as a through working waterway. And the cost at opening in 1824 was ten times greater than Dodd's estimate.

When completed, the canal was 7 miles long, able to take 60 ton sailing barges, with large locks at either end, and an enormous tunnel. Trade was in coal, hops and general merchandise, and a

Maidstone–London run in about twenty-four hours, avoiding the
sometimes difficult sea-passage round N Foreland, had its attrac-
tions. Because of the tides, traffic built up at certain times of day
and too many barges wanted to use the tunnel at once; hence in
1830 it was opened up at the point of lowest cover to make a
passing place. The original length, 3,946yd, made it the second
longest canal tunnel constructed in Britain but far the largest in
bore, being generally 27ft above water level and 26ft 6in wide,
including a towpath. An astronomer's telescope was used to
calculate the line.

Although it does not seem that any dividends were ever paid,
the canal kept reasonably busy during its working life. In the
early 1840s, however, as railway expansion began, the shareholders began to appreciate the potential value of the asset at their
disposal and, turning themselves into the Gravesend & Rochester
Railway & Canal Company, signed a contract for the construction
of a single-track railway alongside the canal from Gravesend to
Higham and then through the tunnels, with one rail laid on the
towpath and the other supported from the canal bed, navigation
continuing meanwhile. A railway station was built at Strood, a
few hundred yards south of the canal basin.

For about eighteen months trains and barges used the tunnels
side by side; then the South Eastern Railway bought the Gravesend & Rochester for rather over £300,000, filled in the canal from
Higham to the Frindsbury (Strood) basin, and laid double tracks
through the tunnel. Renamed the Gravesend & Rochester, the
remaining section of the canal survived for eighty-seven more
years, being used by the local farmers, while the Gravesend basin
was quite busy with the unloading of river craft and boat-repairing
and hiring. In 1934, however, the Southern Railway abandoned
the canal.

The best way to see the canal, apart from the basins, is by train
from Gravesend to Strood, a thirteen-minute journey. After about
a mile, the canal appears, a stretch of weedy water, beside the line
on the north; they run parallel for 2 miles when the canal loops
northwards, rejoining the railway just before Higham station.
Past the station the short cutting before the tunnel begins. After
1,530yd there is a brief flash of daylight as the passing place is
reached; then after another 2,329yd you emerge from the Strood
portal, which has been recently reconstructed. The railway makes

for Strood station, while the course of the canal continues straight on to the basin at Frindsbury. Here the lock gates and mechanism are still in position; the lock was built large enough to take ships up to 300 tons. The cathedral city of Rochester, across the river, still preserves a little of its Dickensian flavour—the city of *Edwin Drood*.

Back at Gravesend, the entrance into the Thames is at the eastern end of the riverside lawns, where the turbans of elderly Sikhs lend additional colour to the scene. The locks are still workable, and part of the basin is still used as a mooring for light craft. By the swing bridge over the lock into the river there is a row of three canal cottages. Standing on the bridge, watching the water lapping at the lock gates, the men busying themselves with their boats, and the Canal Tavern in the background, if you ignore the muddy desolation to left and right it is possible to imagine the Thames & Medway once more as a going concern.

OS sheet 171
The Canals of South & South East England, by Charles Hadfield

THE ROYAL MILITARY CANAL

Here and there, especially in coastal areas, evidence of anti-invasion preparations can be found. Concrete pill-boxes and gun emplacements lurk in corners by road junctions and bridges, forts now for children or refuges for lovers or tramps. A more impressive anti-invasion undertaking, however, dates from the war against Napoleon. The Royal Military Canal loops inland from the coast east of Hythe to Winchelsea Beach, defence against a landing on the Romney and Welland Marshes. It incorporates parts of the Rivers Rother and Brede and, backed by a parapet and a military road, still has a formidable appearance.

The canal was constructed as a result of a report by Lt Col Brown, Assistant Quartermaster-General, who later supervised the building of the section east of the Rother. As well as providing a physical barrier against an invading force, the canal could be used for transporting troops and deploying gun-boats. With the canal as a strong line of defence, it would not be necessary to flood the marshes if invasion were threatened, except as a last resort in

face of overwhelming numbers. Brown's report, supported by
General Dundas, i/c Southern District, and by the Duke of York,
who was Commander-in-Chief, was received with enthusiasm by
William Pitt and work was quickly put in hand. Rennie was appointed consultant and work began with civilian contractors in
1803. It was finished by the end of 1806, military labour having
replaced the civilians who were falling behind time. The total cost
was about the same as the estimate—£200,000.

By the time the canal was completed the war had taken a new
turn and the threat of invasion had passed. The Government set
up an impressive body of commissioners, including the holders of
many of the chief offices of state, to organise the canal on a
commercial basis, while also maintaining it should it be needed
for military purposes. Modest but steady revenue accrued through
the nineteenth century, from canal and road tolls and the sale of
grass from the parapet and surrounding land. In 1837, the canal
became the responsibility of the Ordnance. Commercial traffic
continued until 1909.

The eastern end of the RMC is at Shorncliffe, by the Hythe
boundary on the Folkestone side. It is a few yards from the sea
wall, in the angle of the junction where the Hythe sea-front road
meets A259. There are no impressive works, only a stone landing-
stage and a sluice to take surplus water off to the sea. The canal
runs due west, behind the golf-course of the Imperial Hotel and
through the centre of Hythe, where it is under the control of the
council. The canal has been neatly edged where it runs through
the tidy park in Hythe; pleasure-boats use it in the summer
months. It continues west out of Hythe, with high ground on its
northern side; the Military Road is a footpath along the northern
bank. By St Rumwold's Church it turns south west; the water is
protected for fishing, and fierce notices warn you to keep away
from it.

Between Warehorne and Appledore, the RMC is owned by the
National Trust. This is an especially fine stretch; the canal is more
like a river, wide and healthy-looking, lined with good trees.
From Appledore, a road takes the west bank. Most of the canal
was cut in a series of shallow 'steps', so that guns could be posi-
tioned on each 'riser' to cover a length of canal. The effect of this
(it can be seen on the OS sheet) is very noticeable from this road.

Three and a half miles from Appledore is Iden lock, where the canal joins the Rother. The lock has been replaced by a sluice, but the chamber, 72ft by 16ft, is intact and a substantial cottage stands beside it. The road follows the Rother into Rye, and A259 follows the Brede towards Winchelsea. The western section of the RMC begins where the road to Winchelsea Beach leaves A259, immediately before Winchelsea itself. No lock was constructed here, and it seems as if this western section was never navigated. It is a lesser affair; a comparatively narrow stretch of water leading around the edge of Pett Level and inaccessible by road. It terminates at Cliff End, the west end of Winchelsea Beach. Again there is no basin; the canal just stops by a turn on the Pett–Winchelsea Beach road. The Market Stores are on one side, a white cottage on the other, and a public convenience where the bank of the canal would be if it went on any farther. A few unhappy-looking bungalows have been built on its northern side.

Although the water flows throughout, the RMC would not be fully navigable without the replacement of Iden lock (and the lock on the Rother section) and of various culverts by properly built bridges. It seems at the moment unlikely that anything of this kind will be done. At present the RMC is leased to the Kent River Authority and the provision of drainage, irrigation, fishing, and pleasure-boating in Hythe remain its functions. Last-war pill-boxes on its banks are an odd reminder of its original purpose.

OS sheets 173 (Hythe) and 184 (Winchelsea–5 miles from Shorncliffe)
The Canals of South & South East England, by Charles Hadfield
The Royal Military Canal, by P. A. L. Vine

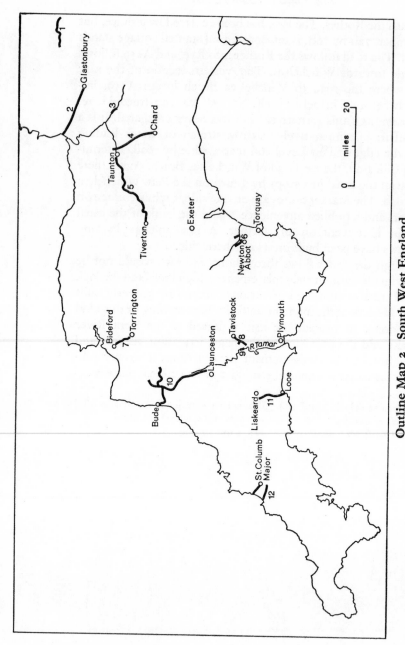

Outline Map 2 South West England

1 The Dorset & Somerset Canal
2 The Glastonbury Canal
3 The Westport Canal
6 The Stover and the Hackney Canals
7 The Torrington Canal
10 The Bude Canal
11 The Liskeard & Looe Union Canal

Chapter 2: *The South West*

THE DORSET & SOMERSET CANAL

The Dorset & Somerset is the archetype of 'the canal that never was'. The scheme was an ambitious one; a 49 mile waterway was to connect the Kennet & Avon, near Bradford, with the region of Sturminster Newton, with an 11 mile branch from Nettlebridge to Frome. Coal, clay and agricultural produce were to be the main cargoes. An Act in 1796 authorised the raising of £150,000. William Bennet was appointed surveyor, and it was decided that the branch, likely to produce the largest profit from coal carrying, was to be constructed first.

The branch, however, or about 8 miles of it, was the only part to be constructed at all. It was estimated to cost just over £30,000, and more than double that amount was subscribed; but by 1803 all that money, and more, had been spent, and work stopped, never to be restarted. Costs had proved far greater than the estimate; prices had risen and priorities altered; local enthusiasm waned and died. A pamphlet published in 1825 sought to revive interest in the canal, listed the works completed and appealed for funds to complete the branch and to build the main line, but it met with no response.

The Dorset & Somerset carried no traffic. Some sections were filled with water for a time, but gaps between sections were never constructed where local contractors failed to start work. Nevertheless, although it disappeared from the 1in OS map in the mid-nineteenth century, a fair amount of it remains and is not too difficult to trace. The section from Nettlebridge, a small village on the Fosse Way, does not seem to have been dug; the canal began at a basin about ½ mile west of Edford, at the bottom of Stratton Common where there was a water supply. Behind the 'Duke of Cumberland' at Edford (ST 669489) you can see a packhorse bridge carrying the old road from the coal pits on the Common; this bridge crosses the canal, which can be followed as a marked depression in the ground to the west until the site of the basin is reached. By the road there is a depression with some masonry lining, which may have been an approach to a bridge. East of the road at Edford the line can be followed along a number of stiles;

it passes through a cutting and emerges at Coleford, a precipitous and partly attractive village. Here, lurking on the eastern side of the north–south road into the village, is what the 1825 pamphlet described as 'a noble and stupendous aqueduct'. It is now smothered in ivy, has lost its parapet, and has acquired the local nickname of 'Hucky Duck'.

A tunnel was planned near Goodeaves Farm, a little to the east, but only some work on a cutting was done; then an old branch railway covers the bed as far as Vobster. It can be found again where the main road crosses it by a well-preserved bridge ½ mile south of Vobster Cross (ST 705492), and then it swings north, being rejoined by the old railway making towards the main line to Frome.

The canal keeps on the 425ft contour as far as Barrow Hill. But here a descent became unavoidable. To reach Murtry, just north of Frome, the canal would have to drop 210ft in little over a mile. Originally, conventional lockage was proposed, but on the plans the words 'by caissons' were substituted. James Fussell's 'Machine or Balance Lock' was patented in 1798, and this was what was intended for use on the Dorset & Somerset.

Before reaching Barrow Hill, the canal line leaves the present railway, heading south east to Frome, and runs roughly parallel to it but higher up the hillside to the north. There is a minor road from the A362 to Mells; if you enter the fields to the east, keeping the railway line below you in sight, you will pick up the line of the canal and come in a few hundred yards to a large depression with trees growing in and around it. This is the site of the first experimental 'Balance Lock', which was in working order and on exhibition in 1800 and 1802. This was a double lock chamber of masonry, 20ft deep, divided by a central buttress. On the approaches at top and bottom the canal was split into two channels. Boats were floated into open watertight caissons, the ends of which were closed by hatches. Stop gates were shut on the canal, and the caissons were raised and lowered like a pair of scales, the beam being mounted on the central buttress and suspending the caissons by wheels and chains. Into the descending caisson water could be admitted, to increase the weight, and then run off at the bottom, while lengths of chain attached to the underside of each caisson compensated for the weight of the suspending chain above. According to the patent, lifts of up to 100ft could be achieved by this method.

From this unlikely scene of industrial adventure, the windswept hillside where thousands once milled to inspect Fussell's engineering masterpiece, the canal can be followed eastward, with a break here and there where the plough has eradicated it, to a small wood, some ¾ mile farther on. Now the cut becomes much more clearly defined and is surprisingly free of weed—possibly because it was puddled with clay but never filled with water. Soon the channel divides at the top of the first of four large pits, each some 20ft deep. The pits are not connected and clearly were never completed, although some masonry work has been done on the first three. Tenders for five 'balance locks' to be built hereabouts had been invited, and there are signs that a little work may have been started on the fifth.

There is now a gap of nearly a mile. The canal as planned would have drawn nearer to the present railway, which would have crossed it about 200yd before going under the A362 Frome–Radstock road. If you cross a stile on the south side of the bridge over the railway, some 2 miles north of Frome centre, you come within a few yards to an attractive, tree-lined stretch of canal cutting (ST 762498). This leads you shortly to the handsome three-arched Murtry aqueduct over the stream that runs north up Vallis Vale. On the near side of the aqueduct is an odd little skew arch and what looks like an overnight stop for vagrants; on the far side is the railway line. Back on the road, a few yards farther north the A362 crosses the stream; looking over the west parapet, you can see the remains of the old road bridge below.

The branch was planned to join the projected main line to the north of the centre of Frome, in the region of ST 774486, the main line being planned to come up from the south east approximately as the railway was later constructed. This area is now being developed with housing schemes and sewer farms; apart from a length of retaining wall (known locally as the 'Roman Wall') which was built, no sign of canal work remains.

Of the works listed in the 1825 pamphlet, including 13 arched bridges and a host of other items, only those mentioned above survive. £66,000 was spent in all on the Dorset & Somerset, most of it on the lock pit excavations and the Coleford Aqueduct. The inhabitants of the cottage beside the latter must have the most expensive garden shed in the kingdom.

OS sheet 166
The Dorset & Somerset Canal, by Kenneth R. Clew (includes itinerary)
Old Mendip, by Robin Atthill
The Canals of South West England, by Charles Hadfield

THE GLASTONBURY CANAL

Born late and dying young, the Glastonbury Canal had a life of only twenty-one years. Very much a Glastonbury project, it was opened in 1833; just over 14 miles long, it linked Glastonbury with the estuary of the Brue at Highbridge, by a tide lock. Costing about £30,000, it was built mainly to the designs of Rennie; there were two aqueducts and one lock, 64ft by 18ft 6in, on the canal, and swing bridges where the roads crossed it. South Wales coal, and manufactured goods from Birmingham and the north were brought inland, and local products, including timber and cider, were exported. The canal also helped to drain the marshy land through which it was cut.

Only thirteen years after the canal was opened, the Bristol & Exeter Railway began negotiations to buy it. There was little trade at this time and the investment looked a dubious one, particularly as the Act authorising the railway's purchase stipulated that the canal be kept operating and in repair. As the peat bottom of the waterway was gradually getting nearer the top, and maintenance had been neglected, the few boats there were found navigation increasingly difficult. Keeping the gates at Highbridge closed to increase the depth of water brought about floods in 1850, and keeping them open to clean the channel made navigation almost impossible. Thereupon the Bristol & Exeter sold the canal to the Somerset Central Railway for the building of its line, except for a short stretch at Highbridge which came under the control of the Commission of Sewers. Through carrying material for the construction of the railway the canal enjoyed a brief period of comparative prosperity, before closure in 1854. The Highbridge portion remained open until abandoned in 1936, and has since been filled in.

Tracing the course of the Glastonbury Canal is not easy as parts of its line through the peaty lands have been used for other artificial waterways. At Highbridge, the tide lock and basin were on the west side of A38, just south of the junction with B3139.

Mooring rings can be found in the wall of a yard behind a public house, and the road bridge with a length of cut beyond it can be defined. For some 5 miles east, the canal followed the line of the Brue; then its line was taken for the Cripps River and the South Drain—which the canal itself had taken when it was constructed. By Edington Burtle the old railway took up the canal line; some remains of the lock still exist west of Shapwick. Through Shapwick and Ashcott the canal course lies on the south side of the abandoned railway. East of Ashcott station the canal crossed the South Drain by a cast-iron aqueduct, of which only the stone abutments remain. Then the railway crossed the canal, which took up the course of the Cuckoo Ditch on its north side. Half a mile east of the crossing at Sharpham the canal crossed the Brue by a double arch iron aqueduct; again, the stone abutments can be seen. Approaching Glastonbury the canal made a sharp right-angle turn, which must have caused its navigators some difficulty, and passed by New Close Farm; the final trace is a depression by the old level crossing on B3151. A timber yard covers the site of the basin, and there are no remains of any of the wharf buildings. Several of the bridges crossed in search of the Glastonbury are modifications of the original swing bridges, narrowed and fixed.

OS sheet 165
The Canals of South West England, by Charles Hadfield

THE WESTPORT CANAL

Four miles from Ilminster, on B3168, is Westport, the terminal of the Westport Canal. This 2 mile canal, opened in 1840, was built as part of a scheme to improve the navigation of the River Parrett, to counter opposition from the Chard Canal, then nearing completion. The whole scheme included rebuilding the old bridge at Langport and making navigable 10½ miles of the river; locks had to be built on the river, but none was needed for the Westport Canal.

The undertaking had some modest success to start with, but the Westport Canal particularly was affected by the opening of the Chard Canal in 1842, its traffic being barely half what had been estimated. Then in the mid-1850s competition from the railway began to take effect, and receipts from tolls began a rapid decline. They ceased altogether in 1875 when Langport lock was ordered to be kept open as the Navigation Company had failed to repair drains, which they had no money to do. Three years later the Somerset Drainage Commissioners took over the navigation, and refused an appeal from local inhabitants to keep the Westport Canal open for trade.

The canal is still maintained for drainage and its accommodation bridges are intact. At Westport on the east side of the road is an attractive group of buildings, including a large warehouse, by the canal basin. Road and canal are parallel for ⅓ mile; then the canal heads north-eastward to the edge of West Moor. At Hambridge, the road bridge has been lowered; from here to the River Isle there is a pleasant ½ mile walk along the towpath, with frisky heifers watching your every step. A floodgate has been constructed 100yd from the junction with the river. The Isle joins the Parrett 1 mile to the north east.

OS sheet 177
The Canals of South West England, by Charles Hadfield

THE CHARD CANAL

With the exception of the Manchester Ship Canal, the Chard was the last of the main-line canals to be made. It was also one of the shortest-lived, lasting a mere twenty-five years before it succumbed to the railway. Several schemes were proposed in the great years of canal construction which would have routed a waterway through Chard; indeed, Moule's Inland Navigation map of 1831 shows Chard comfortably situated on the English & Bristol Channels Canal, a ship canal for which an Act was obtained in 1825 but of which never a yard was dug. However, nothing happened until in 1833 the Bridgwater & Taunton Company became concerned about a rival scheme to improve the navigation of the Parrett and link Chard and Ilminster to it by canal—which would draw off trade from their own waterway—and listened with interest to representations from Bristol merchants on behalf of a Chard Canal Company. This would be formed to build a canal from Creech St Michael, on the Bridgwater & Taunton, to Chard;

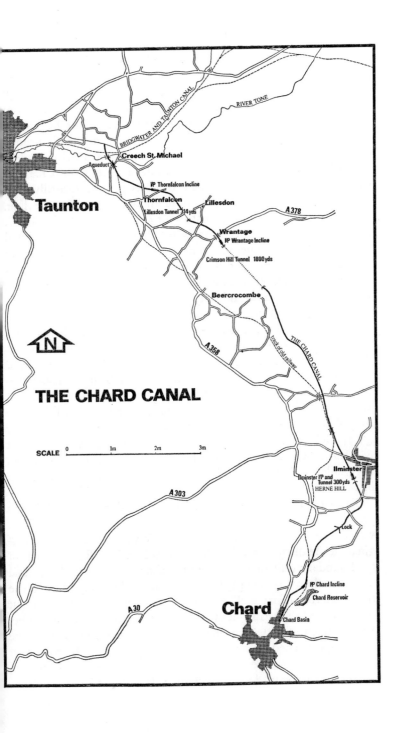

RIVER TONE

BRIDGWATER AND TAUNTON CANAL

Creech St. Michael

Aqueduct

Taunton

VP Thornfalcon Incline

Thornfalcon

Lillesdon

Lillesdon Tunnel 314 yds

A 378

Wrantage

VP Wrantage Incline

Crimson Hill Tunnel 1800 yds

Beercrocombe

A 358

THE CHARD CANAL

track of old railway

N

THE CHARD CANAL

SCALE 0   1m   2m   3m

A 303

Ilminster

Ilminster VP and
Tunnel 300 yds
HERNE HILL

Lock

VP Chard Incline

Chard Reservoir

A 30

Chard

Chard Basin

James Green's survey of a line for tub-boats, replete with lifts, inclined planes and tunnels was accepted. The people of Chard were not very impressed by the plan, and subscribed only a small proportion of the capital required, the bulk of which came from the Bristol backers. Before work began, Green lost his job as engineer; his successor, a young man named Sydney Hall, decided to dispense with the lifts, and action commenced in 1835.

The country was difficult, with a fall of 231ft from Chard to Creech, and the original estimate of costs proved absurdly low. Acts were necessary to raise more money; the 13½ mile line, opened throughout in 1842, cost about £140,000. For their money, the shareholders got three tunnels, totalling 2,414yd, four inclined planes, two major aqueducts, one lock and a stop lock. They did not get any dividends. Trade in coal from S Wales and the Forest of Dean via Bridgwater to Chard developed quite well, but there was little return traffic and only poor trade in other merchandise. Tolls were low, and there was competition from the Bristol & Exeter Railway on the northern part of the route. Moves were soon made to convert the canal, or part of it, to a railway, but as this could not be done until the mortgages had been paid and more capital raised the canal continued in being. Rivalry developed between the Bristol & Exeter and the London & South Western railways over who was to take over the Chard line; the Bristol & Exeter got in first and bought the canal in 1867 for £5,945. The year before, this company had bought the Bridgwater & Taunton Canal, for £64,000, but this waterway is still open and navigable by light craft today. The Chard Canal was shut down in 1868.

The site of Chard basin is now occupied by B. G. Wyatt's premises in Furnham Road, on the north side of the town. Two warehouses have been incorporated in Wyatt's mill, and the original facade of the canal buildings faces Furnham Road. Much of the boundary wall survives from the time of the canal. The canal heads north east beside the line of the disused railway, though the traces are fragmentary. The reservoir constructed to supply most of the water to the canal lies beside the minor road to Chaffcombe, a fine stretch of water screened by trees. Chard Common incline can be approached by a footpath from the Chaffcombe road as it rounds the end of the reservoir. This was a single-track incline, taking the tub-boats down in a cradle 86ft from the Chard summit.

When the canal was being cut hereabouts, a skeleton was dug up, supposed to be that of a certain Hankins, hanged for murder. The incline was operated by a water turbine, the cradle being drawn up the rails by a notoriously fragile rope, later replaced by a wire cable. There is nothing left of the machinery, but the reverse slope at the top may be discerned.

There is not much left of the canal for the next 2 miles, though there is a stretch of cut on the north of the road to Knowle St Giles, ¼ mile west of the telephone box. The remains of the canal's one lock (ST 351123) are near a covert about ½ mile due west of Peasmarsh. For another mile the line continues north east; then just before it is crossed by A3037, by the junction with the Kingstone road, it swings north north west. An embankment is visible from the main road, and a group of cottages by the junction have been built actually on the canal. From the west side of A3037 the bed can be followed towards the slopes of Herne Hill. It leads to the approach to Ilminster tunnel, which can also be reached from the back of a small housing estate on the south of Ilminster. The approach has been filled by tipping, and the tunnel has been recently demolished, apart from some of the brick facing and the wide arch at the northern end. Ilminster tunnel, 300yd long, was wide enough for two boats to pass. It was not on Green's original plan but was added by Hall, after some preliminary cutting had been done, traces of which could be seen on top of the tunnel itself. A few yards from the north portal, the Ilminster inclined plane begins. This, like the remaining two inclines, was double track, with the boats carried in caissons. It took the canal down 82½ft. Now it slopes down behind some newly built houses to the edge of the school playing field. A lock may have been built just north of Ilminster, but this has not been established. The canal then passed by the end of Wharf lane, was crossed by A303 a mile west of the centre of Ilminster, and was carried over the River Isle at the same point later used by the old railway. In the next 3 miles there is little to see. Then there is an embankment south east of Beercrocombe, ¼ mile east of Keysey's Dairy House. Next comes the approach to the south end of Crimson Hill tunnel, the portal of which has collapsed.

The north portal of the tunnel (ST 311221) lies to the south of Wrantage, on A378, ¼ mile south east of the Canal Inn. It can be reached from a short way up the minor road to Curry Mallet. The

E

portal is stone-faced and well shaped; the tunnel is stone-lined, with regularly spaced holes in the sides. The probability is that these were used for drainage purposes. There are shackles in the roof on to which the bargemen could fasten hooks attached to a harness which they wore, so that they could 'walk' the boats through—rather like punting, only pulling on a chain instead of pushing with a pole. A pump has recently been installed just inside the tunnel, to draw out water for use on the local farm. The ruins of the tunnel-keeper's house lie near the portal. Leading down from the portal is the Wrantage incline, lowering the canal 27½ft to a clearly defined pound. A tree-lined stretch of canal leads to an embankment and the abutment of the aqueduct that used to take the Chard over A378. The embankment levels down north of the road; the canal passes under a stone bridge south of Lillesdon, entering a cutting leading to the south portal of Lillesdon tunnel. Because of filling, only the top of the arch is visible. The tunnel, 314yd long, takes the canal under a minor road and emerges as the ground falls away in a field (ST 295235). There is barbed wire around the immediate area, presumably for the safety of cows. The north portal, which in style resembles Crimson Hill, is in fairly good order.

Thornfalcon incline, dropping the canal a final 28ft, is about a mile farther on, on the north of the village, near Canal Farm. There is a bridge over the canal on the road from Thornfalcon to Creech. The aqueduct over the Ruishton–Creech road has gone, but the heavy abutments remain. From here, the Chard continues northwards for its final ½ mile on a massive embankment across the flood plain of the Tone. There are arches for the flood water. The elegant three-arched aqueduct over the Tone survives, though without its parapet. The piers are of stone, the arches of brick. After the Tone comes the railway line; then, on a stone-walled and buttressed embankment, the last few yards to the junction with the Bridgwater & Taunton. A private garden has been planted on the end of the canal, with the towpath as the garden path. The house probably used to be the old toll house. The stop lock and towpath bridge at the junction have disappeared completely.

While at Creech St Michael, it is worth having a look at the Bridgwater & Taunton, and sparing a thought for its future. Now classified as a 'remainder waterway' and, because of fixed bridges, unnavigable except to very light craft, it is one of the very few 'living' canals left in the south west.

OS sheet 177
The Canals of South West England, by Charles Hadfield
The Chard Canal; Chard History Group, publication no 1

THE GRAND WESTERN CANAL

The Grand Western, as originally conceived, was to have been part of an ambitious scheme of the Canal Age for joining the English and Bristol Channels. A Bristol–Taunton line had been proposed; the Grand Western was to be a continuation of this, a wide waterway from Taunton to Topsham, south of Exeter, which could take barges up to 15ft beam capable of sailing between Exmouth and the South Wales ports. There were to be branches to Tiverton and Cullompton as well, and Robert Whitworth, who made the first survey in 1792, estimated the cost at £166,724, although he envisaged narrow locks. The canal committee wanted to get it right. They called in a succession of engineers, including Longbotham, Jessop (who proposed widening the waterway) and Rennie, and the estimate gradually increased.

An Act was obtained in 1796 for a canal 36½ miles long, but the French war, increasing prices and the failure of the Bristol–Taunton scheme combined to ensure that for several years nothing was done. Then the Kennet & Avon company became interested in the possibility of using the proposed canal for extending their own waterway to Exeter, and took over a large proportion of the shares. Work began in 1810, not at either end but approximately in the middle, at Holcombe, on the summit level and on the branch to Tiverton. It looked straightforward enough; no locks were needed on the branch, and the company reckoned there would be a healthy return from the lime and limestone traffic from the quarries at Canonsleigh, by the canal, to Tiverton. But because of difficulties with the ground it took four years to complete the 11 miles of the branch, at a cost of over £220,000, almost three times as much as Rennie had estimated. And it took twenty years before receipts edged up to top £1,000 pa, instead of the £10,000 that had been expected.

Meanwhile, activity had been recommenced to the north east,
and in 1827 the Bridgwater & Taunton (the rump, as it were, of
the Bristol–Taunton proposal) was opened. This reawakened interest in the possibility of continuing, to some extent, with the
original plan for the Grand Western, and James Green, the well-
known West Country canal engineer, suggested to the shareholders that the canal be completed from the branch to Taunton,
and later, if successful, to Exeter. Economy now being a prime
consideration, Green recommended a narrow canal to take tub-
boats 26ft by 6ft 6in, up to four of which could be drawn by one
horse. Seven lifts and one inclined plane would raise the canal
262ft from its junction with the Bridgwater in Taunton to the end
of the Tiverton branch at Lowdwells, near Holcombe, a distance
of 13½ miles. Green's plan and estimate of £61,324 were accepted,
and work on the 'main line' began in 1831, thirty-five years after
the passing of the original Act and very differently from what had
been then envisaged.

Green's lifts resembled Fussell's 'Balance Lock', built experi-
mentally on the unfinished Dorset & Somerset Canal over thirty
years previously. They were masonry chambers of varying heights,
each divided longitudinally by a central masonry pier. Boats were
floated into caissons at top and bottom, and as one went up the
other went down; extra water was introduced to the upper caisson
to start the descent, and a length of chain hung from the caissons
to act as a counter-balance as they ascended or descended. There
was also a braking system on the connecting pulleys. In six of the
lifts Green found it necessary to install 3ft locks at the bottom, as
the descending caissons would not sink to the level of the lower
pound; the more sophisticated engineering of the Greenham lift,
the last—and largest—to be built, enabled the lock to be dis-
pensed with so that this was much quicker in operation than the
others.*

During the next five years, the line inched its way south-
westward. There was trouble at Greenham, where the lift partly
collapsed and had to be rebuilt, and worse trouble at the Wellisford
inclined plane. This, operated by the bucket-in-well system like
the Hobbacott Down incline on the Bude Canal, refused to work;
Green, who ought, if anyone, to have known about inclines,

* Green's description of the lifts, from *Transactions* of the Institution
of Civil Engineers, has been reprinted by the Waterways Museum.

having built seven of them beforehand, must bear the responsibility for faulty design. After having lost both money and patience, the company dismissed Green in 1836, appointed Capt Twisden in his place—and promptly borrowed money from him—and engaged W. A. Provis to examine the works. Provis reported that the buckets on the incline were not nearly large enough to hold sufficient water to raise the 8 ton boats. Money was scraped together to buy a steam engine to power the incline instead, and to complete the Greenham lift, and in 1838 all that was to be built of the Grand Western was opened.

The canal left the Bridgwater & Taunton by a stop-lock at Firepool, near where the Taunton railway goods depot now stands, and within a few yards ascended 23½ft by the first of the lifts. The site of the junction can be seen at the bottom of Canal Road, as can a portion of the retaining wall of the lift, now forming part of the boundary between the gardens of a row of cottages and the goods yard. A goods shed now stands where the lift once was. The down relief railway line has been laid over the course of the canal, and some of the stones of an aqueduct have been used in the railway bridge over Station Road. By the bridge over Staplegrove Road the railway leaves the canal, which curves south-westward but has now been obliterated by allotments. Traces can be found of the line of the 'Parliamentary Cut' which led from the canal to the Tone, but it is not known whether this cut was completed, let alone used.

About a mile to the west of the town the canal passes under the well-preserved Silk Mills bridge, and then runs out across the fields just south of the railway and north of the Tone. South of Norton Fitzwarren the bed is clearly defined; by crossing the footbridge at the station and walking across the field you will come to it, stretching away in each direction. A hundred yards or so to the west (ST 192254) is the site of the Norton lift, the smallest, which rose 12½ft. There is no masonry left, but the change in level is quite clear.

The next lift, Allerford, with a rise of 19ft, is just over a mile farther along the canal, reached from the level-crossing by the 'Victory' inn. The bed of the canal, still holding some water, is approached through two white gates on the road south of the crossing, and the remains of the lift, with some stonework still visible, are a little farther on. The canal continues westward on an

embankment, crossing the Hillfarance brook in ⅔ mile. The Allerford lift is sometimes known as the Hillfarance, which has caused
confusion as to how many lifts there actually were—the same one
being counted twice under different names. There is not much
indication of the canal for the next mile until a road bridge by
Trefusis Farm, north west of Bradford-on-Tone. Half a mile on,
the canal is crossed by the railway on an embankment, and almost
immediately ascends 38ft by the Trefusis lift (ST 161229). This is
in a small copse in the garden of Lift Cottage, on private land, to
the south of the road between East Nynehead and Bradford.
Although the site has been used as a rubbish dump, the high back
wall of the lift is in good condition, with clear indication of the
central dividing pier.

One and a half miles farther west, the canal crosses the Tone by
a fine, though crumbling, single arch aqueduct. The narrow iron
trough which took boats across in single file still remains, with the
towpath beside it. The aqueduct can best be reached from the road
joining Nynehead to A38, 1 mile east of Wellington. This road
crosses the canal a short distance north of the railway bridge, with
the old Wharf cottage at the roadside. The aqueduct is ¼ mile
east; it is easier to walk along the edge of the field than to battle
through the overgrown canal itself, here on a low embankment.
Following the course through a copse on the west of the road, you
come in a few minutes to an impressive masonry chamber—the
Nynehead lift. This has been recently cleared out and surveyed,
and is by far the best preserved of all the lifts, with some of the
original ironwork still embedded in the walls. It took the canal up
24ft. The foundations of the lift cottage are to the right of the lift
as you face it, with a well and the course of the water channel. A
few yards farther along the upper level the canal crosses the old
drive to Nynehead Court by a stately single arch aqueduct.

After Nynehead, the next lift, Winsbeer, is something of an anti-
climax. This (ST 123215) is south of the Tone, about 600yd along
a path 1½ miles north of the Wellington traffic-lights on the B3187
Milverton road. There are no masonry remains, just a hillock to
show where the 18ft lift was, but the course of the canal is clear
again on the upper level. The ruined lift cottage lies to the left.
From here, it is possible to walk through the fields to the foot of
the Wellisford inclined plane, 2 miles on. The incline is ½ mile
north of Thorne St Margaret; a track known as Bughole Lane

runs beside it to Incline Farm at the top. The engine house is by the cottages at the top of the rise, but there seems to be no trace of the wells for the buckets which failed to do their job of raising the boats, though the end of the drainage adit can be found. Cradles were used to contain the boats on the rise of 81ft.

From the top of the incline the canal swings south west to the last, and largest, lift at Greenham. The course can be followed from the southern end of Greenham village, along the bottom of a couple of fields. The ground becomes marshy and the undergrowth dense; at times, there is plenty of water. Soon you come to a wide-spanned accommodation bridge beyond which is a great wall of greenery concealing whatever may remain of the Greenham lift, 42ft high. At the side there is some stonework, possibly the base of the retaining wall or of a buttress. On the upper level is the lift cottage, restored and inhabited. The canal continues for ⅓ mile clearly defined, and then stops at a minor road. Descending to the road, you can see the abutments of an aqueduct partly concealed beneath the ivy; and on the other side, after 100yd of coltsfoot, the watered section—the Tiverton branch—begins. There are no traces of the canal's one conventional lock, but Lock's Cottage marks its site.

On to Tiverton, the canal is indicated on the OS map. There is a short small-bore tunnel, with a length of chain attached to the west portal, under the road by the Greenham/Holcombe/Wellington signpost. The wharf at Sampford Peverell, in the centre of the village just south of A373, is worth looking at, and the Halberton embankment and the aqueduct, brick and two-arched, over the railway a mile south west of Halberton village. The basin at Tiverton is on the right of the minor road that enters the town from the south east.

The Grand Western was never a profitable concern. Receipts never exceeded £5,000 pa, and tolls declined when the Bristol & Exeter Railway opened in 1844. The railway paid compensation for the building of the Halberton aqueduct over its branch line to Tiverton, but after a few years' co-operation a rate-cutting battle began. When the Bridgwater & Taunton began to lose interest in it, the end was in sight. The Grand Western company leased the canal to the railway for £2,000 a year, with an option to buy which the railway took up in 1864. Three years later, the Taunton–Lowdwells section, lifts, plane and all, was closed.

Trade continued on the Tiverton branch for another fifty-seven years. A few thousand tons of limestone were carried annually and the railway did not neglect it, threatening to prosecute 'with the utmost rigour of the law' anyone 'found trespassing, doing any kind of damage or throwing anything in this canal'. The leaks which occurred from time to time in the section near Halberton were repaired, 18 boat-loads of clay being used to re-puddle a 56yd stretch in 1892. There were even signs of generosity; Mr John Lindsay, of Tiverton, being granted liberty to wash his sheep in the canal, apparently for nothing.

In 1962 the Tiverton branch was abandoned by the British Transport Commission. Then in 1970 the Devonshire County Council took over the canal; the towpath walk is still open, and there are proposals for restoring the 11 miles of this very attractive waterway for use by pleasure-boats.

OS sheet 177 (Taunton end) and 164 (Norton–Tiverton)
The Canals of South West England, by Charles Hadfield

THE STOVER AND HACKNEY CANALS

The Stover Canal, almost 2 miles long, was built by James Templer, a local landowner, for the rapidly expanding clay trade in south Devon at the end of the eighteenth century. Work began in 1790, with Thomas Gray as engineer, and was completed in about two years. Templer thought of extending the canal to Bovey Tracey and Chudleigh, but decided to go no farther than Ventiford, where clay cellars were built and where, in 1820, the Haytor Granite Tramway came to its terminus. North of Newton Abbot the canal locked into the Whitelake Channel, and thence into the estuary of the Teign.

The Stover was a busy little waterway. It took boats 54ft long, of 14ft beam, either sailed or bow-hauled. Coal, limestone and sand for manure came up from the estuary, while clay, and later granite, formed the main downward traffic. Templer owned seven of the ten barges working up the canal shortly after it opened, and the family retained ownership until 1829, when they sold both the canal and the tramroad to the Duke of Somerset. The Duke instigated some improvement of the Teign navigation, and the continuing prosperity of the clay trade encouraged another noble landowner, Lord Clifford, to construct the Hackney Canal, to shorten the distance of transporting clay from his excavations north east of the Teign to the estuary. The Hackney, 5 furlongs long, had a tide-lock capable of taking two barges at once, and a wharf and clay cellars were built by the Kingsteignton road.

In 1862, the Stover was bought by the South Devon Railway for £8,000. The top section soon became disused, but the railway continued to rent out the canal, as the Duke had been doing, and some trade continued until 1939. The lessees, Watts, Blake & Co, used it for transporting clay from their own works in barges towed by a tug. In 1943, the GWR authorised its closure. Traffic on the Hackney Canal, which still belongs to the Clifford Estates, had ceased in 1928.

It is possible, though not advisable, to walk most of the length of the Stover; the towpath is not now continuous and the bed of the canal is very overgrown in parts and frequently marshy. The canal locks into the Whitelake Channel about ¼ mile west of where the A380 crosses the railway on the north side of Newton Abbot. Here, at Jetty Marsh, there is a double lock, walled with wood now mostly removed. The canal is crossed by the railway here; for the rest of its length it remains on the north side of the track, and close to it.

There are three features on the canal worth seeing. If you leave Newton Abbot on the A382 Bovey Tracey road, turn right for Teigngrace and continue past the first left turn you will come to a bridge over the canal; on the left are the remains of Teignbridge lock, with the elementary wooden paddle gear on one gate still there, and on the right by the old railway station was the wharf. The clay cellars of Watts, Blake & Co have now disappeared; in 1915 there were cellars 220yd long on the far side of the bridge. Teignbridge itself, a well-proportioned brick and granite structure, has two iron tie-rods driven through it, and has to take a heavy load of holiday traffic.

If you turn back to Teigngrace and take a track on the right on the far side of the village, you come to the derelict station. A few yards along the track to the south is a farm crossing; this also crosses the canal, and here is Teigngrace lock, its granite chamber still in excellent condition. Between here and Teignbridge is Graving Dock lock, if you can penetrate to it through waterlogged

Stover Canal: Teignbridge lock

growth of Amazonian texture. Here the Fishwick feeder runs into the canal, causing flooding at times.

Three-quarters of a mile farther north from Teigngrace brings you to Ventiford (marked Leygreen on the OS map). A few yards to the right and just before the road junction is the depression, now a chicken run, which was once the canal basin. The Jewsbridge feeder no longer supplies it, but still runs from Stover lake to Ventiford brook. The Haytor Granite Tramway ended a short distance away on the south side of the railway.

The Hackney Canal wharf and clay cellars are on the premises of Booker's Autobodies, to the east of the A380 on the Newton Abbot side of Kingsteignton. The basin is filled in, but after traversing an automobile graveyard you come to the clearly defined channel and can follow it as it rounds the racecourse to the entrance lock, now walled across to prevent flooding. The path continues beside the Hackney channel, past the ruined fragments of the clay cellars which were used before the canal was built, and ends at a road along the shore of the melancholy estuary, by a smart-looking pub.

OS sheet 176
The Haytor Granite Tramway and Stover Canal, by M. C. Ewans
The Canals of South West England, by Charles Hadfield

THE TORRINGTON CANAL

A private venture, the Torrington (or Rolle) Canal was the brainchild of Denys Rolle, an important landowner in the Torrington district. Having learnt of the proposals for the Bude Canal, he produced a scheme for a Devon network, to link Bideford, Okehampton, Torrington, and possibly Exeter and Bude. Tub-boats were to carry sea-sand for manure to the farms on route, and gradients were to be mastered by inclined planes. The Torrington Canal was the only part of the scheme to be realised. It was not begun until 1823, twenty-six years after Denys Rolle's death. His son John, who held the revived title of Baron Rolle, employed James Green as engineer of a tub-boat canal to link Torrington with the River Torridge near Bideford, a distance of 6 miles. The canal was opened in 1827, having cost about £40,000. It brought limestone and coal inland, and took agricultural produce to Bideford. From the trade that grew up around it, it seems to have been a flourishing concern, although as there were no shareholders the financial returns were never published.

Lord Rolle died in 1842. His successor, Mark, cherished the canal for ten years and then leased it to a local banker, whose bank shortly afterwards failed. Mark Rolle took it back; then in the 1860s he volunteered to sacrifice the canal to encourage the South Western Railway to build a branch line to Torrington. His offer was accepted; by 1871 the canal was closed, and the railway was constructed over parts of its bed.

Torrington itself is an attractive and historic town. From Castle Hill, high above the Torridge, the line of the canal is clear. In the left foreground, lavishly castellated, is a building of baronial aspect; this is the Town Mill, built by Lord Rolle. Here was the canal basin; A386 crosses the Torridge in front of the mill and there is an extra arch in the bridge under which the canal passed.

Curling round the foot of Castle Hill is the track of an old road, now abandoned. This was built on the bed of the canal. The road ends by a toll house by the next bridge, at Taddiport. At the bottom of Mill Street is the Torridge Inn—this used to be called the Canal Tavern. To the west a factory has been built on the line of the canal, but evidence of it can be found again at the railway station where there is also an additional arch for the canal under the bridge.

The canal turned northward, keeping close to the east bank of the Torridge, through the grounds of Beam House. Here it crossed the river by a stately five-arch stone aqueduct, which now carries the private drive from A386 to the house. A barely legible inscription on the parapet records that the first stone was laid by Lord Rolle himself. Over the river, the canal swung sharply north east, but its course for the next 2 miles has been mostly obliterated by the railway embankment. The descent to river level was made by the Weare Gifford inclined plane, which took the canal down 60ft. It is no use looking for the incline at Weare Gifford, which is a mile away on the other side of the river. But on A386, about 4 miles north of Torrington, there is a lane on the east side, leading to Ridd's Cottage. The line of the incline is across this lane and into the field on its south side (SS 463223). The embankment cut across the upper part of the incline, which was double-track and operated by a waterwheel. Traces of the waterwheel pit can be found by the embankment. At the foot of the incline there is a stone-built shed. A mile farther north, the canal joined the Torridge by a tide-lock.

Road and railway, both abandoned, have used parts of the line of the Torrington Canal. The familiar words 'old canal' cannot be found anywhere between Bideford and Torrington on the relevant Ordnance Survey map. But the great Beam aqueduct, perhaps the least known of the major aqueducts on British canals, is adequate memorial to Lord Rolle and James Green, the West Country engineer.

OS sheet 163
The Canals of South West England, by Charles Hadfield

THE TAVISTOCK CANAL

The Tavistock Canal, 4½ miles of waterway and an inclined plane nearly ½ mile long, connected the Tavy to the Tamar. Its founder was John Taylor who, aged 19, came to Tavistock in 1798 and became manager of the Wheal Friendship copper mine. The purpose of the canal was to convey copper ore from the mines near Tavistock to the quay at Morwellham, on the navigable Tamar. An Act was obtained in 1803; the estimated cost was £40,000, and most of the money was raised locally. Between Tavistock and Morwellham, however, rises Morwell Down, through which a tunnel 2,540yd long had to be dug, and although the first stretch of canal was opened in 1805, it was not until 1817 that the undertaking was completed. Then in June it was opened throughout, to the accompaniment of a band and a 21 gun salute from ships on the Tamar.

The canal cost over £70,000 altogether, and proved a commercial disappointment. The output of the mines did not come up to expectations, and though a profit was made in the early years it averaged only about £600 pa. Limestone, and smaller amounts of pig lead, granite and slate were also carried, but annual tonnage did not exceed 20,000 tons. By the time the railway reached the district, the mines were already failing. To hasten the passage of boats through the tunnel, waterwheels were set up at each end connected with 4 miles of wire rope, but it made little difference. Cutting the tolls proved equally unsuccessful; trade fell off until in 1870 only 1,000 tons passed along the canal. Three years later, the Duke of Bedford bought the canal, together with the Millhill Cut—a 2 mile branch to the Millhill slate quarries, begun in 1817, little used, and abandoned in favour of a tramroad in 1846—for £3,200, and navigation ceased shortly afterwards.

The basin of the Tavistock Canal is easy to find; it is now the car park at the bottom of Canal Road, entered past the old warehouses and cottages. The canal itself is fed from the Tavy a short distance to the north. From the basin it flows with its banks neatly tailored through the municipal park, under the A386, past some allotments, and then, as the ground falls away on the left, through a beautiful wooded section. It is crossed by an arch of the railway viaduct and turns to cross the Lumburn itself by a strong single-arched stone aqueduct. A few yards farther on comes the junction with the Millhill Cut, leading off to the right, and then the canal turns again to enter a deep cutting before disappearing into the Morwelldown tunnel. This makes a walk of a little over 2 miles; except for a short untidy stretch on the edge of the town, the towpath is in excellent condition. The water flows quite swiftly all the way, and is clean and sweet.

The date 1803 is carved over both portals of the tunnel. Only 8ft high and 6ft wide, without a towpath, the tunnel proved extremely difficult to excavate; the conditions in which the men had to work were appalling, and Taylor designed a waterwheel operated pump to clear the air, and another wheel to extract the water which flowed through the workings. Copper lodes were discovered during the excavation, but failed to prove very remunerative. This was the smallest bore tunnel constructed on the English canals, but it is still navigable.

The south portal (SX 448703) can be found about 200yd along a lane forking back on the west side of the road to Morwellham, as the road begins its steep descent to the village. Here the water is diverted through a culvert and two short tunnels built by the West Devon Electricity Board to the reservoir above Morwellham; from here it is piped to the turbines of the big generating station. The Board took over the canal's water in 1933, and its successor, the Central Electricity Generating Board, now rents the canal from the Bedford Estates for £1 a day, although Tavistock UDC now owns the stretch within the town boundary. The course of the old canal, however, now merely damp, can still be followed as it swings to the west after leaving the tunnel and ends about ½ mile farther on at Canal Farm. Here the goods were transhipped from the small iron tub-boats by a crane into special trucks, to be taken down the inclined plane, dropping 237ft to the copper quays at Morwellham. The incline, the greatest in the country, was double-track and operated by a waterwheel; the line is very overgrown, but the waterwheel pit remains and water still sometimes collects in the canal basin and follows its old course round the back of the cottage to the pit. The original stables still stand beside the basin. The incline-keeper's cottage is inhabited, and permission should be sought if you wish to look at the incline. A few yards farther along the path, the Great Devon

Consols tramroad incline used to run down parallel to the canal incline, but this has been recently bulldozed to make a forest ride.

The whole of the Tavistock Canal, although ignored by OS sheet 187, is easily accessible, apart from the interior of the tunnel. The middle of the tunnel, however, can still be seen; a ventilation shaft, known as Bray's, stands in a field ¼ mile south of the Rock crossroads (SX 451709), as one returns towards the A390. Morwellham itself, once a thriving port, was until recently a sad collection of semi-derelict cottages and fragments of industrial archaeology, but it is now being actively reconstructed as a leisure activities centre.

The Millhill Cut

This ran from the junction south of the Lumburn aqueduct to the slate quarries at Millhill. Its bed is clearly defined as far as the A390 (Tavistock–Liskeard); from there it follows the line of the embankment which carried the tramroad as far as Millhill crossroads. A few yards west of the crossroads there is a bridge (SX 453742), now blocked up, that took the cut under the road. Between here and the cottages the other side of the road must be the site of the inclined plane, rising 19½ft, double-track and counterbalanced, with horses assisting the upward traffic. But there is no trace of the incline now, and the exact course of the canal between here and the quarry is conjectural.

OS sheet 187
The Canals of South West England, by Charles Hadfield
The Industrial Archaeology of the Tamar Valley, by F. Booker

THE TAMAR MANURE NAVIGATION

Under an Act of 1796, a waterway, partly river but mainly tub-boat canal, was proposed to join the port of Morwellham on the Tamar with the Bude Canal near Tamerton Bridge. Rennie had supervised the survey; lime, coal and sea-sand were to be the main cargoes; the length of canal was to be over 20 miles, and the estimated cost was some £80,000. For once, the estimate was not exceeded, but only because no more than 2½ miles of the Tamar Manure was made. This comprised 2 miles of navigable river from

Morwellham to Nutstakes, ½ mile south east of Gunnislake, a lock, and about 500yd of canal. The cost was about £11,000, and no work was done after 1808.

The Tamar Manure outlasted commercially all its West Country contemporaries. It traded for nearly 120 years, carrying coal, bricks, lime, manure and granite—the coal mainly for the Gunnislake gasworks, built beside it. The river was not navigable after 1929, but the Tamar Manure Navigation Company survived until 1942, when it went into liquidation.

The granite lock, 70ft by 20ft, with the chamber in excellent preservation and substantial remains of the gates and paddle gear, can be easily found (SX 436710) a few hundred yards down river

Tamar Manure Navigation: gate paddle gear on the lock

from the gasworks. The course of the canal is still clear, and the basin with some ruined cottages is at the foot of a minor road descending from a junction with A390 in Gunnislake. In his painting *Crossing the Brook*, exhibited at the Royal Academy in 1815 and now in the Tate Gallery, Turner gives a rather Italianate view of the Tamar Valley, with a waterwheel and other signs of industrial activity in the distance. Those with keen eyesight or imagination may convince themselves that there also are the lock gates of the Tamar Manure Navigation.

OS sheet 187
The Industrial Archaeology of the Tamar Valley, by F. Booker
The Canals of South West England, by Charles Hadfield

THE BUDE CANAL

The original Act for the Bude Canal, in 1774, envisaged a 95 mile waterway climbing up from Bude harbour with sea-sand for manuring the Cornish farms. This proved too optimistic, and it was not until 1817 that, as a result of a revival of local interest, James Green and Thomas Shearm were asked to produce a survey and report; on the basis of this, a second Act was passed in 1819. This estimated a cost of a little over £90,000 for what was virtually a waterway network, comprising a short stretch of barge canal from Bude to Hele and over 40 miles of tub-boat canal dividing into three branches running roughly north, east and south. Water would be drawn from Alfardisworthy reservoir (Tamar Lake), and Green himself had enough confidence to back the project with £3,000 of his own money. Earl Stanhope, a major shareholder, ceremonially began the work on 23 July 1819; four years later, much of the line was opened, and in 1825 all that was ever to be built was completed. This was 35½ miles of canal, with terminals at Tamar Lake, Blagdonmoor Wharf, near Holsworthy, and Druxton, near Launceston. The works included one major aqueduct, over the Tamar at Burmsdon, a sea-lock, two locks on the barge section, and six inclined planes. Boats 20ft by 5ft 6in were used; they worked in groups and had small wheels affixed beneath them, which fitted into rails on the planes—and which also did no good to the sides of the canal. The undertaking cost about

F

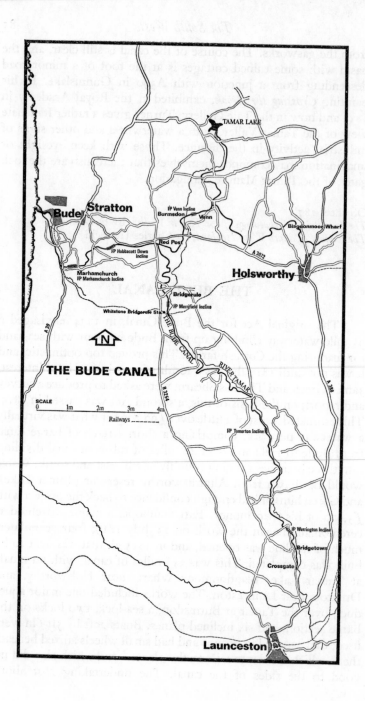

TAMAR LAKE

Bude
Stratton

IP Venn Incline
Burmsdon   Venn

Blagdonmoor Wharf

Red Post
A 3072
IP Hobbacott Down
Incline

Holsworthy

Marhamchurch
IP Marhamchurch Incline

Bridgerule
IP Merrifield Incline

Whitstone Bridgerule Sta's

A 39

THE BUDE CANAL

RIVER TAMAR

THE BUDE CANAL

B 3254

A 388

SCALE
0   1m   2m   3m   4m

Railways _____

IP Tamerton Incline

IP Werrington Incline

Bridgetown

Crossgate

Launceston

£120,000, and it was fifty years before the first dividend was paid.

Although the canal helped the farmers prosper by bringing down the price of sand—by far the most important cargo, though coal, culm and other goods were carried as well—the traffic never approached what had been anticipated; 50,000 tons a year, about one sixth of the estimate, was an average figure. It took all the company's efforts to pay off its debts and keep the canal in working order, and by 1876, when it did manage to pay a dividend, the railways were, at long last, approaching.

In succeeding years traffic declined, and soon only one carrying firm remained trading on the canal. The company was undecided whether to continue or to abandon the waterway; then in 1891 it obtained an Act to enable the closing of all except for the barge section and the feeder branch to Tamar Lake. Land was sold off, most of the staff dismissed, and the machinery of the planes, probably with some relief, dismantled. Until 1901 a little trade continued; then in that year the newly formed Stratton & Bude Urban Council bought the surviving canal and the harbour for £8,000, for the purpose of water supply. In the same year, the Holsworthy–Bude railway was completed, which virtually ended the maritime trade of the Bude Canal. Henceforth it was the railway that conveyed the sand to the farms up country.

The lock gates and sea lock pound at Bude, which is still a registered port, are in excellent condition. Holidaymakers can hire small boats, and the old barge canal is well stocked with coarse fish. Next to the pound are the remains of the track of the old edge-railway, which ran right down to the sand for the easier loading of the trucks. The sand was transferred to the tub-boats at the wharf. The two locks towards Helebridge have been converted to weirs. At Helebridge the canal is crossed by the A39; the now overgrown wharf is on the east of the bridge, with a canal house opposite it. A few yards on is the foot of the Marhamchurch inclined plane.

The Marhamchurch incline, like all six on this canal, was double-track. It was 836ft long, rising 120ft, and is now a slope of overgrown scrub in between two hedges. There is a footpath on one side and the road to Marhamchurch on the other, but no visible remains of the engineering works or buildings at the top. All the Bude inclines were water-powered, and all, except Hobbacott Down, worked by waterwheel, the one at Marhamchurch being 5oft diameter. To raise a boat up Marhamchurch took five minutes.

The course of the canal, now dry, can be found again under a road bridge in the village, a few yards north of the crossroads. It turns north-eastwards through fields to Cann Orchard and comes, in about 1½ miles, to the foot of the next incline, Hobbacott Down, the greatest on this canal and second only to Morwellham, on the Tavistock, in the whole country.

Hobbacott Down (SS 244049) can best be seen from the top, on the south side of the A3072, halfway between Stratton and Red Post. The incline is in the grounds of Thurlibeer Farm, from where permission to see it should be obtained. Hobbacott Down, 935ft long and rising 225ft, was the only one of the Bude planes worked on the bucket-in-well system, simple in theory but often disastrous in practice. There were two buckets, suspended in wells the same depth as the rise of the incline. As the full bucket, holding 15 tons of water, descended, so the boat was drawn up by a chain. At the bottom of the well, the water escaped through a valve in the bucket and flowed along the adit (the horizontal channel) to emerge in the lower pound. All was well as long as nothing broke. When it did—usually one of the chains—either boat or bucket descended with frightening speed. Replacements were expensive and often slow to arrive, and Hobbacott Down was a constant drain on the company's resources. A steam engine was installed to operate the plane when the buckets were out of commission, but this too was costly to use. The engine house, the incline keeper's cottage and the well still stand at the top of the Down, which commands a superb view to the coast. The course of the canal below can be easily discerned. The incline-keeper, when he had time to look at it, can have enjoyed some of the finest scenery in England—some compensation for the poor wages and the frequent wrestling with recalcitrant ironmongery.

The course of the canal runs east to Red Post, just south of which it diverges. The main line soon swings north, parallel to the Tamar. A good bridge survives at Anderton. It turns east again to cross the river by a sturdy single-arch aqueduct at Burmsdon (SS 281065), and arrives at the foot of the next of the inclines.

The Venn, or Veala, incline (SS 285065) 500ft long, takes the canal up 58ft to its summit level. At the head of the plane are the filter beds of the N Devon waterworks. The northern feeder branch of the canal still brings water down from Tamar Lake which, after filtration, is led beneath the incline and the canal for about a mile, thence being conveyed to Stratton by underground pipeline. This branch can be followed on the OS map through Puckland to the Lake, about 4 miles to the north.

The main line (SS 293071) follows the contours eastward, much of it being marked on the map as 'old canal'. The A388 north of Holsworthy crosses it at Stanbury Wharf (house and warehouse), and the minor road running due north from the town brings you within a few yards of a good stretch of embankment. The line ends just beyond Blagdonmoor Wharf, 1½ miles north east of Holsworthy, with its group of small warehouses and cottages, in a cutting, at the beginning of an intended tunnel.

As for the southern, and longest, branch, most of this has vanished under the plough. Even the 1907 OS map does not record the top few miles. From Red Post, it worked along the contours south-eastward towards the Tamar, and from Bridgerule south it kept within ½ mile of the river for the rest of its course. But while there are few traces of the waterway itself, the three remaining inclines can all be found.

The Merrifield incline (SS 271012) lies off the B3254 Red Post–Launceston road. This road crosses the old Holsworthy–Bude railway, 3 miles south of Red Post. A lane to the east, immediately after the railway bridge, leads to Whitstone Bridgerule station, now disused. A few yards walk along the line, which has been closed for some years, brings you to a point from where you can see the incline, 360ft long with a fall of 60ft, over to the north between two lines of hedges.

For the fifth incline, Tamerton (SX 324957), it is necessary to return to the B3254 and continue south for about 4 miles to a turning to the east leading to North Tamerton. Here a house called 'Bude Canal' shows where the canal once crossed the road by an aqueduct. Shortly before this, there is a turning to the south. By a farm on the left at Tamerton Town there is a lane; following this to its end and then keeping to the line of the hedges brings you in a mile to the foot of the plane. Its measurements are almost identical with those of Merrifield. In the undergrowth at the top of the rise is the waterwheel pit and a short stretch of clearly defined cut with masonry sides. There is a feeling of remoteness here; the Tamerton incline must have been a lonely place to work.

The last incline, Werrington, (SX 338905) is rather different from the others. It is near Tamartown—one must be careful hereabouts if asking directions locally. Return to the minor road, and continue south some 4½ miles to Bridgetown. At the T junction turn left; a road sign warns of a low bridge, headroom 8ft 6in, ½ mile ahead. This bridge is, in fact, the Werrington incline crossing the road. It is now part of a farm, and permission should be asked to look at the waterwheel pit opposite the cottage. The Werrington plane was 259ft long, falling 51ft, and is now frequented mostly by pigs.

The journey is nearly over. Back through Bridgetown, heading south you come in 1½ miles to the end of the canal by the crossroads at Crossgate, within 3 miles of the attractive town of Launceston, with its granite church and castle. Touring the Bude Canal—and even in the holiday season the roads and lanes that lead you to it are mostly unfrequented—is a revivifying experience. James Green may not have been the greatest of canal engineers, but his work in more than one way enhanced and enriched the countryside through which it passed.

OS sheet 174
The Canals of South West England, by Charles Hadfield

THE LISKEARD & LOOE UNION CANAL

The Liskeard & Looe was exceptional among West Country canals in that, for a few years, it made a profit. The first proposal for it was made in 1777, following the opening of the St Columb, but the difficulties of the undertaking deterred supporters until 1823, when a committee met in Looe to examine means of improving communication between the towns. James Green was consulted; he thought a canal was a practical proposition, and recommended a tub-boat canal with inclined planes to effect the descent of some 200ft from Liskeard to the coast. However, his advice was not taken; the line was surveyed again, and a locked canal, almost 6 miles long, was decided on, to take boats 50ft by 10ft, from Moorswater, 1½ miles west of Liskeard, to run alongside the River Looe, crossing it and then widening at Sandplace and eventually joining the river at Terras Pill. The Act was obtained in 1825, giving authority to raise £13,000, most of which came in from local shareholders in comparatively small amounts. Robert Coad was appointed engineer, and the canal was completed in three years, paying a dividend of 6 per cent in its first year of work.

Although originally envisaged as carrying mainly agricultural produce and coal, the canal became almost wholly industrial on the opening of copper mines in the neighbourhood. Copper became the principal cargo, followed by coal, granite and limestone. So busy did the canal become—carrying 48,000 tons in 1856—that the water supply was unable to cope with the demands of the heavy lockage—there were 25 locks—and congestion was becoming a major problem. The canal company, with no shortage of money in the bank or of suitable land adjacent to the waterway, therefore built its own railway line alongside the canal to Terras Pill and then on farther into East Looe. The line opened in December 1860, and within a year or two the canal, apart from the broad section at Sandplace, ceased to be used. A little traffic survived between Sandplace and Terras Pill until about 1910.

River, railway and canal, and for some parts of the distance road as well, are squeezed together in the narrow valley. The canal can be followed from an untidy, semi-derelict industrial area south of Moorswater until it becomes lost in the marshes south of Sandplace and reaches the river lock, where the narrow Looe widens into its estuary. Although it is not marked on the modern OS map, it is easy to find; every bridge that crosses river and railway also crosses canal. At the tails of some locks are the original road bridges; the present road bridges are double-arched to take railway, canal and river in their stride. The scenery is spectacular, with the hills rising sharply on either side, and except in high summer there is little traffic. The bed of the canal is mostly dry now, but the river bubbles along beside it. Much of the lock masonry still stands firm.

OS sheet 186
The Canals of South West England, by Charles Hadfield

THE ST COLUMB CANAL

The St Columb is about as disused as a canal can be. Work began probably in 1773, but it was never completed; traffic on it ceased about ten years later.

John Edyvean, of St Austell, planned the undertaking, which was intended to be some 13 miles long in a rough semicircle, each end terminating on a headland overlooking the sea. The purpose was to supply the farms inland with sea-sand for manure, and also with coal, while stones were to be exported. From each end of the canal an inclined plane was planned down to the beach, up which the sand and coal were to be hauled in boxes and down which the stones were to be shot out.

Edyvean died in the 1780s and his canal seems to have died with him. A description of one of the inclined planes exists, but it is not certain which it refers to, nor indeed if both were built. But the end of the canal can be distinguished at Trenance Point, a few miles north east along the coast from Newquay, just above Mawgan Porth. A cliff footpath crosses the shallow depression, now full of gorse, some 200ft above sea level and ending a few yards short of the cliff edge. Inland it becomes part of the gardens of cliff-top bungalows, a convenient site for greenhouses and garden sheds. No trace can be found of the inclined plane.

The St Columb was designed as a tub-boat canal. There were no locks, but the rock at Lusty Glaze was excavated for the incline; apparently this was laid on planks with a rise of about 200ft. As neither boats nor trucks used the incline, rails would not have been needed. Work was begun on the southern arm first, extending for about 2½ miles; a little more was completed on the northern half, but the two never met. Edyvean himself became blind, but knew his canal well enough to conduct visitors along it.

The other end of the canal comes out at Lusty Glaze, by St Columb Porth, nearer Newquay. Much of the sea end has been obliterated by buildings, but a good stretch of canal bed can be found by following a path beside St Columb Minor church. About 200yd along, this path crosses the canal. Immediately on the left is a bridge—the only one left on the St Columb—though only the stones of the arch are now above ground level. From here, the bed can be followed clearly in either direction for about a mile.

As planned, the canal would have been 13 miles long, but the two ends were never joined and the total length dug was not more than 6½ miles. But no canal can have had more spectacular terminals than Trenance Point and Lusty Glaze, part of the rugged splendour of the North Cornwall coast.

OS sheet 185
The Canals of South West England, by Charles Hadfield

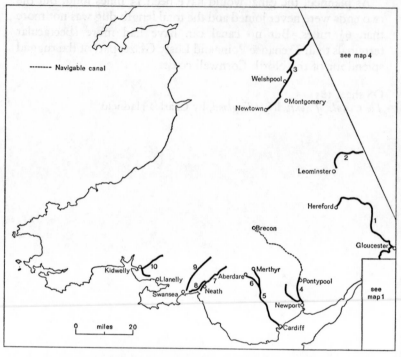

Outline Map 3   The Border Counties and Wales

Chapter 3: *The Border Counties and Wales*

THE HEREFORDSHIRE & GLOUCESTERSHIRE CANAL

One of the last main line canals to be completed, the Herefordshire & Gloucestershire was opened throughout in 1845. This was fifty-four years after its Act of authorisation; but only thirty-seven years before its demise.

A group of local gentry appointed Josiah Clowes to survey a line from Hereford to Gloucester in 1790. Enthusiasm was quickened by the discovery of a new vein of coal at Newent the following year; a committee was appointed, the Act obtained, and £50,000 collected. Then there was a lull; some bricks were made, the committee pondered, and the line was re-surveyed. Digging began, and in 1796 the canal was opened from Gloucester to the tunnel at Oxenhall, reaching Ledbury, the far side of the tunnel, two years later. Coal prices at Ledbury dropped by nearly half; however, the 16 mile stretch of canal, with a 2,192yd tunnel, 13 deep locks and a short branch at Oxenhall, cost over £100,000—and there were still a further 18 miles to go. Shortage of funds was matched by shortage of water, of which the supply was sufficient to operate the canal for only a few months in the year. The committee, with half a canal and receipts about one-tenth of the estimated £10,000 pa, rapidly lost interest.

Until 1827, the H & G staggered on, kept in being by the exertions of a superintendent and one assistant, and a lock-keeper, Thomas Hatchett, who received no pay for thirteen years (he did get £20 eventually). In that year, Stephen Ballard was appointed clerk. He brought back some of the project's original enthusiasm, and with a new committee revised the tolls and began to raise funds to complete the canal to Hereford. Money was slow to accumulate, and the line had to be revised, but in 1840 work began again, with Ballard himself as engineer. 500 men were employed in cutting the 7 miles to Canon Frome, where the canal connected with a feeder which greatly improved the water supply. The

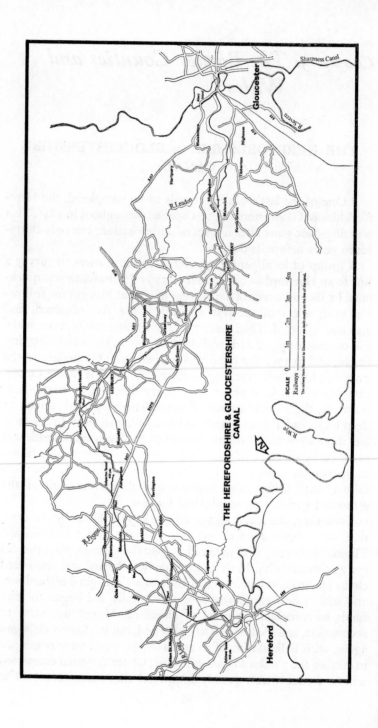

THE HEREFORDSHIRE & GLOUCESTERSHIRE CANAL

SCALE

0   1m   2m   3m   4m

Railways

The railway from Newent to Gloucester was built nearly on the line of the canal.

ambitious tunnel at Ashperton, originally planned to be over 1,000yd, was reduced to 440yd, with deep cuttings at either end. Withington was reached in 1844; the last of the tunnels was cut through Aylestone Hill, and Hereford basin was opened in May of the following year. The H & G was finished; 34 miles, 22 locks, three tunnels and an enormous debt.

No sooner was the canal completed than the West Midland Railway approached the committee with a proposal to take it over. Parliament refused an Act; so the company had to make the best of it and try to improve the canal's profitability. In 1848, when the Monmouthshire Canal over the Border was handling nearly 800,000 tons, the H & G's figure was 43,080. Various companies advertised as carriers, but the canal's largest receipts came from carrying materials for the Worcester & Hereford Railway in 1860. There were troubles too; twice the banks burst, and entry into Gloucester was made more difficult by the closing to navigation of one branch of the Severn, so that the canal boats could now only get in at high tide.

The company continued to encourage railway interest, and in 1862 arranged to lease the canal to the GWR for £5,000 pa, although it was not until 1870 that the necessary Act was passed. Despite denials that they intended to convert the canal into a railway, the GWR did that very thing a few years later, closing the Ledbury–Gloucester section in 1881, draining it, and using its line, except for the sharper bends, for its track. Though it has been suggested that the Ledbury–Hereford section was engineered with the possibility in mind of its later being converted for railway use, this never happened. The GWR sold off some portions of it, but continued to pay shareholders the £5,000 a year until nationalisation. This section became disused in or soon after 1882.

The H & G was a narrow canal with exceptionally deep locks, taking boats 70ft by 7ft 6in. The site of the Hereford basin, in front of the present railway station at Barr's Court, has been built over; the canal line is on waste ground or, as with the Aylestone Hill tunnel, on industrial property and inaccessible. But outside the built-up area, much of the line can be traced. It ran north out of Hereford, then swung east to cross the Lugg near Shelwick Green; the aqueduct has been demolished, but the piers are visible when the river is low (SO 532438). The embankment that used to be here has been recently levelled. Most of the bridges have gone, but by the site of the bridge on A465 at Withington Marsh the wharfinger's house (the legend 'William Bird, Wharfinger' just legible on the end wall), the weighing house and a canal cottage still remain. On the road ½ mile north of Withington church is a bridge with the date 1843 on the keystone, and the remains of a lock now incorporated in a private garden. About 2 miles farther along the canal, at Kymin, there is a well-defined length of canal and a wharf house. A4103 crosses the canal south west of Newtown. In another ⅓ mile, at Monkhide, the H & G returns briefly to life; it is crossed first by a fine, sharply angled skew bridge and then, under the next bridge, appears as a wide watered stretch, clean and navigable, with an empty house on the bank. But only for 220yd; then it is back to a scrubby, tree-lined ditch.

The line continues south-eastward; an old warehouse, with the word 'Salt' still discernible, is by A417, a mile south of Stretton Grandison; on the other side of the road a low embankment cuts across a field, to end at a bridge by the gates of Canon Frome Secondary School. The canal can be followed for a mile to the Ashperton (or Walsopthorne) tunnel; the stonework of the north end has gone, but the south portal is in quite good condition. Canon Frome cricket ground is on top of the tunnel. By the south portal, which emerges into a deep cutting, there is a derelict cottage. After the next road bridge, the canal turns east to Staplow, where there is a typical H & G cottage—red brick, high for its width, with windows, now bricked up, which once looked along the line of the cut. Behind Prior's Court, ¼ mile farther on, is all that is left of the last lock gate—a top gate, the heavy timber disintegrating, but with some of the ironwork intact. Most of the masonry has gone, and the bed of the canal is here very overgrown, with tall trees and nettles head-high. There are two single-arch aqueducts within the next ½ mile, the first over the Leadon, the second crossing a stream. A reputedly savage pig may lurk nearby.

The canal turns south; there used to be a wharf at the next road crossing. Wellington Heath bridge still stands; then A4154 crosses the line of the canal, which continues under a double-arched railway bridge and so into Ledbury. The town's swimming pool is on the canal bed.

The track of the railway that replaced the H & G in Ledbury has been long taken up but its course can be followed on the west side of the town, curving to cross A449 by an engineering works—originally a well-proportioned canal warehouse. At hand, with recently added extensions, is the wharf house that marked the terminus of the canal until work restarted towards Hereford in 1840. Canal and railway coincide for nearly 3 miles southwards towards Dymock. They diverge a mile north of the village; from a point (SO 692324) on the Roman road B4215 a cross-section of embankment can be seen to the south west, the far side of a potato field. More of the embankment is on the other side of the road. Canal and railway rejoin to take the same route past Dymock, but their builders chose different methods to cope with the higher ground to the south. The railway dodged round through a cutting; the canal tunnelled for over 2,000yd. There is water in the cut approaching the north end of the Oxenhall tunnel, in the grounds of Boyce Court, where the drive crosses by a red-brick bridge. The north portal, with rough brickwork exposed as the stone facing has gone, has been reduced by silting to about half its original height; the horse path comes down on its left under a stone footbridge. The portal is in a wooded cutting below an orchard on the north side of M50. Spoil heaps can be seen on the south side of the motorway. The south portal (SO 7092$78\frac{1}{2}$), a squat, stone-faced opening, is in good condition; it is behind Holder's Farm and can be reached through the farm or by walking for a short distance north beside the canal from where it is crossed by a minor road past Hilter's Farm. Recent exploration has proved the tunnel intact, though delicate, for at least half its length. Near the south portal there is a large 'cave' carved into the side of the cutting, which may have been used for stabling. Half a mile south, by the minor road east of Oxenhall, is the junction with the short Oxenhall branch on the north side of a collapsed bridge. The branch curls around a hill on which the church stands, ending by a road; there is no sign of a basin here but there are indications on the ground that the branch may have continued for several hundred yards farther. Alongside the main line the towpath leads to Lock Cottage, with its lettering above the front door beautifully restored, and the remains of four locks, the chamber of the top one being mostly intact. At some times of the year there is water here, which runs off through a hole made in an aqueduct over a brook a little lower down.

Canal and railway meet again by a timber yard near the remains of Newent station, and apart from some deviations where the railway straightened the sharp bends of the canal they coincide to the outskirts of Gloucester, keeping close to B4215, which crosses them twice. The canal ran into the Severn just south of its junction with the Leadon and crossed the meadows to the eastern arm; its shallow depression can be seen from A40 entering Gloucester, winding away to disappear near the power station. Introducing its explorer to the gentler countryside of the border counties, the H & G, commercial failure though it was, has a fascination and appeal all its own. Its 34 miles traverse some of the least despoiled landscape of England.

OS sheets 142 (Hereford–Ashperton)
             143 (Ashperton–Gloucester)
The Canals of South Wales & the Border, by Charles Hadfield
Transactions of Woolhope Naturalists' Field Club, vol XXXVI pt 2, pp 167–79: 'Herefordshire & Gloucestershire Canal', by I. Cohen

THE LEOMINSTER CANAL

The Leominster Canal, intended to run from Kington via Leominster to Stourport, was a disastrous commercial failure. Only 18½ miles of the proposed 46 were ever constructed; the waterway reached neither Kington nor Stourport, and never paid its shareholders a single dividend.

The proposition, in 1789, was to link the market town of Leominster with Stourport-on-Severn, opening Leominster to manufactured products from the Birmingham area via the Staffs & Worcs, and providing an outlet for north Herefordshire's agricultural produce. Coal from the Pensax collieries, near Newnham, could also be transported to Leominster.

Thomas Dadford, jun, surveyed the route. He proposed opening the line from Kington, about 12 miles to the west of Leominster, crossing the River Lugg by an aqueduct, then from Leominster cutting roughly north to Woofferton, and thence easterly to Stourport. There would be three tunnels, the longest, at Pensax, to be 3,850yd, and two more aqueducts, over the Teme and the Rea. Lockage would be heavy—there were to be three summit levels—and the canal would descend to the Severn by a flight of 17 locks in 3 miles. In 1791 the Act was obtained for this

Page 101 (above) *St Columb Canal: bridge, St Columb Minor, built about 1775;* (left) *Herefordshire & Gloucestershire Canal: restored plaque at Lock Cottage, Oxenhall*

Page 102   (above) *Leominster Canal: the Rea aqueduct;* (below) *Leominster Canal: Wharf House, Marlbrook*

ambitious undertaking, authorising a capital of £150,000 to start with, and soon after work began.

The first boat, the *Royal George*, was launched at Tenbury in May 1793, and the waterway from Woofferton to Marlbrook was opened a year later. Delays occurred, however, over the building of the short Putnal Field tunnel to the south of Woofferton. The longer Southnet tunnel, 1,250yd, near Mamble, was completed, and work began on the Lugg aqueduct; but a great deal of the money raised had already been spent. Then the north end of the Southnet tunnel, which had not yet come into use, fell in, reputedly entombing three workmen. Called in to advise by the worried proprietors, John Rennie criticised the tunnel design, which is not surprising, and also the design of the aqueducts—which is, as the Rea aqueduct still stands and the Teme aqueduct was only destroyed, with much difficulty, during the last war.

In 1796 the proprietors obtained a further Act to raise more money, the Putnal Field tunnel was completed at last, and the canal was opened to the Wharf House, a mile north of Leominster. Coal boats from Sir Walter Blount's mines near Mamble began to arrive, and the price of coal in Leominster dropped by half. But that was all. In the following years, a little digging was done east of Southnet, including, it is now known, a short length of Pensax tunnel, but Southnet was never repaired. A ceremonial sod was cut at the proposed entry to the Severn, but the 17 locks were never even started. By 1803 all work had stopped; the canal was as long as it was ever going to be and the company was £25,000 in debt. Jonathan Williams' *Leominster Guide* of 1808, with its lyrical description of the canal 'at length descending into the Severn by 17 locks and thereby opening a communication with every part of the kingdom, and of the world' was, to say the least, misleading—and misled subsequent writers as well.

In the following decades, several proposals were made for adding to the waterway by means of tramroads, and even for linking it to the Herefordshire & Gloucestershire, but no action was taken and, as railways began to penetrate the area, the company began negotiations for the sale of its property. In 1858, it was sold to the Shrewsbury & Hereford, for £12,000—a mere £16 for each original £100 share. It took a lawsuit to compel the railway company to complete its purchase; their lack of enthusiasm may be partly explained by the fact that receipts on the canal for five

G

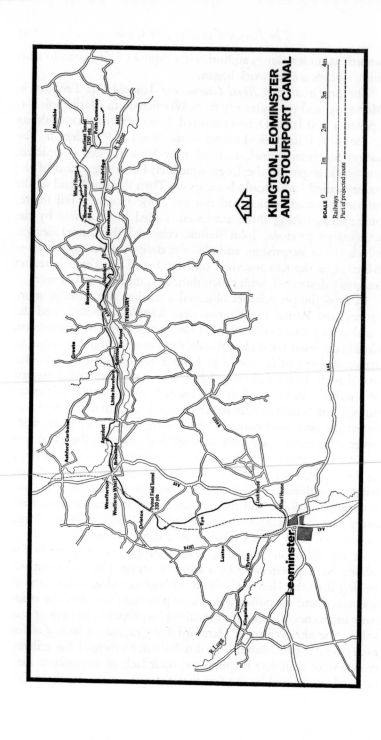

KINGTON, LEOMINSTER AND STOURPORT CANAL

SCALE 0   1m   2m   3m   4m

Railways ———
Part of projected route ———

months in 1858 were only £29. The following year the canal was drained, and various parts of it were sold off, some to the Tenbury Railway which laid its line over part of the bed.

To summarise: the Leominster Canal took over five years to make, cost just under £100,000 at opening and never paid a dividend. It contained 16 locks, three tunnels (one short one not mentioned on the original plan), and two completed aqueducts. A product of the canal mania of the 1790s, one can see now that it was doomed from the start. Even had it been completed, in the hilly and irregular countryside water supply and maintenance of the engineering works would have presented enormous problems, which the trade carried could never have justified.

The Leominster Canal ran through some of the most beautiful countryside in Britain, and rediscovering it is a pleasure though sometimes a muddy one. About a mile out of Leominster on the left of the A49 Ludlow road is the Coal Wharf house, and the line of the cut can be seen from time to time as you head northwards. The bridges and locks on this stretch have all gone; the first engineering work you come across is found by taking the left turning to Orleton, about 3 miles along the main road. A mile and a half along here you come to a bridge over the railway; Putnal Field tunnel is on the far side of this bridge, parallel to the railway line and about 50yd from it. Both portals can be found, one on either side of the road. By the southern portal, there is a beautiful watered stretch through the trees.

Returning to the main road, continue to the Salwey Arms, at the junction with the A456. Turning left, stop at the disused Woofferton railway station, cross the road and go through a white gate, across a field. In about 200yd you reach the canal bed; turn right along it, under the railway line, and shortly you come to the last remaining piece of lock masonry on the Leominster, the north wall of a set of three locks. The heel post of a lock gate, still bolted to the masonry, has taken root and is now a tree some 20ft high—an almost poetic comment on mutability. A few yards farther on, signs of more locks can be seen, and a lock-keeper's cottage, still inhabited, and a few stables.

Back on the road, take the A456 towards Worcester. A mile along, one can easily find the disused Tenbury Railway track. Follow this—it is to the left of the road and there are plenty of access points—until you become aware of the canal course swinging away to the left on an embankment. This embankment leads to the Teme aqueduct, originally a three-arched brick construction, but the centre arch was deliberately blown up during the war, presumably to stop the enemy seizing it and thereby getting control of Britain's inland transport system.

On the road towards Tenbury, and continuing on to Newnham, most of the left turns bring you to evidence of the cut. At Newnham Bridge, the minor road past the old railway station leads to a farm road just over the railway. The canal bed runs beside this lane, but the short tunnel which Mr Cohen found on his survey in 1957 has now been filled in, though it is easy to see where it was. The course can be followed across a large field, past two small cottages in the style of the architecture of this canal's buildings, across the track of the railway and up a track the other side to the top of the single-arched brick aqueduct over the Rea, still safe but beginning to look rather fragile in places from river level. One can either continue walking along the canal bed for nearly 2 miles, past the sites of seven locks, although only one or two traces are visible, and a lock house, which has been restored and added to, until you reach Wharf House, or you can return to the road via the railway track, continue along the A456 for about 2 miles to the Broom Inn, and approach Wharf House less muddily along a lane from the other direction (SO 673705). Wharf House is a beautifully preserved red-brick building; the 'docks' where the boats were repaired are now filled in and used as cellars, and the wharf itself turned into an attractive garden, despite the coal dust permeating the soil. At one time the canal in front of the house was used as fisheries, but few traces of this enterprise remain. Here, where once a tramroad brought the coal from the Mamble pits, the canal ends.

There is, however, one more sight to see. Although the north end of the Southnet tunnel has disappeared, the south portal is still there. From Newnham Bridge, take this time the A443 Worcester road, for about 3 miles. Turn left at the Nag's Head, and stop at the second farm entrance on the left, nearly a mile up the hill. A few yards towards the farm, over the first gate on the right, a few more yards through the long grass—and there it is. But it may not be there much longer; the brickwork is crumbling away, and when the tree roots at the top dislodge the keystone of its peculiar tall and narrow section, it won't be long before vegetation conceals for good this desolate and unlikely relic.

OS sheet 129
The Canals of South Wales & the Border, by Charles Hadfield
Transactions of Woolhope Naturalist Field Club, vol. XXXV: The
Leominster-Stourport Canal, by I. Cohen.

THE MONTGOMERYSHIRE CANAL

Many travellers along the Llangollen Canal, now thanks to
the development of pleasure cruising one of the busiest of the
inland waterways, will have seen a notice stating 'The Montgomery Canal Starts Here', some 3½ miles south west of Ellesmere.
The notice, placed there by the Shropshire Union Canal Society,
stands at the head of the four derelict Welsh Frankton locks. It is
a simplification, rather than a statement of historical accuracy, but
it serves to remind all who see it that 35 miles of waterway,
stretching into the beautiful countryside of mid-Wales, lie behind
it, waiting to be restored. For the Montgomeryshire is not yet
'lost'; rather is its future uncertain, depending to a great extent on
what impression the arguments and enthusiasm of those who want
it restored as an amenity can make on the responsible authorities.

What is today regarded as the Montgomeryshire consists of
three branches of canal. The northern 11 miles are the Frankton–
Carreghofa branch of the Shropshire Union, originally of the
Ellesmere Canal; then come 16¼ miles of the Montgomeryshire
Canal Eastern Branch, to Garthmyl, with a short branch to
Guilsfield; finally the Montgomeryshire Canal Western Branch, a
further 7⅜ miles to Newtown. Jessop, with Telford as resident
engineer, built the Ellesmere Canal section, which had seven locks,
taking narrow boats, and was opened in 1796. The Eastern Branch,
engineered by the Dadfords who also engineered some of the
South Wales canals, was opened a year later; lime and limestone
were the main traffic, the limestone being burnt in kilns by the
canal and then distributed via the canal for agricultural purposes.
Soon the undertaking became modestly prosperous, and in 1813
the company decided to extend the line to Newtown. Complications arose, as some shareholders foresaw this might mean a
reduction in their dividends; eventually, agreement was reached
that the extension be built by a separate company with its own

proprietors, the companies not to unite financially until the Western Branch dividends reached 5 per cent. Which, in fact, they never did. John Williams was the engineer for the Western Branch, which was completed in 1821. From Frankton Junction to Newtown there were 26 locks, falling to Carreghofa and rising to Newtown. Two major aqueducts were built on the Eastern Branch.

Railways were slow to penetrate the area, and the Eastern Branch continued to trade with profit. Tonnage carried edged over 100,000 a year in the mid-1830s. The company was still doing well when, having reached agreement with the Ellesmere & Chester, it decided to join the SU. The cash in hand was shared out, and negotiations were completed on 1 January 1847. For a time, the Western Branch stayed independent, but it too joined the SU in 1850.

In 1861, the railway reached Welshpool and Newtown, and the canal's prosperity was now in decline. A few years before this, however, the Montgomeryshire itself provided a link for passengers to the railway system; in 1853, a flyboat service was initiated to connect at Rednal station, 4 miles east of Oswestry, with trains for Liverpool, Birkenhead, Chester and Shrewsbury. According to the timetable, the journey from Newtown to Rednal took five hours twelve minutes, the return journey taking seven minutes less, the distance being 32 miles. With 22 locks to negotiate, and many stops en route, the speed achieved reflects great credit on the designer of the flyboats, the maintenance of the towpath, and the quality of the horses—though the teams must have been changed several times during the journey.

The Montgomeryshire survived an attempt to close it in 1887; it was returning a profit of something over £400 pa at the time. Trade continued to decrease and the canal's condition worsened, but it was still carrying a few hundred tons of coal a year when in 1936 there was a breach in the bank near Frankton Junction. The LMSR, now the canal's owners, refused to foot the bill for repair and, despite objections, nothing was done. Three boats were cut off by the burst, and have been quietly rotting away ever since. With much of the SU system, the Montgomeryshire was abandoned officially in 1944.

Apart from some 2½ miles at the north end and about ½ mile in Newtown, the Montgomeryshire is still watered. Most of the lock chambers are in good order, with much of the machinery intact. However, some of the road bridges have been flattened and the canal culverted; restoration would not simply be a matter of clearing and dredging but would also involve civil engineering. The Newtown basin has been filled in and built over; behind the 'Wool Producers of Wales' factory on B4568, on the north side of the town, there are the remains of a bridge, with an old warehouse near it. The basin was sited south of this bridge. The chimney of the pumping station that used to raise water from the Severn to feed the canal is on the outskirts of Newtown by the line of the cut. The bed is clearly discernible behind Llanllwchaiarn church, on B4568. It rounds the churchyard and passes under a bridge with an iron railing parapet. It can be followed on foot as it skirts a steep hill, keeping close to the Severn, as it does for some distance. B4389 crosses the Montgomeryshire by bridge no 152, reinforced in 1862 with a massive iron girder. The canal is now watered, and crosses a minor tributary of the Severn by a small aqueduct, which can be reached by walking along the towpath to the north east. A483 keeps close to the canal to Welshpool, crossing both it and the Severn 2 miles farther on. Just after the crossing is bridge no 146, on the right of the road, with Bryn-derwen lock, a neat white lock cottage and an adjacent red-brick building; there is also a corrugated iron shed still bearing the legend 'Shropshire Union Railway and Canal. General Carriers'. Restoration between here and Garthmyl would present several problems; the canal has been culverted under the main road twice, and in various places parts of it have been used for widening corners. One such place is by the 'Nag's Head' at Garthmyl, where bridge 131 stands parallel to the realigned road, on its left.

Garthmyl marks the junction between the Western and Eastern Branches. A mile north, the canal turns north west away from the Severn, but soon turns north east to cross the Rhiw by the ponderous-looking Berriew aqueduct, which was rebuilt in 1889. Two 30ft arches take the canal, here piped, over the river, and a third arch takes it over the minor road alongside. Having passed the village of Berriew, the Montgomeryshire keeps on the west side of A483 until shortly before Welshpool, and can be reached by any of the tracks or minor roads off to the left. Limekilns Lane, a few yards south of A483/A490 junction, leads to the Belan locks, one each side of a bridge, with a lock cottage by the northern one.

Here it is worth studying the ground paddles, a type unique to this canal. An exceptionally large gear wheel is supported by a substantial iron framework, with an elegant curve to the outer posts. The paddles were fitted horizontally in the canal bed, and were made of cast iron. Some of the lock gates on the Eastern Branch were made of cast iron, installed after 1819; a pair of these is at the Waterways Museum, Stoke Bruerne, on the Grand Union. The remains of one of the boats marooned by the burst in 1936 may still be visible in the growth between the two locks. The locks have been converted to weirs, but a massive lock key lies in the grass by the southern one.

The canal enters Welshpool on the east side of A483. The wharf, in Severn Street, was cleaned out by a volunteer working party in 1969; the lock at least looks operable, and the warehouse is in good condition. Occasionally a boat may be seen on the canal hereabouts; there is also an extraordinary craft, a squarish punt with an outboard motor on one end and a legless wire bedstead on the other, which the local enthusiasts use for clearing weed and debris. A483 again crosses the canal, culverted, on the north of Welshpool, and keeps in close company for the next few miles. Pool Quay, with its lock, is 3½ miles farther north: Bank lock, at the summit, is another mile on. The canal deserts A483, looping westward for a couple of miles; conveniently for the motorist, it soon meets B4392, near the two Burgedin locks and the junction with the 2¼ mile Guilsfield Branch. The branch, much overgrown and now a Nature Reserve, runs south west alongside B4392 to Tyddyn Basin, where timber used to be shipped for Liverpool.

Three miles north from the junction, the main line crosses the Vyrnwy by a five-arch aqueduct, with a smaller three-arch aqueduct over the flood plain next to it. One of the 39ft arches collapsed soon after construction, and had to be rebuilt; in 1823 the whole structure had to be repaired, and the iron bands used for strengthening it stand out against its white finish. It is leaking again today. The aqueduct is by the junction of B4398 and B4393, 1½ miles south west of Llanymynech. Between the aqueduct and Llanymynech are Carreghofa locks, the junction with the old Ellesmere Canal section. Several limestone quarries are in this area. There is a pleasant watered stretch with some bridges to the west of the village; on the north side, A483 occurs for the last time as the canal heads north-eastward for Frankton. Some lengths here are short of water. Crickheath Wharf is 2¼ miles on from Llanymynech; then B4396 crosses the canal at Redwith. Maesbury Marsh has a Navigation Inn, and an old crane by the canal, here narrow and reedy. A5 crosses the Montgomeryshire by the 'Queen's Head', near the junction with the Oswestry road A4083. A minor road to Rednal runs north east from this point, alongside the canal. Just before the railway crosses the road, there is a brick roving bridge, no 74, and beside it a small two-storey, half-timbered building, almost overhanging the water. It has been suggested by Mr J. Horsley Denton (see below) that this was the 'canal passenger station' where the flyboat passengers, having left the train at nearby Rednal station, could buy their tickets for Newtown (25p first class, 15p second) and wait for their craft. The towpath leads to a larger warehouse building on the far side of the railway.

Another 2½ miles, mostly dry, brings the Montgomeryshire to Lockgate bridge and the junction with the Weston Branch of the Ellesmere. From here the towpath leads to the two single and one double Frankton locks, looking as if it would not take too much work to put them back into commission, and a cottage beside them. At the top is the junction, and the waters, busy in summer, of the Llangollen.

OS sheets 128 (Newtown–Garthmyl)
      117 (Berriew–Llanymynech)
      118 (Crickheath–Welsh Frankton)
The Canals of the West Midlands, by Charles Hadfield
'By Rail & Canal to Mid-Wales in 1853', J. Horsley Denton; RCHS
    Journal vol XVI no 2, April 1970
'The Montgomery', by H. Arnold; IWA *Bulletin*, no 93, May 1970

THE MONMOUTHSHIRE CANAL

The two arms of the Monmouthshire Canal stretch up from Newport into the valleys of the Usk and the Ebbw. The eastern arm, the main line, meets the Brecon & Abergavenny Canal at Pontymoile Basin, near Pontypool. Here begins 33 miles of one of the most beautiful waterways in Britain, much of it terraced on the hillside above the River Usk and recently restored and re-opened as a navigation into Brecon. The only canal within the boundaries of a National Park, the Brecon & Abergavenny has been fortunate in its saviours: the gentleman whose possession of a lock pass brought about the restoration of the locks in the 1930s, the devoted local engineer of BWB, and the Monmouthshire and Brecon County Councils who contributed generously to BWB's restoration work on the canal in the last few years. But the Monmouthshire Canal, with its far heavier lockage, has met a different fate; although even here all has not been lost.

The Monmouthshire Canal, mostly completed by 1796, was constructed chiefly to serve the blast furnaces of Abercarn, Ebbw Vale, Nantyglo and Blaenavon. It cost about £220,000; this included the building by the Canal Company of a considerable mileage of tramroads linking the canal with the various works, many of them situated high on the hillsides. The main line ran from a junction with the Usk in Newport to Pontnewynydd, to the north of Pontypool. There were 42 locks, taking it up well over 400ft. The western, or Crumlin, branch left the main line at Malpas, 2 miles from Newport, and ascended by 32 locks to Crumlin, 11 miles to the north west. The locks on the Monmouthshire, like those on the other South Wales valley canals, were built to their own peculiar dimensions, in this case to take boats 64ft 9in by 9ft 2in (the first boats, which cost £28 each, were slightly smaller than this)—dimensions shared, by perhaps uncharacteristic foresight, by the locks on the B & A. Boats used on these canals, certainly in their later years, were double-ended and essentially workmanlike, with no pretensions to elegance; the gay reds and greens of the English narrow boats did not penetrate to the dour valleys of South Wales.

The Monmouthshire was engineered by Thomas Dadford, jun, who worked also on the Glamorganshire and Leominster canals. He grouped many of the locks in flights, the greatest being the Fourteen at Rogerstone, on the Crumlin Branch. There were no major aqueducts and only one short tunnel, on the main line. Coal and iron were the principal cargoes, and within a few years Newport became an important coal-exporting port; 7,000 tons were shipped in 1797, and 148,000 tons in 1809. In the early nineteenth century the canal was twice extended in Newport; new wharves were constructed and another lock added, at Potter St. But for the first few years the company did poorly and dividends were either small or non-existent. Receipts rose about 1810; then trouble arose for the proprietors in 1812 with the completion of the B & A, which charged lower tolls. The Monmouthshire company paid the B & A £3,000 to make a junction with their canal at Pontymoile, instead of bypassing to cut into the Usk lower down. The Monmouthshire charged 5d per ton per mile for iron, while the B & A's price was 2d per ton; eventually the Monmouthshire agreed to charge no more than its neighbour on goods which passed over both canals. But, although it was compelled to reduce tolls from time to time, it remained always a relatively expensive canal.

Receipts rose again after the agreement with the B & A, reaching over £40,000 in some years. The canal was very busy, over 800,000 tons a year being handled in the peak period of the early 1840s. Newport at this time was exporting more coal than Cardiff, despite the Taff Vale Railway already serving the latter port. A railway from Newport to Nantyglo had been proposed; chary of competition, the Monmouthshire company decided to act themselves, and surveyed their own line from Newport to Pontypool. After a deal of complicated manoeuvring, the company in 1845 obtained a Bill to turn itself into a railway company; the tramroads were relaid with track suitable for locomotives (limited to 10mph), and tolls were reduced to 1½d a ton on iron and ¾d a ton on coal. For the Monmouthshire Railway & Canal Company the first few years were disappointing; work was delayed and accusations of incompetence were made. Then in 1852 a virtually new committee was elected and the Newport–Pontypool Railway opened at last.

Traffic was now leaving the canal, which by 1864 was very little used, more being spent on maintenance than was taken in tolls. The next year the company raised money to buy the B & A, thus bringing more traffic to the railway. Receipts fell to £738 in 1878; the following year part of the canal in Newport was closed and railway lines laid over it. In 1880 the Monmouthshire Co amalgamated with the GWR; canal trade declined still further: 1915 saw the last regular Newport market boat; 1930 the last cargo on the Crumlin Branch; 1938 the last cargo on the main line. The branch was closed in 1949 and the main line finally abandoned in 1962.

Like the Glamorganshire Canal in Cardiff, the Monmouthshire in Newport has now been nearly entirely eliminated. Much of its course has been covered by car parks here as well. At the time of writing, the Town Lock can be found in Mill St car park but this, with the stretch of cut as far as Barrack Rd, is due to be filled in. North of Barrack Rd the canal has water and a towpath, and rounds a wooded hillside to the junction with the Crumlin Branch at Malpas. Here the main line turns north; the M4 motorway has been lifted over it, optimistically leaving full navigational headroom; a pair of swans disturb the surface weed on the far side of the motorway. It is possible to follow the towpath through to Cwmbran and Pontypool. Some stone bridges remain, and short stretches of the canal can be used for canoeing. The locks, however, are now weirs; in Cwmbran, some of them have been converted into waterfalls or cascades, attractive enough in their way. Cwmbran UDC was the first local authority in Britain to take over a stretch of canal within its boundary from BWB and develop it as an amenity. Hence most of the Monmouthshire has been saved from becoming a linear rubbish-dump.

By Cwmbran's northern boundary, Five Locks Road has been constructed over the top of the five locks, thus cutting off the top 2 miles. There are no locks on this stretch, which includes the 80yd Cwmbran tunnel, which would be passable if the silt were cleared. North of the tunnel, the canal passes into the area of Pontypool, and its condition is greatly deteriorated. Parts of the channel are nearly blocked by weed; beneath each bridge old bicycles and bedsteads accumulate. The water, which is drawn off and used by factories, has to be kept flowing; but it has a struggle. Short-sighted alterations at Crown Bridge, Sebastopol, involving the insertion of a corrugated iron 'pipe' too narrow to admit the passage of boats, have cut off prospects of restoring navigation on the section and, by encouraging silting, cause flooding of the towpath and the adjoining properties from time to time. Properly maintained, this stretch could prove a valuable amenity to a heavily industrialised area, with easy access from the roads, and two canalside pubs; as it is, it is more of a disgrace. But soon the Monmouthshire debouches into Pontymoile Basin, with its attractive white-painted bridge and toll-house by the site of the stop-lock that once divided its water from that of the B & A. The section from Pontymoile to Pontnewynydd was closed by 1853, much of it having been used for the line of the railway. A few scattered traces of it can be found, including part of a lock preserved on a new traffic roundabout on the east side of Pontypool.

From Malpas Junction the Crumlin Branch continues westward, parallel to the motorway. It preserves a rural atmosphere, despite the proximity of heavy traffic. It runs beneath the hill called Allt-yr-yn, 'the declivity of the ash-trees'. Of this place, W. H. Davies, the Super-Tramp and poet, born in Newport, wrote:

> Thy water, Alteryn,
> Shines brighter through my tears,
> With childhood in my mind;
> So will it shine when age
> Has made me almost blind.

Allt-yr-yn lock, with its cottages and small stone bridge, is dear to Newport hearts, holding memories of many childhoods. There are five single locks on this stretch as it winds through the fields. Then the canal turns north-westward, is culverted under the motorway, and reaches the foot of the fourteen Rogerstone locks. These locks, some of them double, have deep stone chambers, lifting the canal over 150ft. There is a lock cottage about halfway up. One of the locks, known as the 'sea lock', was built wide at the top to provide a passing-place for boats. The skeleton of one of the boats lies in the grass near the top of the flight, between the side-ponds.

The remainder of the branch lies on the north-east side of A467, easily accessible from several minor roads. Although close to a busy main road and to the heavily populated Risca district, much of the canal is in rural surroundings. It is culverted three times as it passes by the Ty Sign housing estate, the least attractive stretch, but otherwise the bridges and towpath are mostly in good repair. Steep hills and woodlands border the canal on the top section, north of Risca quarry. In all, nearly 6 miles of the branch, as far as Pontywaun, survive. North of here, through Abercarn, the canal either has been or will be used for road widening; there is nothing to see except bits of muddy ditch. Crumlin has lost its canal as well as its great and famous viaduct. A Planning Study has been recently made of the watered section of the branch which, among other recommendations, suggests that where it passes through the housing estate the canal should be treated to provide an 'intimately detailed arcadian setting'. The Fourteen Locks may be filled in to give only a few inches depth (the old lock-keeper's comments on this are unprintable even in this permissive age), and the side-ponds may become paddling pools for children.

Bertram Baxter (in *Stone Blocks & Iron Rails*, 1966) lists 24 tramroads (the old horse railways using L-shaped rails, known as 'dramroads' in Wales and the Forest of Dean) that connected with the Monmouthshire Canal. About half of these were privately owned. A further nine connected with the B & A. With the two canals, these tramroads formed an integrated transport system for the industries of the Eastern Valleys. In his novel, *Rape of the Fair Country*, Richard Llewellyn dramatically reconstructs the perils and pleasures of the use of Hill's Tramroad, which descended from Garn Ddyrys to the B & A at Llanfoist. Of the Monmouthshire Canal's tramroads nearly all traces have now been obliterated; Baxter could find no more than sixteen items, and by now several of these have probably disappeared.

OS sheet 155 (Newport–Pontypool)
        154 (Crumlin Branch, Rogerstone–Crumlin)
The Canals of South Wales & the Border, by Charles Hadfield

THE GLAMORGANSHIRE CANAL

The story of the Glamorganshire, the greatest of the South Wales canals, is entwined with the history of the Taff Valley. The canal was cut from Merthyr Tydfil to Cardiff; its beginning is within sight of Cyfarthfa Castle, family home of the Crawshays, and its last traces in Cardiff skirt the walls of Cardiff Castle, once the home of the Marquesses of Bute. Between, it runs through mining villages: Abercanaid, Troedyrhiw, Mount Pleasant and Aberfan.

Opened in 1794, the Glamorganshire was the creation of the Merthyr ironmasters, led by Richard Crawshay, who raised the money, appointed the Dadfords and Thomas Sheasby as contractors, voted each other on and off the committee, wrangled among themselves and with the common enemy, the Marquess of Bute, and made themselves very rich indeed. The canal was 24½ miles long, falling 543ft to Cardiff through 49 locks, most of them well over 10ft deep, taking boats 60ft by 9ft carrying up to 25 tons each. The result of one of the quarrels of the committeemen was

the famous Penydarren tramroad which met the canal at Abercynon and on which Trevithick's first locomotive ran in 1804.
This was built by the Dowlais ironmasters, who had had the
temerity to try to circumvent Crawshay and were thrown off the
canal committee as a result. As well as fractious committeemen,
the Glamorganshire company had another problem, one not often
met with among canal undertakings. They had more money than
they knew what to do with. This was a consequence of a clause in
the Act, limiting dividends to 8 per cent. Even in the canal's early
years the profits exceeded this; so tolls were progressively reduced
and large percentages of them were also returned to the traders.
As the traders were mostly the ironmasters who owned the canal,
this was fine for them; but their generosity did not extend to their
employees, who suffered reductions in wages and the stopping of
their supply of beer.

As traffic increased—reaching, in the early 1850s, almost
600,000 tons a year—congestion grew and new problems arose.
The Marquess of Bute prevented the company improving their
basin and wharves in Cardiff, as he had his own schemes for
developing Cardiff docks. Delays occurred at the Treble Locks at
Nantgarw, where 'working turns' became necessary to conserve
water, as well as at Melingriffith where Blakemore, owner of the
tinworks, refused the company's request to widen the cut at a
particularly notorious narrow stretch, for fear his works would
lose water thereby.

In 1836, the Taff Vale Railway Co, formed, as might have
been expected, by a group of ironmasters who had fallen out with
the reigning Crawshay, got its Act, bought the Penydarren tramroad, and opened its line from Merthyr to Cardiff in 1841. This
became for a time the most prosperous line in Britain; yet, as the
coal trade increased, the canal continued to prosper as well. It was
not until the 1860s that the canal's trade began to fall off; new
collieries were now connected directly to the railway, as were new
steelworks which replaced the old ironworks, and the canal company's plans to improve their property in Cardiff were again
defeated. By 1882 the company was hardly able to pay any dividend, and Lord Bute's offer to buy all the shares was accepted. For
Bute, control of the canal removed one of his old enemies,
strengthened his hand against the other, the Taff Vale Railway,
and gave him an additional water supply for his own dock im-

provement projects. On Bute's canal committee there was no representative of the Crawshay dynasty.

The first section of canal to be abandoned was the short Cyfarthfa–Merthyr length, in 1868. In 1898, the stretch from Merthyr to Abercynon was abandoned; the section to Pontypridd closed in 1915, and a burst at Nantgarw in 1942 saw the end of the canal as a navigable waterway. Until very recently, almost all of the line of the Glamorganshire could be followed quite easily, but improvements to the main road down the valley are obliterating certain lengths. There are few traces in Merthyr itself; the site of the basin is opposite the Barley Mow by the Georgetown round-about, near the bus depot. The lock cottage has been recently demolished, but a warehouse carries on a tenuous existence. In Cyfarthfa Castle, now partly a college and partly a well-kept museum, there are examples of the Penydarren track and the numberplate of a Glamorganshire boat. In the Castle grounds the descendants of the Crawshays' workers eat ice-cream, sail small boats on the lake and relax to enjoy the view over industrial Merthyr.

South of Merthyr is the village of Abercanaid; the canal runs along the west of the village and can be followed for some miles. Here also are traces of the Cyfarthfa Canal, most of which lies beneath tips and old workings. This short waterway, which ante-dated the Glamorganshire by some ten years, was used to take coal into the Cyfarthfa works in strings of small tub-boats drawn by men, sometimes by women or children. It was out of use by 1840. At Abercanaid there are the remains of two docks on the Glamorganshire, the lower one over 80yd long with the stone-work well defined. The pumping engine at Pontyrun, built in the early nineteenth century to improve the canal's water supply, was demolished many years ago. Dressed stone from its housing was used in the building of a church at Aberfan, itself recently demo-lished. There are two bridges on this section, one an old swing bridge, now fixed; farther south, the canal passes by the fan house and Cornish beam engine house of the Gethin mine. The towpath can be followed down the valley to Cefn-glas, north west of Quaker's Yard, where there is a cottage and a bridge with most of its parapet missing. A fine railway viaduct by Brunel can be seen to the south east. The canal passes through Aberfan, where sight-seers still come to gaze at the scene of disaster. At 14ft 6in, one of

Page 119 (above) *Montgomeryshire Canal: the suggested 'interchange' station at Rednal;* (below) *Glamorganshire Canal: the pump at Melingriffith. Operated by a waterwheel, it returned to the canal water taken out by the tin plate works*

(above) *Tennant Canal: the aqueduct over the River Neath at Aberdulais, seen through the arches of the railway bridge;* (below) *Neath Canal: the Giant's Grave extension, crossed by the viaduct taking A483 over the valley*

the Aberfan locks was the deepest made in Britain, greater by 6in than the top lock at Tardebigge on the Worcs & Birmingham Canal.

Eight and a half miles from the Merthyr basin is the junction with the Aberdare Canal, at Abercynon. This is at the top of the town near Incline Top, the head of the fall by several double staircase locks through Abercynon. A smart modern house, with a carefully preserved lock wall in its garden, has been built almost on the site of the junction; in front of it the Glamorganshire descended through the middle of the town, the lock sites being discernible on a grass and rubble slope between the backs of houses. Boats were once built at Abercynon. At the foot of the descent, the canal used to cross the Taff by an aqueduct, which it shared with a turnpike road. The aqueduct is now replaced by a bridge carrying A4059; the junction with the Penydarren tram-road, where there are some traces of the basin and wharves, is on the north side of the road between the bridge and the Navigation House.

Much of the canal south of Abercynon is—or will shortly be—obliterated, replaced by a new road. The greatest loss, from the point of view of industrial archaeology, is the great Nantgarw Treble Locks. Each about 14ft deep, the chambers were in excellent condition, with the remains of gates and footbridges, before demolition. These locks were lit by gaslight for round-the-clock working in the busiest days of the canal. Now, as no Preservation Order could be obtained, they have gone, though it is hoped that a model of them will be displayed in the National Museum of Wales, Cardiff.

At Tongwynlais, nearly 2 miles down the valley road and to the west of it, a stretch of the canal has been preserved as part of a nature reserve. There is a firm towpath, two lock chambers, and the water is full of roach. The canal joins the Melingriffith Works feeder at the end of this stretch. Here was the famous 'narrow place' which caused so much trouble. By a path around a car park, just past the end of the main building of the works, is the major engineering relic of the canal; the waterwheel and pump, installed about 1809 as a result of Rennie's recommendations for improving the water supply to the canal. It pumped back to the canal the water that had been taken out by the Melingriffith Works.

The canal continues into Cardiff, although traces are rapidly

H

Glamorganshire Canal: balance beam and paddle gear, Nantgarw locks (now demolished)

disappearing under building sites. Its course now forms part of the car park along the east side of Cardiff Castle. The pedestrian subway under Kingsway incorporates a canal bridge, with towpath under it; on the parapet by the Castle are the bases of the original gas lamps. The 115yd tunnel beneath Queen Street, through which boats were hauled by chains fixed to the walls, has gone, but the course of the canal can be followed through East and West Canal Wharf, the Custom House, and the New Sea Lock Inn. After a series of car parks there is a levelled grassy stretch, with an old warehouse and an iron bollard. Some of the bollards on the Glamorganshire were cannon barrels, rejected because of some flaw in the casting. Part of the sea lock remains, leading into a silted arm of the estuary, but the lock itself has been walled off, the pound filled in and lorries are parked where the sailing ships used to moor. The barge weighing machine from Cardiff has been installed at the Waterways Museum, Stoke Bruerne.

OS sheet 154
The Canals of South Wales & the Border, by Charles Hadfield

THE ABERDARE CANAL

Nineteen years elapsed between the Act authorising the construction of a canal joining Aberdare to the Glamorganshire Canal at Abercynon and the completion of the work. The canal itself, a straightforward waterway 6¾ miles long, with three locks and no major engineering works, took only two years to build. The delay was due to disagreement among the ironmasters about priorities. The Aberdare Canal Company built a tramroad towards Hirwaun, in the opposite direction to Abercynon, in the first instance, which paid a 1 per cent dividend, and some of its members also sponsored a turnpike road from Abercynon through Aberdare to the head of the Neath valley; but it was not until 1809 that the major shareholders became impatient and the company began to fulfil its *raison d'être*.

John Dadford had surveyed the line originally; Edward Martin had another look at it, Thomas Sheasby, jun, became engineer (he, was succeeded by George Overton before the canal was completed), work began in 1810 and the canal was opened in the summer of 1812 at a cost of a little over £26,000. It took boats of the same dimensions as those on the Glamorganshire. It followed the north side of the Cynon valley and joined the Glamorganshire by a stop-lock.

For some years trading figures were disappointing, but they began to improve after tolls were reduced in 1819 and the Crawshays took over the Hirwaun works and also bought shares in the canal. As Crawshay interest grew so efficiency increased, but for twenty years the iron traffic remained at about 60,000 tons a year and dividends were correspondingly low. It was the steam coal trade that eventually justified the canal's existence. By 1840 this was beginning to make an impression; by 1846 there was not enough water to cope with the traffic and a pumping engine was installed to raise water from the Cynon; and by 1848 the canal was carrying almost 160,000 tons a year.

Although by this time the railways had reached the valley, for the next sixteen years the canal continued to flourish, with the annual tonnage increasing to over 200,000 and dividends to £10 per £120 share. But when a third railway, the Aberdare Valley extension, arrived in 1864, the canal began to suffer. Trade fell off by over 50 per cent, and as receipts and dividends declined so the Company became pessimistic about its future. In 1883, with dividends down to about 1½ per cent, they sold out to Lord Bute, who had recently purchased the Glamorganshire. A plan to convert the canal to a railway fell through, the coal and iron trade ceased completely, and in 1900 defeat was acknowledged and the Aberdare Canal was closed. In 1923 the Aberdare and Mountain Ash UDCs bought the property, and it was used for road widening. The B4275 (Aberdare–Mountain Ash) and A4059 (Mountain Ash–Abercynon) show where the Aberdare Canal used to be. About 200yd of the bed can still be traced at Abercynon, westward from the junction with the Glamorganshire, and the remains of the stop-lock are concealed in the undergrowth. What used to be some canal-side cottages at Mountain Ash now back on to the road, but otherwise there are now few traces left.

OS sheet 154
The Canals of South Wales & the Border, by Charles Hadfield

THE NEATH CANAL

A river, a road, a railway and a canal run down each of the four South Wales valleys leading to Newport, Cardiff, Neath and Swansea. According to a Welsh international fly-half, the necessity of learning to side-step at an early age to avoid being either run over or drowned is the reason why Welsh rugby players are so nimble-footed. In the Taff and Tawe valleys the road has in many places been widened over the bed of the abandoned canal; but in the Neath valley this has not yet happened, and the course of the Neath Canal can be followed almost without interruption.

The Neath was the second of these canals to be completed, about 1795. It was 13 miles long, with three short private branches, and descended by nineteen locks taking boats 6oft by 8ft 10in. Thomas Dadford, jun, was the surveyor, followed by Thomas Sheasby; coal for export and iron ore for the Neath Abbey works were the main cargoes. A tramroad connection was made to furnaces at Aberdare, Abernant and Hirwaun, but trade from this source declined when the Aberdare Canal, connecting with the Glamorganshire, opened in 1812. However, the company did well; the canal was cheap to construct and it was not long before it was carrying over 200,000 tons of coal a year, as well as other products. At first the coal was transhipped into sea-going vessels at Neath; later some of it went to Swansea via the Tennant Canal. The canal was extended from Neath in various stages by the privately-built Giant's Grave & Briton Ferry Canal, which served wharves and works farther down the estuary.

The Vale of Neath Railway opened in 1851, but as mostly it ran on the other side of the river from the canal, the latter survived the competition for over twenty years. But it could not go on indefinitely; new collieries preferred the railway and the older ones made connections to it by building bridges. Although the canal was not closed until 1934, there had been very little traffic on it for many years. It is still owned by the Neath Canal Company; the lower portion is in good order and, with the Tennant Canal, supplies most of the industry in the area with water.

The canal begins at Glynneath, about halfway between Merthyr and Neath on A465. The site of the basin is near the end of

Oddfellows Street, on the south-east side of the main road. A wall and a ruined house mark the end of the basin, and there is a muddy length of cut with a broken bridge through an opencast coal site. The canal keeps very close to the road, which crosses it twice south of Glynneath; there are several bridges and lock chambers along the route, many of them in sound condition. Fed by streams from the hills, the canal at times holds water north of Resolven; south of the village it is watered throughout. Just over 2 miles from Resolven the canal crosses the river by the Ynysbwllog aqueduct, stone-built with three low arches. This can be seen from the road, but is not quite so impressive on closer inspection as, although there is a towpath across it, the water is piped and the farther parapet has fallen away.

At Aberdulais is the junction with the Tennant, which crosses the river so that the two canals arrive in Neath with the river between them. South of Neath the canal is hemmed in by railways. By turning west at the traffic lights in Briton Ferry and following Brynhyfryd Road round to Zoar Chapel, you come to the Giant's Grave bridges, built in 1930 by Neath Council, which cross the canal a few inches above water level. Here is where the Giant's Grave extension begins in the shadow of the hill of that name; there is the Ship Inn and a few cottages, and the Neath Canal winds away under a bridge northwards around the foot of a hill and into railway territory. The canal arm leading to the pill is cut off and dry. The Giant's Grave Canal runs southwards between the High Duty Alloys rolling mill and a steep rocky bluff. By the entrance to the works the great viaduct carrying A483 over the estuary crosses high overhead, the Vernon Arms nestling beneath it. There is a footbridge over the canal and then the water is taken off underground at the entrance to another works. The remaining few yards of its course have been filled in.

OS sheet 153
The Canals of South Wales & the Border, by Charles Hadfield

THE TENNANT CANAL

The Tennant Canal is the subject of one of our best examples of bad verse. Two stanzas will suffice:

O! Could I make verses of humour and wit,
George Tennant Esquire's great genius to fit;
From morn until even I would sit down and tell,
And sing in the praise of Neath Junction Canal.

To his noble genius, great merit is due,
The increase of traffic, he'll daily pursue;
Employ to poor labourers, it is known full well,
He gave them by making Neath Junction Canal.

And so on for nineteen verses. It was written by a Neath poetess, Elizabeth Davies, on the opening of the canal (often called the Neath & Swansea Junction) in 1824.

George Tennant wanted to develop the land on the western side of the River Neath. He took over a short existing canal, the Glan-y-wern, in 1818, and cut the Red Jacket Canal from the west bank of the estuary to join it. It was now possible for boats to come off the River Neath and voyage by canal to Swansea. But there was no direct connection with the Neath Canal; so, instead of making a difficult river crossing, Tennant decided to extend his canal northwards to join the Neath Canal at Aberdulais. This he did as a private undertaking, at a cost of about £20,000. At Port Tennant, on the east side of the Tawe estuary, he built a tidal dock with extensive wharves.

The project was successful. Trade, mainly in coal, was steady and in the peak years of the 1860s, later in time than with most other navigations, rose to over 200,000 tons a year. Even the opening of the Swansea & Neath Railway had little effect on receipts. For several years there was a service for passengers and parcels. Because it was tidal, however, Port Tennant had obvious limitations, and in the early years of this century it was absorbed by Swansea Docks and the canal was truncated. Some little commercial traffic continued for a time, navigation ending at the same time as on the Neath Canal, about 1934. The Tennant Canal is still in the family's ownership and is well maintained as a source of industrial water supply.

The Tennant–Neath junction is at Aberdulais and can be reached by walking northwards along the Neath towpath from where this canal is crossed by the road to Tonna. The bridge that takes the Neath towpath over the Tennant is of remarkable construction—a skew bridge with massive stepped stonework on one side of the arch. The Tennant heads south through trees for 50yd and crosses the river by a fine aqueduct, 340ft long, with eleven low arches. At the south end of the aqueduct, by the Tonna road, is a lock, the only one on this canal. On the aqueduct, Elizabeth Davies is, if regrettable, also irresistible:

> The stones that are in it, are the best of all,
> They came from the rock of Dylais water-fall;
> These stones of all others, in strength do excel,
> To bear up the waters of Neath Junction Canal.
>
> The work it is finished, and now is complete,
> And no man did there with an accident meet;
> Though there was great danger, yet nobody fell,
> By building the aqueduct of Neath Junction Canal.

The canal is the westmost of the three waterways through Neath; it then runs parallel to the river through factory estates and criss-crossed by railways. There is a long deep cutting where the canal passes to the south of Neath Abbey. B4290 on the south side of Jersey Marine crosses the canal, which heads westward across the edge of Crymlyn Bog to terminate by works and railway sidings south of the housing area of Port Tennant. For many years there has been no connection with the docks.

The achievement of George Tennant and his engineer, William Kirkhouse, was no mean one. The Tennant was one of the most successful of the private canal undertakings, and there is no doubting the prosperity it brought to the areas it was constructed to serve.

OS sheet 153
The Canals of South Wales & the Border, by Charles Hadfield

THE SWANSEA CANAL

Like the other South Wales valley canals, the Swansea Canal was a profitable undertaking. It obtained its Act, and was opened in 1798, three years after its eastward neighbour, the Neath Canal, several of whose shareholders also promoted the Swansea venture.

It ran 15 miles down the Tawe Valley, from a point south of Abercrave to a wharf in Swansea, and incorporated the short Trewyddfa Canal south of Morriston, built about 1796 by the Duke of Beaufort. There were 36 locks, to take boats 69ft 2in by 7ft 6in (all the Welsh canals had their local variations in lock dimensions), and the surveyor and chief engineer was Thomas Sheasby, who had also worked on the Neath.

From 1804 to 1895 the canal never failed to return a profit. Although it never reached the figures of the Monmouthshire or Glamorganshire, trade in the peak years of the 1830s and 1850s approached an annual figure of 400,000 tons, and dividends rose to 18 per cent. Coal, culm, and later iron were the chief cargoes, and the valley and the port prospered with the canal. Railway competition caused the company to reduce tolls to maintain trade at a reasonable level, but in 1873, while still a going concern, the company sold the canal to the GWR for over £107,000, about twice the construction cost of the waterway. The lower end continued to run profitably for over twenty years, and some short-haul traffic continued until 1931, but trade ceased on the upper stretch before the turn of the century.

The A4067 Sennybridge–Swansea road runs alongside the canal for the whole of its length. The terminal basin was near the southern namepost of the village of Abercrave (or Abercraf); there is a bridge to the west of the road, and the remains of a lock and some cottages along the second turning to the right. It passes by the Castle Hotel at Caer Lan, and keeps to the west of the road towards Ystradgynlais. There (SN 790110) it crosses the Gledd, a tributary of the Tawe, by a single-arch stone aqueduct; a path follows the canal in either direction. It stays on the west side of the village, steps opposite the side of the Yniscedwyn Arms Hotel leading up to the canal on an embankment. There is a lock chamber where a minor road crosses the canal by the new industrial estate, and a skew bridge beside the Aubrey Arms—so far, following the Swansea Canal is greatly a matter of proceeding from pub to pub. For the sake of variety, as it were, the next landmark is a small white cinema at Ystalyfera. Behind this—there is a convenient car park—is the largest artefact on the canal, a substantial three-arch stone aqueduct over the Afon Twrch which comes tearing down from the hills towards the Tawe. A footpath also goes under the canal. The towpath can be followed southward to the remains of a lock and a derelict flour mill, which used to be operated by the canal water.

South of Ystalyfera, the canal loops towards the main road and locks into it by a signpost to Godre-graig. There are the walls of two locks, with a seat in the lower one; then for a mile or so road and canal virtually coincide. The tops of the lock walls have been preserved on the grass verge on the right of the road, where there is a narrow water channel. Just before Cilmaengwyn the canal leaves the road, to swing westward, and crosses under it in the village. The towpath leads under a bridge and past a derelict tinplate works; the water pours down through two well-preserved lock chambers. From here onwards it really looks like a canal, as it passes on the east of Pontardawe under a bridge and then under the Neath road and across a small single-arch aqueduct. Approaching Clydach, the main road crosses the canal twice, the old red diamond signs still marking the bridges. By the second bridge a pair of lower lock gates remain in situ, with short balance beams, because of their nearness to the parapet, worked by ropes and pulley wheels. In Clydach there is another single-arch aqueduct, over the Clydach River; it is found by following the 'Gentlemen' sign beside the Public Hall. The amenity itself is furnished with splendid brown porcelain by Duckett & Son, Ltd, of Burnley.

The canal now, as wide as when first made, keeps close to the road through Morriston and into Swansea. There are proposals to utilise it for road widening, and proposals to reopen it for light pleasure boating as a kind of water park—which would certainly brighten up this not particularly attractive part of the valley. It terminates on the northern side of Swansea, behind the British Electrical Repairs factory. The final stretch runs past the backsides of several factories and under some shaky-looking bridges; then the canal stops, railway sidings begin, and water is led off through a culvert towards the Tawe. Rebuilding has obliterated the last mile or so to the Docks, which themselves have been reconstructed so that the old pattern has gone.

Cheaply built—it cost less than any other South Wales valley canal except for the Neath—and efficiently run, the Swansea Canal, like the others, brought the initial prosperity to its port. Now that so much of the Glamorganshire has disappeared, it is perhaps the best surviving example of its kind, and one hopes that because of this its preservation will be assured.

OS sheet 153
The Canals of South Wales & the Border, by Charles Hadfield

THE KIDWELLY & LLANELLY CANAL

There is a sizeable collection of old canals in south west Wales, most of them unpronounceable by the Englishman and all but invisible to the naked eye. Investigating their remains demands time and dedication; it is easier to discern their traces after heavy rain—when, of course, it is more difficult to approach them because of the morass thereby created. The most considerable of these canals was the Kidwelly & Llanelly—inappropriately named, as it turned out, as it merely skirted Kidwelly and got nowhere near Llanelly at all.

Included in the K & L was an earlier canal, Kymer's, the first Welsh canal to obtain a Parliamentary Act, which opened in 1769. This was made by Thomas Kymer to connect his mines and quarries with the quay at Kidwelly and avoid the uncertainties of navigation on the Gwendraeth Fawr. Although only 3 miles long, it proved to be useful, and when in the early nineteenth century proposals were made to develop Kidwelly harbour and improve communications generally, Kymer's Canal was seen as an integral part. Llanelly and Kidwelly were to be linked by a canal which would incorporate Kymer's, and a branch was to be built up the Gwendraeth valley for several miles. Other branches or tramroads were also suggested, the whole to form a transport network. But not all the necessary funds were forthcoming, and work proceeded in fits and starts. What was to be built of the K & L was finished about 1838. This comprised a line from Kymer's Canal up the valley as far as Cwm-mawr, and another from a junction near Spudder's Bridge, 1½ miles south east of Kidwelly, to Burry Port. The best way to comprehend what was built is to look at the single-track railway line on the OS sheet, as this was built generally on the bed of the canal.

The first plan was to use locks for the descent down the valley to Kidwelly, but when, after some interval, work restarted in the 1830s, the plan was altered. That interesting engineer, James Green, was called in, a man who, as his work on the West Country canals shows, would never use a lock if he could think of an alternative. He proposed three inclined planes with a total fall of about 200ft; and three inclined planes there were. But, to be fair, it cannot be proved that the substitution of inclines shortened the canal's life. For it was a short life; in 1865, aware of the threat of loss of traffic to competing railways and troubled by problems of maintenance and the difficulties of keeping a channel in Kidwelly harbour, the K & L turned itself into a railway company, joined with the company running Burry Port, and within a few years built railway lines over its canals.

Evidence on the ground of the existence of the K & L is fragmentary. Opposite Kidwelly church a road leads to the railway station. On the far side of the level-crossing the northernmost of two tracks leads to a sewage farm and also to a bit of the Kymer's section of the K & L—the last few yards with a small stone-walled basin. There was no connection with the estuary, a silted expanse with something of a hopeless air about it. Back a short distance along the canal there is indication of a branch that was intended to go to Kidwelly bridge, but may not have done so.

There are a few things to see in the vicinity of Spudder's Bridge, on B4308, one of which is the old bridge itself, now bypassed. About ½ mile downstream, the branch line to Burry Port crosses the river using the aqueduct constructed for the canal in 1815, according to its inscription. A short walk south-westward is the end of the Moat Farm branch of the canal, which was connected by tramroad to collieries at Trimsaran. Farther up the valley there are signs of the canal bed by the bridge over the railway at Pont-newydd. At Ponthenry was the first of the inclines; again, the railway indicates the site on the south side of the village. Little is known about the K & L inclines, except that they seem to have been worked by water power and took small tub-boats. Goods were presumably transhipped into larger boats somewhere on the canal's lower reaches. The head of the Ponthenry incline is conveniently marked by the Incline Hotel in the village. Another incline was at Clos-isaf, 1½ miles up the valley from Pontyberem (the incline used to be called Hirwaun-isaf); the stone structure marking the head of the incline is beside an ungated level-crossing a few yards along a minor road on the north side of B4317. This was the top incline; Mr Charles Hadfield believes that it was never used and that the canal after Pontyberem was no more than a water channel. Between the two inclines mentioned was another one, which has disappeared under coal workings.

The canal ended at Cwm-mawr, near the derelict railway station. It has been suggested that it crosses the river to a basin on the north side, but this does not look likely and evidence on the ground is lacking.

Of the southern arm of the canal there are some traces south of Burry Port, at the east side of the golf links. There are also a few traces of the Pembrey Canal, which lost most of its purpose when the K & L was made. These include a bridge over Pembrey Halt and a terminal building, Glo-Caled, north of A484 between Pembrey and Burry Port. The bridge over the railway just before B4317 joins A484 was adapted from a K & L canal bridge.

One feels that there should be a lot more to add, but it would need research of a microscopic kind. The results of an aerial survey of the region would be invaluable to the earthbound scrutiniser.

OS sheets 152 (Burry Port–Kidwelly–Ponthenry)
　　　　　153 (Ponthenry–Cwm-mawr)
The Canals of South Wales & the Border, by Charles Hadfield

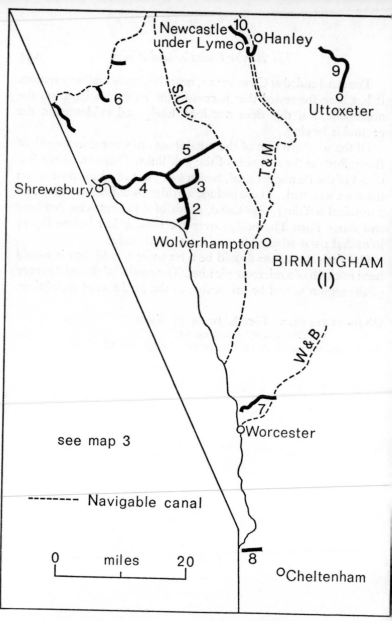

THE BIRMINGHAM CANAL NAVIGATIONS

Birmingham, it has been very often said, has more miles of canal than Venice. In 1905, before closures began, there were 159 miles, as well as several hundred short private branches and basins. Since then, commercial traffic has dwindled away and over 50 miles have been abandoned. But the canals of Birmingham, unlike, it seems, those of Manchester, have a future as well as a past.

Today, Birmingham seems to sprawl, a shapeless conurbation, over most of the West Midlands. Originally a village on high ground, lacking a river and of little importance compared to nearby Coventry, Warwick and Worcester, it grew to surpass its neighbours for three reasons. Firstly, it had beneath it a plentiful supply of water; secondly, it stood on the line of the two most practicable routes linking the neighbouring towns and villages; thirdly, its lords of the manor and their servants had a good nose for trade. Its Bull Ring market was of early importance and, as industries developed, a large number of smaller trades were drawn to Birmingham because of its geographical position and it soon became a manufacturing centre in its own right. By the mid-eighteenth century it was clear that the further prosperity of the town was being hindered by the expense and limitations of waggon transport. The success of the Sankey Brook Navigation and the Bridgewater Canal gave the cue to the Birmingham businessmen; in 1767 a meeting was called to consider the making of a Navigable Cut, an Act was obtained in the following year, and in 1772 the Birmingham Canal, from Newhall to a junction with the Staffs & Worcs at Aldersley, was completed. Matthew Boulton and Samuel Galton were on the first committee, and Brindley was the engineer. The line, a devious one, was probably laid out by Samuel Simcock, working at first under Brindley's supervision. Although the winding line involved some lockage, one advantage was that it served a larger number of works than would otherwise have been possible; when the canal was later straightened, the works remained on the loops of the original line. The price of coal in Birmingham fell dramatically; pig-iron, limestone and industrial materials of all kinds were also carried. In the following decades, branches, basins and wharves were constructed both by the Birmingham Canal Company and by private firms; the Birmingham & Fazeley Canal, 21 miles long, opened in 1789, and the Wyrley & Essington joined the Birmingham system with the Coventry Canal in 1797. The Dudley and Stourbridge canals linked the BCN with the Staffs & Worcs at Stourton, west of Birmingham. Against the opposition of the BCN the Worcester & Birmingham built its line from Gas Street Basin to the Severn, and the Warwick & Birmingham, now part of the Grand Union, formed the essential link with London. All this did not happen without many legal and financial battles. But the significant thing was that, in the words of Professor Gill, in his *History of Birmingham*: 'The problem of cheap transport had been solved, and the solution was so thorough and important that the period from about 1770 to 1830, a time of extraordinarily rapid growth in this town and in many other centres of industry, might well be called the age of canals.'

The 'old' main line, as it came to be known, was surveyed by Brindley on two levels—the Birmingham level at 453ft and the Wolverhampton level 20ft higher. There was also a short summit level at Smethwick. John Smeaton, engineer of the Eddystone lighthouse, who also worked on the Birmingham & Fazeley, replaced the summit section by a cutting in 1790. But the major improvements were carried out between 1825 and 1838, when Telford constructed a new main line from Birmingham to Deepfields, reducing the distance by 7 miles. Telford's great waterway, 40ft wide with a double towpath, striking through the massive cutting at Smethwick beneath that engineer's superb Galton Bridge, was a formidable weapon for the BCN against railway competition. Following Telford's improvements came the last major additions to the system: the Tame Valley Canal (1844), the Rushall Canal (1847), and the Cannock Extension (1863), the last two being part of the Wyrley & Essington which had itself joined the BCN in 1840.

In 1846 the Birmingham company leased its canals to the London & North-Western Railway. The LNWR would guarantee a dividend of 4 per cent, but the canal company would retain control of its waterways as long as the guarantee was not called upon. Railway–canal interchange basins were built, and there was a great deal of short-haul traffic between these and works and

Page 137   (above) *Birmingham Canal Navigations: balance beam of the top lock on the abandoned Upper Level at Smethwick;* (below) *Wyrley & Essington Canal: n/b* Corona-tion, *decomposing in the canal near Huddlesford*

mines on the BCN network. Tonnage carried, mostly short-haul, rose to over 8½ million a year by the end of the nineteenth century. By then there were 26 interchange basins, and the narrow boats were performing similar functions to lorries in the earlier days of mechanised road transport. Tolls were kept low to retain trade, but gradually the LNWR took greater control over the canals. Commercial traffic on the BCN endured longer than on most other canals and over a million tons a year was still being carried immediately after World War II. Closures of branches accelerated in the late 1950s; Thomas Clayton's fleet of tar boats stopped working in 1966; 1968 saw the end of the Cannock coal boats and the closing of the last interchange basin. The Transport Act of 1968 put about 65 miles of the BCN into the category of 'remainder' waterways whose future, at this moment, is still in doubt.

Examination of the 'lost' sections of the BCN is no easy matter. Some have been completely built over, some have been filled in, and some have been cut off by motorway construction. Many derelict loops and branches are best approached by boat, and for this purpose the 'Cruising Guide' to the BCN by K. D. Dunham and R. B. Manion is invaluable. But we must await the full 3 volume study of the BCN now planned. Here I can do no more than indicate a few of the more interesting 'lost' elements of the system.

Much of the new Civic Centre area of Birmingham is built on the site of old canal basins. Baskerville House, the city administrative centre, and the Hall of Memory stand on the site of Gibson's Basins, and the Old Wharf was filled in in 1929 to make a car park in an area which is now being redeveloped. The Newhall Branch, which took the canal deepest into the centre of the city, has been filled in; but on a section of this branch and the adjacent Crescent Wharf something rather unexpected has happened. This area, which lies between King Edward's Road and Summer Row, on the south side of the top of the Farmer's Bridge flight of locks, has been recently developed by the Birmingham City architects in a unique fashion. It is now Birmingham policy 'to integrate the neglected urban canal environment into the life of the City as a recreational and amenity asset'. A landscaped walk, called James Brindley Walk, has been constructed on the line of the Newhall Branch, with a finely restored wharfside crane as a feature and a plaque commemorating the opening of the Walk

I

on the bicentenary of the BCN, in 1969. At the west end of the
Walk, the old Cambrian Wharf has been cleaned out and forms an
excellent mooring. Beside the wharf a public house, very popular
at lunch-times, has been built; although the interior, with its relics
of the Willow Wren fleet which one would rather see afloat, may
strike some as slightly aggressive in its canal associations, the
exterior fits in well with the scale of the waterway outside.
Another crane stands outside, and the beer is (apparently) de-
livered by narrow boat. Beyond the pub, in Kingston Row, a
group of BCN cottages have been restored and re-modelled with
tact and close regard for the environment; a BWB Information
Centre is now housed in this terrace. The short approach to the
Row is paved with the setts taken during alterations from the
locksides. On the far side of the canal, BWB have restored a pair of
lock cottages. The south side of the area is dominated, but not
over-awed, by four tower blocks of flats. On the north side of the
canal old warehouses survive; that they still seem an integral part
of the scene is proof of the imaginative rightness of the development. This is one of the few places in the new Birmingham where
man is comfortable in the scale of his surroundings.

A walk, or voyage, along the main line from Farmer's Bridge
Junction to Smethwick will give a good idea of what remains and
what has been lost of at least part of the BCN. First on the left is
Oozell's Street Loop, still open; then a few hundred yards farther
on Brindley's main line winds across left and right, forming first
the Icknield Port Road Wharf Loop, which leads to Rotton Park
reservoir, one of the BCN's four major reservoirs, and on the right
the Soho Loop, which is in danger of becoming derelict. On
either side of the main line some short cuts into works, most of
them now stopped off, can be seen. As you arrive in Smethwick
the main line continues on the lower level, but Smeaton's upper
level is also accessible through the three Smethwick locks. These
locks were originally duplicated, but the three on the northern
side are now abandoned and, together with the pounds between
them, are due to be filled in. These three were the old locks; the
others were built on account of the heavy traffic over the summit.
Past the top lock the short Engine Branch, so called after the first
Boulton & Watt steam engine, which the company bought to
pump water to the old summit, leads off from the upper level and
crosses the main line by a fine cast-iron aqueduct, called Telford

aqueduct after its designer. The next bridge, Brasshouse Lane, spans both levels. From this bridge—or better from the adjacent railway footbridge—the engineering history of the main line can be seen, as it were, encapsuled. On the left, as you look north west, is Telford's firm line, with the single arch of Galton Bridge spanning the 150ft wide cutting in the distance. In the centre is the upper level, Smeaton's line, with one of the BCN's thirteen pumping stations beside it. Then on the right, high on the hillside below the wall of the 'Boatman's Rest', you can detect the line of Brindley's short summit level which used to be three locks higher than Smeaton's line and was replaced by the latter in 1790.

One of the more interesting abandoned branches of the BCN is Anson Branch, opened in 1830 to serve the Bentley collieries and the Bentley limestone quarry. This branch, less than 1½ miles long, is at Darlaston Green, on the west side of Walsall, and leads off the Wyrley & Essington. Map reference for the junction is SO 987978. A cemetery is on the south side of the junction, and a steel works on the north. The branch soon crosses the Tame, here not much more than a stream, by a brick single-arch aqueduct. Then comes the junction with the Bentley Canal, abandoned in 1961. This canal, with the short section of the Anson Branch, formed a bypass of the northern loop of the w & E; the upper section, not abandoned, is in fair condition, but the Anson end is derelict and weeds are encroaching on the water. Just north of this junction a minor road crosses the Anson Branch, which is soon culverted to pass under M6 and then under the Wolverhampton–Walsall road. On the northern section of the branch remains of the limestone wharves can be found; there is also a tramroad tunnel in a quarry and a pump house at the end of the branch, though this is on private property. For nearly fifty years the water from the Anson Branch has been used by Birchills electricity generating station.

The present termination of the w & E is at Anglesey Wharf, by the Chasewater reservoir. The length from Ogley, at the junction with the Anglesey Branch by B4153 north of Brownhills, to the Coventry Canal at Huddlesford was abandoned in 1954. This stretch, which included thirty locks, passes south and east of Lichfield through pleasant countryside, much of it within sight of the three spires of Lichfield Cathedral. Several sections, including the top three locks, have been filled in and more seem destined to go, either for road widening or under the plough. It seems a pity that now the BCN is attracting an increasing number of pleasure cruisers this valuable link with the waterways of the East Midlands has gone beyond hope of recovery.

The Ogley–Huddlesford length is accessible from several points along A461, between Brownhills and Lichfield, and from the roads south of Lichfield itself. Scenically perhaps the most attractive part is the last mile before the Coventry Canal. A minor road heading north west from the village of Whittington crosses the canal, although the bridge has recently been levelled. On the south-west side the towpath leads to the bow half of the narrow boat *Coronation*, embedded in the mud of the cut. A few yards farther on is a well-proportioned red-brick lock house and the chamber of the last lock of the descent to the Coventry. Much of the wood and ironwork remains. In this rural setting it takes an effort to realise that one is still on a part of the BCN. A mile north east is the junction with the Coventry, near the 'Plough' at Huddlesford crossroads. The final yards of the W & E are used as moorings by a cruising club; there is a cottage at the junction, which is quite a busy area in the summer.

As contrast, and also for its own interest, the western part of the BCN is well worth investigating. It is best to explore this by boat, by turning off the Staffs & Worcs at Stourton, ascending the sixteen Stourbridge locks, restored to navigable standards in 1967, and joining Dudley Canal No 1 at the foot of the Delph Eight. There were originally nine locks here (the eight are still sometimes referred to as nine), and the site of the old flight is clear on the east side of the present locks, which were built by 1858. The old locks ran in a curve, with side ponds at right angles as on the Bratch staircase on the Staffs & Worcs. The top and bottom of the old locks were reconstructed to form part of the present flight. From the top of Delph it is a short distance to Park Head locks, gradually being restored, which lead to Dudley tunnel. This tunnel, which has its own Trust, is navigable and with its basins, caverns and branches is perhaps the most intriguing of all tunnels on the waterways. Until the locks are in working order, however, craft must use the Netherton tunnel to get to Birmingham. There used to be a short branch known as the Two Lock Line, which cut off the loop to Park Head on the way to Netherton. The entrance to this is marked by a roving bridge past Round Oak steelworks, but the line suffered from subsidence, was closed in 1909, and the site has been developed for industrial use. There are also an abandoned loop and branch at Bumble Hole, by the southern portal of Netherton.

Dudley Canal No 2 begins at Park Head, approaches Netherton, and then strikes off southwards. The 557yd tunnel at Gosty Hill is still open, but the canal now ends before the third and longest of the BCN's great tunnels, Lapal (or Lappal), 3,795yd, is reached. This was completed by 1798 and took the canal under the higher ground on either side of the present M5 to within 2 miles of Selly Oak, where a junction was later made with the Worcester & Birmingham. The west portal of Lapal was near an abbey and the east portal near Weoley Castle; however, both portals, with the approach cuttings, have been obliterated since the abandonment of this part of the canal in 1953. Parts of the parapet brickwork are visible, and some of the line of the tunnel can be traced by the horse path over the top. BWB are still responsible for the bore of Lapal.

The more one knows of the BCN, the more one wants to know. Although there may be more losses on the outer sections of the system, it does seem that the enlightened attitude of the Birmingham authorities will lead to the careful preservation, and even enhancement, of the older sections within the city. There are plans for revitalising Gas Street Basin—one hopes with the same sense of functional beauty that has been applied to the work at Farmer's Bridge. Birmingham is still the centre of England's waterway system; the more boats that visit it, the better for the health of the system as a whole.

OS sheet 131 (Birmingham)
   120 (Wyrley & Essington, Ogley–Huddlesford)
The Canals of the West Midlands, by Charles Hadfield
The BCN: a Cruising Guide, by K. D. Dunham & R. B. Manion
History of Birmingham, by Conrad Gill
Information from Mr Philip Weaver

THE SHROPSHIRE CANAL

William Reynolds, the ironmaster of Ketley, was the founder of three of the canals of the East Shropshire tub-boat network.

The Wombridge Canal, 1¾ miles long, was built about 1788 to take coal and ironstone from Wombridge to the Donnington Wood Canal, for the furnaces at Donnington Wood. When the Shrewsbury Canal, with which Reynolds was also concerned, was being constructed, it bought the length of the Wombridge which it connected with at the top of the Trench incline. This section became disused soon after 1900, outliving the part which had not been bought by some eighty years. Of the Wombridge Canal very little is left; traces of the cut near the top of Trench incline and a rough path round the gardens of a nearby housing estate are about all.

It had been possible to cut the Wombridge Canal on the level; but this was not so with the Ketley Canal, which Reynolds was building at about the same time. This was needed to supply the Ketley Works with coal and ironstone from Oakengates, 1½ miles away. There was a drop of 73ft down to the works, and not enough water available to supply the number of locks that would be needed. So Reynolds constructed an inclined plane—the first to be operated on a British canal. It was double-track and self-balancing; boats locked into the top of the incline, settled on to a cradle, and descended the slope, either being braked on the descent or counter-balanced by an ascending boat. Ketley Works closed in 1816, and the incline was reported as being disused two years later.

The Ketley Canal has been fairly thoroughly obliterated; so thoroughly in parts that only a recent study of an 1813 estate plan of the Lilleshall Estate proved the canal had actually been constructed from the bottom of the incline into the works. The incline itself is near Ketley Hall. It lies at the back of a new housing estate opposite the *Shropshire Star* offices on the southern arm of a crossroads on A5 by the 'Seven Stars' inn. Another inn, the 'Wren's Nest', is opposite the foot of the incline, evidence of which can be found behind the houses ascending the hill. An older house, 'Hillside', stands near the top of the incline, and the course of the upper level of canal alongside the garden of Ketley Hall can be seen. There are traces of brickwork on the slope, and an intricate network of small tunnels near the top, which apparently extends under the Hall.

Reynolds' third and largest waterway undertaking was the Shropshire Canal, envisaged before he built the Ketley, and connected with it. For this, Reynolds joined with a group of local industrialists, including the Darbys of Coalbrookdale, the Marquess of Stafford (formerly Lord Gower), brother-in-law of the Duke of Bridgewater and builder of the Donnington Wood Canal, and Thomas Gilbert, brother to the Duke's agent John, a principal mover of the Bridgewater Canal itself. Work started about 1789 from the junction with the Ketley Canal northwards to the Donnington Wood. Again, the contours made a heavy demand, and the Wrockwardine Wood inclined plane was constructed to link the two canals. At the foot of the incline the Wombridge Canal met the Donnington Wood. South of Oakengates, the Shropshire Canal made for Coalport, on the Severn, past several ironworks and furnaces. To bring it down to the river there were two more inclined planes, at Windmill Farm, near Stirchley, the longest, and at the Hay, Coalport, with the greatest fall. Above Windmill a branch, 2¾ miles long, wound away westward to a point above Coalbrookdale, known as the 'Wind', on Brierly Hill. Here two shafts were made for lowering crates of coal and iron by cranes, and raising limestone. These shafts were used from 1792–4, when they were replaced by an inclined plane. This counts as a railway incline, however, as boats were never taken down it.

The Shropshire Canal cost a little under the £50,000 raised to build it. It was economically run, serving as it did its proprietors' own industries, and returned healthy dividends during its independent life. The last mile of the branch, however, proved unnecessary once the incline was built at Brierly Hill, as it proved more sensible to extend a tramroad to Horsehay Works along the towpath, rather than to have to bother with transhipment from boats.

With the Shrewsbury and other canals, the Shropshire became part of the Shropshire Union concern in 1845. In the next few years its condition began to deteriorate, partly owing to subsidence. The tunnel at Snedshill and the Wrockwardine Wood incline both suffered collapses. The su obtained power to convert the canal to a railway, but this power was not transferable to the lnwr, the lessors of the su. It took some years before the lnwr obtained a Bill to buy the canal outright and close part of it, and build their own branch railway to Coalport. In 1858 the canal from the foot of the Wrockwardine Wood incline to the foot of the

Windmill incline was closed, with the remaining part of the branch. The section above The Hay survived until about 1894. The last section to close was 1¼ miles of the pound south of Windmill, used for carrying coal to Blist's Hill furnaces for some years. It outlasted the furnaces and was not abandoned until 1944.

Housing development, including the new town of Telford, new roads and factories have eradicated much of the old Shropshire Canal. The inclines, however, can still be traced. Wrockwardine Wood incline, now a rough stony track, rises from the junction of Furnace Lane, Plough Road and Moss Road, 1¼ miles from Oakengates. The Bellevue Inn is beside it. Some 40ft of it lie beneath the crossroads and housing estate. The incline rose 120ft; at the top there is an old cottage, and bits of brick and stonework can be found amongst the scrub. Two hundred yards down Furnace Lane there are slight traces of the Wombridge Canal; at the top of the incline the course of the Shropshire can be followed for a short distance, though it is very overgrown. The tunnels at Snedshill and Stirchley have both gone, although the site of a short tunnel under A5, where the railway coincided with the canal, is clear. The course of the canal generally shares the track of the old Coalport branch railway, passing east of Dawley. The junction with the Coalbrookdale branch has been obliterated by A442. This was by the scattering of houses—it can hardly be called a village—called Aqueduct (SJ 694060). The aqueduct itself, which took the branch over what was once the main road and is now a dead end, has survived, a sturdy, single-arch stone construction, with iron railings on the parapet. The railway incline at the end of the branch is on the hillside west of B4375 at Coalbrookdale. It is very overgrown, and parts of it have fallen in. At the top there are two cottages, one recently restored, said to have been built to Telford's design. The canal can be followed for a mile or so along the fields, with a bridge where a farm road crosses it.

From Aqueduct the main line swings west into Windmill Farm, then turns south to descend the incline, dropping 126ft. This can be seen from the railway on the south side of the farm, its slope ending at the railway embankment. After dry weather one used to be able to discern the marks of the rails on the grassy slope. South of the railway the canal can be found on either side of A442, by a bus-stop ¼ mile north of the crossroads with B4380. At times it holds a little water here. A factory and the gardens of houses have almost overwhelmed it, but it emerges again under B4380 on the north-east side of Madeley, where a bridge parapet can be detected. South east of Madeley the canal appears again towards the bottom of a grassy slope opposite a new housing estate, and above the sewage farm. At the south edge of the slope there are the remains of a bridge, from which the Shropshire Canal emerges. There is a lot of weed and a little water; it can be followed by path for its final mile to the top of the Hay incline, trees lining its banks, and with derelict factories on both sides.

The Hay incline, in the grounds of Hay Farm, has recently been tidied up and is preserved as a monument of industrial archaeology. It falls 207ft on a gradient of 1 in 5. The canal leads into the upper basin along the top of the hill; the tub-boats were then manoeuvred 90° in preparation for the descent. As on the other Shropshire Canal planes, there was a short reverse slope to the highest point, to obviate the necessity for a lock. This slope is evident at The Hay. In both the docks are the iron rails of the track. There are three thick stone walls, one separating the docks and the others on the outside of them, which used to carry the drums for the chains to which the boat-carrying cradles were attached. The foundations of the engine-house, with two semi-circular brick chambers which housed two haystack boilers, and about half of the chimney, stand on the far side of the docks from the canal. The tub-boats, 18ft long and 5ft beam, were brought along the canal in trains of twelve, sometimes more, drawn by a single horse. Each boat, weighing $1\frac{1}{2}$ tons empty and carrying 5 tons of cargo, usually coal or iron, was detached and lowered down the incline in a wooden-framed cradle. It was estimated that about 100 boats could be handled in twelve hours.

Halfway down the slope, now cleared of scrub and debris, are the crumbling blue and red-brick parapets of a bridge over the track of the old Coalport railway. A road bridge crosses the foot of the incline, and a rough and ready car park takes the place of the lower basin. Looking up the grassy slope, you see two cottages on the left, the far side of the bridge, and the Shakespeare Inn on the right. Behind you is the Severn, crossed by an iron footbridge. The canal did not connect directly with the river but turned at right angles again to continue for $\frac{1}{2}$ mile along the northern bank, which used to be lined by wharves and warehouses. There are two kilns there now (late 1970), but the course of the canal is being bulldozed for future development. Of the docks at the foot of the incline there is no trace.

The prosperity of Coalport was founded on the Shropshire Canal. John Rose established his pottery before 1799, and its fine porcelain, with brightly coloured floral decoration in high relief, soon became widely known. One of the first chain-making factories was also established there, which supplied chain for colliery winding-houses and also for the incline, originally operated by rope. Coalport today is a site of relics of industry, rather than activity; a place of that slightly melancholic interest so often associated with derelict industrial canals.

OS sheet 119
The Canals of the West Midlands, by Charles Hadfield
Industrial Archaeology, vol 2 no 3: 'The Canal Inclined Planes of E. Shropshire', by W. Howard Williams (1965). (This contains E. A. Forward's translation of the detailed report on the working of the Hay I/P by two German mining engineers who visited the site in 1826/7)
Newcomen Society *Transactions*, vol 28: 'Canal Lifts and Inclined Planes', by D. H. Tew
Also articles in *Shropshire Magazine* during 1954, by W. Howard Williams

THE DONNINGTON WOOD CANAL

The Donnington Wood Canal, sometimes known as the Marquess of Stafford's or, even more gloriously, as the Duke of Sutherland's, was of appropriately noble origin, having been built by Lord Gower, brother-in-law of the Duke of Bridgewater. It was a canal for small tub-boats, designed to convey coal from Lord Gower's mine at Donnington Wood to a wharf on the main road 2 miles south of Newport. Like the Bridgewater Canal at Worsley, it connected with navigable levels in the mine. The Gilbert brothers, John, the Duke of Bridgewater's agent, and Thomas, joined Lord Gower in Earl Gower & Co, and the canal was completed in 1768. The main line was a level 5½ miles; a few years later, a branch was added, with three short arms, connecting with limestone quarries and limeworks at Lilleshall and Pitchcroft. The branch left the main line at Hugh's Bridge, near Lilleshall

Abbey. The main line was higher than the branch. The original connection was by two vertical shafts with a tunnel below. Coal was crated and lowered by crane down one shaft to boats in the tunnel below, while a compensating weight of limestone would be lifted up the other shaft. By 1797, however, this system had been abandoned, and an inclined plane, rising 42ft 8in, was substituted to carry the tub-boats without the necessity of their being unloaded.

Lord Gower rose a degree in nobility, and as Marquess of Stafford formed the Lilleshall Co to which the canal was leased. His son's elevation to become Duke of Sutherland accounts for the canal's third alternative name. The canal retained its independence and remained in full use until the 1870s, when the closing of Lilleshall limeworks made the branch redundant. When the Lodge furnaces were shut in 1888 the arm leading to them went out of use, and a few years later a stretch of the main line was filled in to make a carriage drive to the Duke of Sutherland's Lilleshall Hall. There was now virtually no traffic east of Muxton. The western end of the canal became disused by 1904.

The Donnington Wood connected with the Shropshire, and also the Wombridge, near the foot of Wrockwardine Wood inclined plane. This area has been built over, and one has to go to Muxton Bridge, at the end of a minor road from Muxton on A518, to find traces of its bed. From here it runs north east for a mile to Abbey Farm, where pigs root about in it. The ruins of Lilleshall Abbey, well kept and heavily buttressed, are circled by the canal as it turns to head due north for ½ mile. A rough road heading south east from the village of Lilleshall crosses the canal at Hugh's Bridge, about ¾ mile along. There is water here, and a sign points to Incline Cottages along a track beside the canal on the north side of the bridge.

The incline, 123yd long, is now a grassy slope running down between the cottages and sheds; there is a farm gate near the top. The engine house has gone and the upper basin filled in; there is no trace of the bridge that carried the path across it. The shafts of the original connection have been filled in, but the mouth of the tunnel can be found in the grounds of the cottage on the east side of the slope. Measurements on the site indicate that the incline was probably double-track. Like the Shropshire Canal inclines, it was worked by a steam-engine. According to the recorded memory of an old lady who used to live there, the incline last worked in 1879.

From the foot of the slope, the branch heads north west towards Lilleshall, where it divides; traces hereabouts are fragmentary and not likely to last much longer. There is a bridge over the canal on a rough road heading east from the north end of the village. One arm peters out in the grounds of a farm; much of the other, which included seven small locks, has been ploughed in. This ended at Pitchcroft, off A518, where there are the remains of a bridge with traces of the cut on its southern side by some cottages. The wharf has been filled in.

The main line continues north east for a short distance from Hugh's Bridge until its incorporation with the drive to Lilleshall Hall. It ended at Pave Lane, on A41, where coal used to be sold from the wharf, but now there is nothing of the canal to see there.

The Donnington Wood was the first of the tub-boat canals which enabled the rapid development of the industries of East Shropshire. From what is left of it, it is difficult to gain much idea of its significance. For a better realisation of this, it is worth visiting the Duke of Bridgewater's Canal at Worsley, which gave Lord Gower and Thomas Gilbert their inspiration.

OS sheet 119
The Canals of the West Midlands, by Charles Hadfield
'The Canal Inclined Planes of E. Shropshire', by W. Howard Williams
    (*Industrial Archaeology*, vol 2 no 3)

THE SHREWSBURY CANAL

The Shrewsbury Canal has suffered less from later development than the other canals of the East Shropshire network and still has several features of great interest. It obtained its Act in 1793 and was open throughout four years later. Originally a tub-boat canal, it was built to bring coal from the Oakengates area to Shrewsbury; the line included eleven locks, eight lifting bridges, a tunnel, an inclined plane, and the famous iron aqueduct at Longdon-upon-Tern. On the higher ground south of Trench it connected with the short Wombridge Canal and the Donnington Wood; it descended by the inclined plane to circle to the north of Wellington and, having crossed the Tern, ran roughly parallel to it on the northern side to enter Shrewsbury from the north east, though it did not connect with the Severn. Locally financed, the Shrewsbury was engineered by Josiah Clowes and, after his death, by Telford. For many years it returned reasonable profits from coal, much of which was sold from the several wharves, lime from Lilleshall, and other commodities; these profits reached their highest level in the mid-1830s, when the Birmingham & Liverpool Junction Co opened their branch through Newport to join the Shrewsbury—and through it the rest of the East Shropshire system—at Wappenshall. Complications now arose over boats, as the Shrewsbury locks were not wide enough to take the narrow boats in general use. Two locks and the bridge holes towards Shrewsbury were widened, but the company could not afford to alter the others and narrow boats only 6ft 4in beam had to be specially built for the traffic between Wappenshall and Trench. Tub-boats still had to be used for the Trench incline and the canal system above it, so cargoes had to be transhipped at Trench. All this may have contributed to the relatively high tolls charged on this canal.

In 1846, the Shrewsbury Canal became part of the amalgamation of transport undertakings known as the Shropshire Union Railways & Canal Co. Its valuation was put at £75,000, a few thousand more than it had cost to construct. Although shortly afterwards the LNWR moved in with the Shropshire Union, and as the years passed bit by bit the East Shropshire canal system was closed down, the Shrewsbury remained inviolate until 1921. In that year the Trench incline, the last at work in the country, was shut, and in 1922 the basin in Shrewsbury was abandoned. Commercial traffic, the last being in sulphuric acid for Shrewsbury gasworks, ended in 1931. The canal was officially abandoned in 1944, part of the 175 miles of waterways shaken off by the LMS, for many years their legal guardian.

Today almost all of the Shrewsbury Canal can easily be found. The first 1½ miles or so out of Shrewsbury have been built over, though a short stretch remains by the gasworks. Uffington, to the south of B5062 some 3 miles from Shrewsbury, is a good place to begin exploration. The road crosses the canal at the entrance to the village; to the west the bed is dry but on the east it holds water. One and a half miles south, opposite a pair of houses on a minor road to Preston, is the north portal of Berwick tunnel, accessible over a stile. It is now bricked up above water level. The tunnel, 970yd long and the first major tunnel to have a towpath built into it, runs south-eastwards under fields, a road and a small wood, there being comparatively shallow cover. A ventilation shaft can be found about halfway along.

The south portal is open, and more interesting. It can be found on the west side of the road between Uffingham and Atcham, under which the canal is culverted, by a white house just before Berwick Wharf. A gate just past the house leads to the overgrown towpath. First there is an accommodation bridge; then, after about 400yd, the tunnel. The date 1797 is discernible in elegant freehand inscription on the keystone; the tunnel itself is brick-lined, but both portals are stone-faced and beautifully proportioned. The arch is over 10ft wide; the towpath through the tunnel, which had been made of wood, was dismantled in 1819.

Some of the buildings at Berwick Wharf remain, including a warehouse with the inscription 'Lilleshall Co., Ltd., Corn & Salt Merchants, Cornflower, Meal and Malt Stores', giving some indication of the goods carried. After the wharf, the canal turns sharply north-eastward for Withington, 3 miles on, where it is culverted under the road and only a few traces of the wharf are left. At Rodington, the canal heads south of east to cross the Roden by a three-arched aqueduct near the road; beyond the village, on the right of the road to Longdon, is a fine wooden lifting bridge, taking a farm track over the canal.

In 2 miles the road from Rodington meets B5063 as it approaches Longdon-upon-Tern. There is a Shropshire Union Canal Co warehouse, with a distinct railway look to it, beside the road where it crosses the canal at the site of Longdon Wharf; and ¼ mile on, to the north of the road, is Telford's famous iron aqueduct over the Tern. Although the idea for using iron may not have been Telford's, he certainly supervised its construction. It was built to replace Clowes' original stone aqueduct, destroyed by floods before completion. The masonry abutments of this support a 62yd long trough made of cast-iron plates from Ketley. It stands 16ft above the river. The Longdon aqueduct looks serviceable rather than elegant. It carries a towpath, but the canal holds no water here and the trough serves as a continuation of a farm track along the top of the embankment. The small aqueduct in Derby pre-dated Longdon in the use of iron by a month or two, but it was the successful use of the material at Longdon that led Jessop to recommend cast iron for the trough of Pontcysyllte, where the Llangollen Canal crosses the valley of the Dee, which Telford was later to build so magnificently.

The Shrewsbury continues on an embankment, but parts of this are being levelled and a small aqueduct over a stream to the east has been recently demolished. A neat little iron footbridge still stands, but its future is problematic. The canal is crossed by A442, and begins to swing southwards across Eyton Moor. The two Eyton locks were the only ones widened to take boats off the Newport branch; one of them can be reached along a lane through Eyton upon the Weald Moors, where there is also a lock cottage. The junction with the branch at Wappenshall is a mile farther along the canal. A minor road signposted to Preston leads to an attractive group of buildings behind a bridge which used to take the road over the canal. The road has been widened here and the lock that used to stand on the south side of it demolished, while the canal is now culverted. On the north side, the Newport branch comes in from the east to join the Shrewsbury, under a substantial roving bridge. By the junction, accessible with permission through a coal yard, is a well-preserved warehouse under which boats moored to be loaded or unloaded from above. The warehouse is now empty, apart from a hoist on each of the two floors. A toll office stands next to it, and a canal cottage nearby.

South of the road, the towpath can be followed to where the tall framework of the bottom gate of a lock can be seen 400yd away. The Shrewsbury locks are particularly interesting; not only were they the narrowest to be built, but they were all fitted with lifting, or guillotine, lower gates, those which remain looming over the shrubbery like ominous gibbets. On this particular one little of the mechanism survives on the wooden supporting frame, but a mile farther south along the canal there are two more locks, by the private road leading to Hadley Park. The lock beside the road is the only one which retained the mechanism of the original pattern, operated by a counterweight suspended over the canal. Its remnants now sway grotesquely in the wind. The other locks were altered so that the weight came down the side of the frame-work and sank into a pit beside the lock, as can be seen in the second Hadley Park lock, a short but rough walk to the south. The object of this type of lock was to save water; the stop-lock at

Shrewsbury Canal: guillotine gate, Hadley Park lock

King's Norton, where the northern section of the Stratford joins the Worcester & Birmingham, has a good example of a guillotine gate with all its constituent parts in place.

The canal continues through factory grounds, then turns east and south again to be crossed by the railway and A518 Wellington–Newport road. Trench lock—which no longer has its lower gate—is on the south of the road by a signpost pointing to the Shropshire Arms. A short walk between the canal and Trench reservoir, which used to feed it, leads to the inn, which stands by the foot of the inclined plane. Now a steep, rough path, this used

Page 155 (above) *Weston Branch of the Shropshire Union: Westonwharf;* (below) *Droitwich Canal: lock cottage in Dutch style*

(above) *Cromford Canal: the west portal of Butterley tunnel;* (below) *Chesterfield Canal: Tapton Mill bridge, near Chesterfield*

to be a double-track incline, 223yd long with a rise of 75ft, operated by a steam-engine. Although it lasted till 1921, all the works, including the engine house, have now disappeared. At the top, there are a filled in well and two fragments of curved brick walling, the entrance to the upper basin from the Wombridge Canal. Workings and dumping have destroyed everything else except for part of the old Wombridge channel which can be followed for a few yards. New housing estates ring the rough area at the top of the incline; below, few of the old factory chimneys are left today; the air is clearer, and the water of the Shrewsbury Canal, undisturbed by coal-carrying tub-boats, reflects the sunlight.

OS sheet 118 (Shrewsbury–Wellington)
   119 (Trench)
The Canals of the West Midlands, by Charles Hadfield
Articles by W. Howard Williams, in *Shropshire Magazine* during 1954

THE NEWPORT BRANCH OF THE
SHROPSHIRE UNION

Norbury Junction on the Shropshire Union is busy these days. It provides a good mooring for pleasure cruisers; there are the headquarters of a hire firm, and an inn which serves meals. On the west side is a white painted bridge, with a short stretch of water used as a permanent mooring, and a pair of lock gates, firmly shut. This is the entrance to the Newport Branch, 10½ miles long, falling by 23 narrow locks to meet the Shrewsbury Canal at Wappenshall.

The Newport Branch was opened in 1835, part of Telford's Birmingham & Liverpool Junction Canal, which became the spine of the Shropshire Union system. As the Shrewsbury Canal had particularly narrow locks, special narrow boats had to be used; the Shrewsbury planned to widen its locks to accommodate the normal boats, but work was completed on only two of them. Although transhipment from tub-boats at the Trench incline caused some delay, the Newport Branch enabled iron from the Coalbrookdale area to be sent throughout England, and brought increased revenue to the Shrewsbury company. A short arm,

K

known as the Humber Arm, was built to Lubstree Wharf, connected first by road and then by rail to Lilleshall, principally for coal traffic.

The Shropshire Union was formed in 1846, and the Newport Branch passed with it into railway control. The Humber Arm became disused in 1922, when Lubstree Wharf was closed by its owner, the Duke of Sutherland. In that year, the London & North Western Railway took over the Shropshire Union company, very shortly before itself became absorbed by the LMS. During the next twenty years trade steadily declined, until in 1944 the LMS obtained an Act to abandon 175 miles of canal, including all the Shropshire Union system except for the main line, though the Llangollen branch was later saved. Commercial traffic between Wappenshall and Newport had ceased five years before.

Wappenshall Junction, with its group of canal buildings, is described in the section on the Shrewsbury Canal. The canal runs north-eastward past Preston upon the Weald Moors; ¾ mile farther on is the junction with the Humber Arm. The site of the wharf is due east of Preston; from the road (SJ 693153) can be seen a warehouse, still used for storage, and a cottage. The basin has been filled in, but much of the outline can be traced. There is a bridge with a broken parapet ¼ mile from the road.

Duke's Drive aqueduct, with its iron trough and railings and fine stonework, has been demolished; it used to carry the canal over the drive between Kynnersley and Hincks Plantation. From here on parts of the canal have been filled in, and much of it is dry. Only the top of the lock chamber by the bridge over the canal south of Edgmond is visible. In Newport, where the wharf was on the north side of the town, the canal is being filled in, although to date the wharf buildings—or some of them—are still standing. One and a half miles north east of Newport, near Meretown, there is a good skew bridge over the canal, which itself crosses a stream by a small stone aqueduct. In just over a mile is the head of the flight of 17 locks down to the main line. The chambers, of stone with some brickwork on the approaches, are in firm condition; the top gates have been removed, and the bottom gates are crumbling away. Deeply incised rope marks on the iron posts protecting the stonework of some of the bridges are evidence of the heavily laden boats which once used the Newport Branch.

OS sheet 119
The Canals of the West Midlands, by Charles Hadfield

MINOR BRANCHES OF THE SHROPSHIRE UNION CANAL
(Whitchurch, Prees and Weston)

The Ellesmere Canal, which in 1846 became part of the Shropshire Union, was intended to link Ellesmere Port, Chester, Ruabon and Shrewsbury. It ended up as something rather different; two main lines, one from Ellesmere Port to Chester, the other from Pontcysyllte to Weston, with eight branches of varying lengths. Navigable today are the Ellesmere Port–Chester line (comprising, with the Chester Canal from the Dee to Nantwich, part of the su main line), the branch to Middlewich, and what is now known as the Welsh or Llangollen branch, via Welsh Frankton and the Chirk and Pontcysyllte aqueducts into the Welsh hills.

Commercial traffic on the Whitchurch and Prees branches ended just before the last war. Both branches were legally abandoned in the lms 'holocaust' of 1944. The Whitchurch Branch is now waterless, and much of it has been filled in. The site of Whitchurch Wharf is near the Victoria Jubilee Park; the Wharf Gun Shop conveniently marks the position, and there are a few of the canal buildings standing. The canal ran north-westward out of the town; the filled-in bed is now part of the park by the boundary, with gasometers on the other side. It remains filled in as far as the village of Chemistry, on the outskirts of the town. In the village, which lies on the north of A525, is bridge no 1, carrying the road to Chemistry Farm, with a derelict cottage beside it. On the cottage side the bed is used as a car graveyard; the cut is still defined to the west and remains so as far as the junction with the main line. The junction can be reached by walking along the towpath of the Llangollen Canal from the A525 road bridge, by the Bridge Canal Cruisers depot. There is a lifting bridge by the junction, which is now a soggy, reeded inlet.

The Prees Branch never got to Prees; work on it stopped at Quina Brook, 6 miles south of Whitchurch on A5113. Here lime-kilns were built (lime and limestone were important cargoes on the Ellesmere Canal, together with coal and building materials).

The limekilns, on the west of the road opposite a road junction, are today inhabited by pigs. The canal runs south west for ¾ mile and then turns north west towards the main line. At Edstaston, by the turn, there is a su warehouse and wharf; the canal is dry and the road bridge blocked. There is an accommodation bridge by the approach to the village of Waterloo, and a brick bridge (no 5) by the T junction signposted Wem/Whixall/Edstaston. Here the canal holds some water, and there are a few houses along the banks. A mile farther north (SJ 492343), by the next road bridge, there is an attractive watered stretch; the towpath is accessible and in good condition for walking, leading northwards to two lifting bridges and some su notices off which the blue paint has not yet flaked. No 1 lifting bridge is on a track leading to Moss Farm; from here it is ¼ mile walk along the towpath beside the fully watered canal to the junction with the main line. There is a red-brick cottage with stabling behind it by the junction, a favourite reach for the local anglers.

What became known as the Weston Branch was originally, as has been indicated, part of one of the main lines of the Ellesmere. It is 6 miles long, from a junction at Lockgate bridge, near the foot of Frankton locks, to Westonwharf. The junction is with what is now regarded as the derelict Montgomeryshire Canal, which used to be part of the Hurleston–Frankton–Carreghofa branch of the Ellesmere.

The Weston Branch was little used after 1870, and various proposals for its closure were made in the following years. It survived mainly because the LNWR did not solve the legal problems associated with closing it, until in 1917 it burst its banks at Dandyford. Only the top ¾ mile was thereafter usable; this length was closed in 1937. Although restoration of the whole branch had previously been sought, the Board of Trade decided against it in 1920.

The line terminated at Westonwharf, a group of houses along a rough road 2½ miles north of Baschurch. The area of the wharf is still defined by low stone walling; there is an old warehouse by a bridge, and a sluice which has been bricked up, though some of the iron paddle gear is still there. The canal extended a short distance beyond the basin. There are the ruins of limekilns in the farmyard by the warehouse, and the dry bed of the canal is clear on the north side of the bridge. Some parts of the cut hold water as you follow it northwards, but much has been ploughed up. Between Bagley and Wycherley Hall, a bridge stands isolated in the fields (SJ 414272). A stone cottage marks where the road crossed the canal about 500yd north of this bridge, at Shade Oak.

The northern half of the canal, from Lower Hordley to the junction, is easier to discern. Dandyford, where the Weston Branch died, is ½ mile north of the village. The site of the basin at Hordley, on the west side of the road running northwards out of the village, is easy to find; a notice stating 'Shooting Rights on the Canal are the property of Hardwick Estate' stands in the middle of it. Lockgate bridge, a ferociously hump-backed construction notable even in an area which has plenty of such, is on the minor road from Hordley to Welsh Frankton. The junction is on the east side of the bridge; one can reach it either by forcing through a few yards of dense growth or by walking down the towpath from Welsh Frankton locks.

OS sheet 118
The Canals of the West Midlands, by Charles Hadfield

THE DROITWICH CANALS

The history of the Droitwich Canal—the senior of the two waterways which eventually linked Droitwich with the Severn and the Worcester & Birmingham—is a long and complicated one. Attempts over the previous century to make the River Salwarpe navigable had failed; therefore in 1768 an Act was obtained for a canal to be made roughly parallel with the river from Hawford on the Severn to Droitwich. Most of the shareholders were local men. Brindley supervised the works, with John Priddey as engineer. The canal was 6¾ miles long rising through eight wide locks; the boats could carry over 60 tons, salt and coal being the main traffic, and in the early years were either under sail or bow-hauled, no adequate towpath for horses being constructed.

The canal opened in 1771, having cost £23,500—almost double the original estimate. With no rivals for the traffic the canal in its early years prospered; £100 shares rose to £160 in 1777. A few years later, some of the Droitwich shareholders wanted to link their canal with a proposed extension of the Stourbridge Canal to Worcester, but the plan fell through. In 1791, however, the Worcester & Birmingham promoters obtained their Act. Their line was to pass within 2 miles of Droitwich, and with the w & b the Droitwich company began a somewhat uneasy relationship. The interests of the Droitwich company seem to have been looked after by a large w & b shareholder, a Mr W. A. Roberts, who appears to have acted the part of a double-agent. Through his machinations, the w & b became involved in an arrangement which led to their virtually subsidising the Droitwich, while the prosperity of the latter company was declining owing to the improvement in local roads and the failure to use horses to draw the barges. Urged by the w & b, the Droitwich company reduced tolls and improved the towpath; then in 1810 they handed over the running of their navigation to the w & b (whose own waterway, incidentally, was not yet near completion) under their own supervision.

The loss of trade to the Droitwich Canal consequent on the opening of the w & b in 1821 was compensated for by an increase in salt traffic when the salt duties were ended, and for some years both canals, although in rivalry, continued in business to some purpose. But with the coming of the railways in the 1840s, both companies began to suffer. The Birmingham & Gloucester Railway got a grip on the salt trade from Stoke, on the w & b's line. Then in 1852, to try to defend themselves from the threatened competition from the Oxford, Worcester & Wolverhampton Railway (later notorious as the 'Old Worse & Worse'), the w & b set up the Droitwich Junction company which obtained an Act to cut a canal joining the w & b at Hanbury Wharf with the Droitwich Canal in Droitwich. Both Droitwich canals were then leased by the w & b for a total of £2,745 a year.

The Junction Canal, 1¾ miles long, was built with seven deep narrow locks, like those of the w & b. It locked into the Salwarpe in Droitwich and then out of it to join the Droitwich Canal. The w & b now had the upkeep of 65 narrow locks in 32 miles of canal plus the eight broad locks of the Droitwich. Each of these eight it lengthened by 7ft 6in, so that narrow boats could use the whole of its system to the Severn.

Twenty years of disputes, offers and lawsuits followed, mainly with the owwr, while the canal trade slipped away and the liabilities grew. Rescue came in 1874, when the Sharpness New Docks Company took over the three navigations for £6,000 a year, renaming itself the Sharpness New Docks and Gloucester & Birmingham Navigation Company, a cumbersome title still discernible on the remaining iron bridge plates. Over the years, the Sharpness company fought a long, hard but losing battle. The Droitwich was thoroughly dredged, the locks deepened to take larger craft off the Severn, but the receipts fell annually and by 1914 the Droitwich canals were falling into decay. In 1939 the long-suffering and patient Sharpness company admitted final defeat, and the Act for abandonment of the Droitwich and Droitwich Junction was passed. The W & B, now owned by British Waterways Board, is still open and busy now in the summer with pleasure traffic, but the old salt canals are closed. There are, however, plans to reopen them, despite the considerable work involved.

The Droitwich Canal locked into the Severn at Hawford lock. The remains of this are in the garden of the Lock House—now a smartly rejuvenated private dwelling—at the bottom of Lock Lane, a turning to the west of the A449 about 4 miles north of the centre of Worcester. The canal is piped under the A449 by Hawford Lodge School, and emerges on the other side south of Judge's boatyard, where there is a mill on the River Salwarpe. Now holding a full width of water, the canal runs for a short distance close to the river, divided from it only by its towpath. In ½ mile it passes under an attractive high red-brick accommodation bridge. It continues winding eastward under two road bridges, each with a lock; by the second, there is a restored lock cottage with a beautifully kept garden. From here the next mile of bed is virtually dry; then there is another bridge with a lock and small cottage just to the west of Ladywood.

Heading now north east, the canal, in a deep cutting, reaches Salwarpe, passing under a bridge beside the church. The small iron lozenge-shaped sign of the Sharpness Co is intact in the centre of the parapet; but more attractive is the superb Elizabethan Salwarpe Court, one of the finest examples of half-timbered houses in a richly endowed countryside, on the opposite bank of the canal from the church.

As Droitwich is approached, the condition of the cut deteriorates. On the outskirts of the town it passes under a rebuilt bridge on the Ombersley road; it survives for the best part of a mile, and then is no more. Until recently it used to enter Droitwich under two railway bridges and the Kidderminster road, beside the Railway Inn; but now it has been filled in and the water piped underneath. The course across the pleasure gardens by the river can be easily deduced, and an old salt warehouse which has been in recent years a cinema and a furniture store still stands, ramshackle and desolate—but not for much longer.

At the east end of the gardens, by the river, is the remainder of the lock of the Droitwich Junction, which used to have two sets of gates facing each way so that it could be used regardless of the relative height of the river and canal. The Droitwich Junction used the river to take it under the Roman Road (A38) and then locked up on to its own course. There is a bridge over it behind the Barley Mow, 200yd along the B4090 (the old Salt Way, also a Roman road), but for the next ½ mile the course has been intermittently built over. It continues along the north side of the road towards Hanbury Wharf, on the Worcester & Birmingham; through the hedge and brambles are the seven narrow and deep locks by which it ascended. At the top there is a bridge, now bricked up, and where the Droitwich Junction met the w & b is now wholly overgrown. The water in the Droitwich canals, though it does not look very tempting, still tastes of salt.

OS sheet 130
The Canals of the West Midlands, by Charles Hadfield

THE COOMBE HILL CANAL

A pleasant but rather undistinguished stretch of waterway, the Coombe Hill Canal runs from Coombe Hill, 7 miles north of Gloucester on the A38 Tewkesbury road, almost in a straight line 2¾ miles westward to the Severn. Its purpose was to improve the carriage of coal to Cheltenham, by cutting down the distance it needed to be carried by road. It was opened in or shortly after 1796, with two locks into the Severn and capable of taking barges of up to 70 tons. It cost about £5,000 to construct, but despite high tolls of 12½p a ton it made little, if any, profit. Between the basin and the main road at Coombe Hill there is a short but steep hill, and this added to the cost and difficulty of transporting the coal off-loaded at the wharf on towards the town.

Plans to extend the canal to Cheltenham, or to build a connecting tramroad, came to nothing. But the coal trade was worth fighting for, and a Worcester & Birmingham group leased the canal and traded on it for about twenty-five years, reducing the tolls and maintaining the traffic. In 1849, the Staffs & Worcs took over the lease and held it for seventeen years; but they lost money on it and when they gave it up tonnage fell right away. For four years the Coombe Hill company themselves tried to run it. They gave up in 1871, selling the undertaking for £520. Two years later, it was resold to Algernon Strickland for £1,000. In 1875 he had it examined; the report on its condition was highly critical, and shortly afterwards the lock gates were swept away by the Severn flooding and the surrounding countryside was swamped. This was enough for its owner; despite protests from the Severn Commissioners and other interested parties, he obtained an abandonment Act, and the canal was closed in 1876, having taken only £8 in tolls in its last six months of operation.

There are an attractive group of cottages and a warehouse at Coombe Hill, found at the foot of a No Through Road opposite the A38 junction with A4019. One can walk beside the canal, which still holds water, through the fields to the Severn. Here a floodgate has replaced the old locks, and summer picnickers disport on the river bank.

OS sheet 143
The Canals of the West Midlands, by Charles Hadfield

THE UTTOXETER BRANCH

A Chinese temple, a Roman bath and a Swiss cottage have all been built within a few miles of Stoke-on-Trent. With many other remarkable monuments they can be found in the grounds of Alton Towers, and may be inspected by the public in the summer months. Charles Talbot, 15th Earl of Shrewsbury ('he made the desert smile', said his son) in the early nineteenth century converted a vast stretch of wilderness and farmland into an ornamental park. Along the southern border of the park runs the River Churnet—and the Uttoxeter Branch of the Caldon Canal.

The Caldon, opened about 1779, runs in a semicircle from Etruria, on the Trent & Mersey in Stoke, to Froghall, with a short branch to Leek. An Act for its extension from Froghall to Uttoxeter was obtained in 1797. The Uttoxeter Branch was intended to serve the copper and brass works at Oakamoor and Alton, and to transport coal and lime. It was $13\frac{1}{4}$ miles long, with 17 narrow locks and was completed in 1811. But its life was short and there are very few references to the trade it carried, except that it is said to have brought prosperity to Uttoxeter. In 1846 the North Staffordshire Railway bought the Trent & Mersey, including the Caldon, and one year later it closed the Uttoxeter Branch in order to use some of it for its line through the narrow Churnet Valley.

The narrowness of the valley has helped to preserve the remnants of the Branch from destruction. From Froghall to Denstone access to the canal by road is difficult. Where, infrequently, roads cross the course, the explorer must take to the railway track, the lines having been lifted, and trudge across the ballast. The canal keeps near the 300ft contour; the Churnet is always close at hand; for much of the journey the hills rise steeply on either side, and the scenery is glorious.

Froghall Basin is $\frac{1}{4}$ mile along the road to Foxt, which turns north off A52 on the east side of Froghall. At the moment, the top $7\frac{1}{2}$ miles of the Caldon are unnavigable and the basin is a sad place, with the skeleton of a boat resting on the silt and the warehouse crumbling away. Notices warning of the 'dangerous land' surround the site. Plans for restoring the Caldon, an interesting and mostly beautiful waterway, are in hand, and it may not be long before boats once more negotiate Froghall tunnel and moor near the entrance lock to the Uttoxeter Branch. This deep lock, on the east side of Foxt Road bridge, leads down into another basin out of which the branch descended by three locks to cross A52 near its junction with B5053. A railway siding was built over this part of the canal, and a works car park covers its course immediately south of the main road. Lime was burnt at Froghall, brought down by tramroad from quarries in the hills; there are kilns remaining in the area around the basin.

South of Froghall, canal and railway coincide for a distance. By following the track for rather over a mile one can find some watery remains by and just past Ross Bridge. A little farther on is the site of a coal wharf where coal was brought by tramroad from the Kingsley Moor collieries on the west side of the Churnet. A well-preserved lock chamber soon occurs, locally known as California lock. There were three more locks between here and Oakamoor, but there are no signs of them now. There were locks also at Oakamoor, but a railway siding was built on the canal here.

A narrow road runs along the west side of the Churnet between Oakamoor and Alton. At Alton the track is accessible from the bridge over the railway by the entrance to Alton Towers. On the west side is the neo-Gothic railway station; the track leads to a weir on the river and to Lord's Bridge, where the canal can be seen quite clearly. There used to be a short canal tunnel near where the present road bridge is at Alton; also a wire mill, supplied with water from the Churnet. The leat accompanies the track for a distance on either side of the bridge.

East of Alton, the canal soon appears at the bottom of Abbey Wood, part of the Earl of Shrewsbury's park. On the other side, Alton Castle dominates the scene. A mile along, the ruins of Gig Cottage, once a public house, stand on the canal bank. For the next mile, the canal is watered. Emerging from the wood, it swings away from the railway; the towpath can be followed to a stone-built accommodation bridge with most of its parapet missing, known as Seventy Bridge. Drainage pipes are being laid across the canal here, and the bridge helps to keep the workers' boots dry; 250yd on is Weir lock, which has lost much of its masonry. The canal has been filled in at its old entrance to the Churnet, by the present pumping-station. The boats used to be towed across the river above Crumpwood Weir into Flood lock, which can be seen on the far side. The horses crossed by a bridge now gone, though there is a footbridge by the pumping-station By Flood lock is the old lock-keeper's cottage.

South of the weir the canal's course can be discerned for about ¼ mile, first on one side of the railway, then the other. It has disappeared on the approach to Denstone, where the church, vicarage and school have all been built upon it. There is a clear stretch past the railway bridge south of Denstone; then it coincides again with the railway, as far as Rocester. Here, J. C. Bamford's impressive factory (whence come the JCB's so well known to canal reclamation workers) has been built over much of the line, and further developments are in progress. There used to be two locks and a warehouse near the road from Rocester to Hollington. B5030 from Rocester to Uttoxeter has the line on its west. In front of the roofless shell of Woodseat, a large mansion, the canal was widened to form an ornamental lake, with a wooded island in it. Accessible from the road ½ mile from Rocester, it is very attractive still, ringed with shrubs and providing a home for swans.

Canal and railway combine for over a mile. Then the railway turns south, but the canal keeps straight. It can be seen beside a white cottage on a minor road ¼ mile due east of Stramshall. It looped westward along the 300ft contour (the towpath can be followed) to an iron aqueduct which took it across the River Tean. This was 35ft long; just the abutments and some of the central pier remain. The canal was crossed by A50 and entered Uttoxeter from the north west. A housing estate has been built on the course. The warehouse at the north end of the High Street was converted into a factory, and the basin filled in.

More, then, is left of the Uttoxeter Branch than might appear from a glance at the modern OS maps. It has something for most tastes. For the industrial archaeologist there are the area around Froghall, memories of the wire and copper factories, and tramroad remains; for the ecclesiastic there is Denstone Church in the canal bed; for the criminologist there is the Round House in Alton, the 16th Earl's circular lock-up. The connoisseur of country houses has Alton Towers and the ruins of Woodseat; the lover of spectacular beauty has the Churnet Valley; the lover of the macabre has Slain Hollow, Dead Waters and Gallows Green, all within a mile of each other. It is a canal to walk beside, and to linger by.

OS sheets 111 (Froghall)
       120 (Oakamoor–Uttoxeter)
The Canals of the West Midlands, by Charles Hadfield
'The Froghall–Uttoxeter Canal', by A. E. & E. M. Dodd, in *N. Staffordshire Journal of Field Studies*, Vol 3, 1963
The Caldon Canal, pub by the Caldon Canal Society

THE NEWCASTLE-UNDER-LYME CANALS

There is little evidence today in Newcastle-under-Lyme that

three canals once existed there. Entering the town from the north was Sir Nigel Gresley's Canal, 3 miles long, opened about 1776. Joining this near its southern termination was the Newcastle-under-Lyme Junction Canal, just over a mile in length. And from the Trent & Mersey at Stoke, looping round for 4 miles to enter Newcastle from the south, came the Newcastle-under-Lyme Canal. Between them they had not a lock nor a single major engineering feature.

Sir Nigel Gresley built his canal from his mines at Apedale to a wharf and basin by the Liverpool Road on the north side of the town. By the Act the proprietors of the canal were bound to supply Newcastle with coal for 25p a ton for twenty-one years, and for 27½p (or under certain conditions 30p) for the next twenty-one years, and were under obligation to keep an adequate supply readily available. There is no reason to doubt Priestley's statement that the canal 'added considerably to the interests of the inhabitants of Newcastle by the regularity wherewith they are supplied with coal at a moderate charge'. The Newcastle-under-Lyme Canal, authorised in 1795, was forbidden to carry coal, except for the manufacture of earthenware, while Gresley's agreement lasted. A main cargo was limestone off the Caldon Canal.

Gresley's son helped to promote the Junction Canal in 1798. This was planned to extend Gresley's Canal and provide a connection with the Newcastle Canal, which was on a lower level, by means of a railway running on an inclined plane. But the finances were shaky, the railway was not built, and the canal did little more than bring Gresley's coal nearer to the town centre.

The Junction Canal and Gresley's both stopped trading in the 1850s. The Junction company seemed to have taken little interest in its property until the North Staffordshire Railway began planning a line through Newcastle. The company closed its canal and sold a part of it to the railway in 1851, afterwards disposing of the rest in bits and pieces. Gresley's Canal, now owned by R. E. Heathcote, became disused after 1856, when a branch railway was built to Apedale collieries.

The fortunes of the Newcastle-under-Lyme Canal, however, were rather better. Revenue was only a few hundred pounds a year, and few dividends were paid. But in 1863 the company leased the canal to the North Staffordshire, who already owned the Trent & Mersey. The shareholders did well out of the deal, and the canal continued working until 1921. Part of it was then abandoned, the remainder following in 1935.

Building and road improvements have eradicated nearly all traces of the Newcastle canals. Apedale Road, which leaves A52 at Chesterton, 3 miles north of Newcastle, leads to the quarries of the Apedale Mineral Co. Bits of Gresley's Canal survive in this area of mud and despoliation, north and south of the collection of pot-holes that is the road, but the area is well churned up and uninviting. A section of the Junction Canal has endured a mile nearer Newcastle, behind houses on the east side of the Liverpool Road A34. Mayer Avenue, south of where B5068 crosses the main road, leads to St Michael's Infants School. A path beside the school within 100yd reaches a chunk of the canal, a depression between two raised banks, which runs for about ¼ mile across an area of rough ground ringed by suburban houses. Traces can be found along Station Walks, and where it crossed Brunswick St. The end was what is now Stubbs Walks, and the line of the proposed inclined plane is now Occupation St.

Much of the Newcastle Canal was used for road widening. It entered Newcastle along the west side of A34 London Road. Some of it is still there, providing the all-too-characteristic function of the disused urban canal—a convenient tip for rubbish. It can be found opposite the hospital, about a mile south of the centre of Newcastle. Behind a bowling green and a small cemetery the canal lurks in a cutting, a wide, muddy ditch. Its basin was in the railway yard. Further traces of the Newcastle canals there may well be; the explorer, nimble and intrepid—two qualities essential for coping with the traffic of the Potteries—is welcome to look for them.

OS sheet 110
The Canals of the West Midlands, by Charles Hadfield

The map on page 171 shows the Birmingham canal system as it was in 1811. The 'proposed extension' is the Tame Valley Canal. The Birmingham Canal as shown is the old main line, before Telford's improvements.

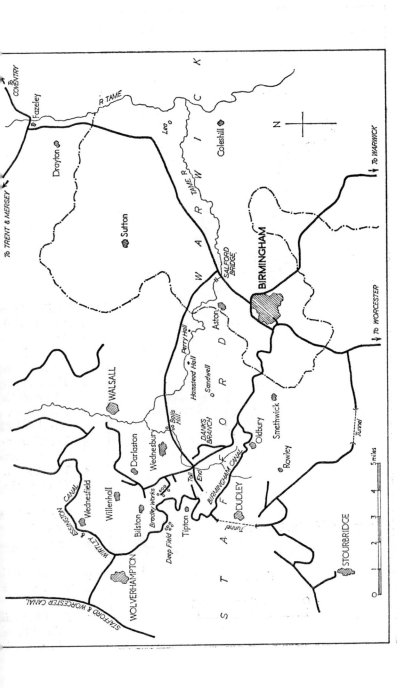

-------- Navigable canal

0 miles 20

Chapter 5: *The East Midlands*

THE OLD STRATFORD & BUCKINGHAM BRANCH

'This stupendous and most useful line of navigation' is how Joseph Priestley describes the Grand Junction Canal. With a main line of 93½ miles from the Thames at Brentford to Braunston, and nearly 50 miles of branches, it was indeed a massive undertaking for the canal age. It bought the old Grand Union and Leics & Northants Union in 1894, and continued as an independent body until 1928 when it combined with the Regent's Canal to form the Grand Union. In subsequent years the Loughborough Navigation, the Leicester Canal and the Erewash were added to the Grand Union network. The GUC, which included its own large carrying company, fought valiantly and not unsuccessfully for inland water transport during the 1930s and 1940s and when nationalised after World War II was still a profitable concern.

Nearly all of the Grand Union's waterways are still navigable; even the Erewash, nearly given up for lost, is coming back to life. One loss, however, is the 10½ miles branch to Buckingham, part of the old Grand Junction. This branch was cut from Cosgrove on the main line to the London turnpike road, now A5, at Old Stratford as a result of the canal's first Act in 1793. It was extended to Buckingham by the 1794 Act, which also authorised the branches to Aylesbury and Wendover. The Buckingham Branch was opened in 1801, coal to Buckingham being the main traffic, and closed down in sections during the twentieth century; 1910 saw the first closure, from Leckhampstead Wharf to Buckingham, and 1961 the last, from the main line to Deanshanger. Now, apart from a short length off the main line, the branch is waterless and much of it has been filled in.

The Buckingham Branch leaves the main line immediately above Cosgrove lock near the fine stone bridge in the village. It looks a pleasant stretch of water, but this is deceptive; the water does not last for long. There is a good accommodation bridge south west of Cosgrove before the canal arrives at Old Stratford. The extension to Buckingham authorised by the 1794 Act leaves what was known as the Old Stratford Cut at the north-east side of the village. The cut continues for over 100yd to the site of a wharf, which is connected to A5 (Watling Street) by Wharf Lane. Here the brick-walled basin and about a half of the original large brick warehouse survive. This was built about 1805; beneath it are considerable vaults, reminiscent of a church crypt but solidly constructed of brick, which were used for storage. In 1870 the warehouse became the property of a local boatbuilding firm, Edward Hayes & Co, and a scene, from time to time, of much excitement. The hulls of the boats—tugs, barges, confections for Eastern potentates, but all with one thing in common: a beam of maximum 2in less than the width of the Grand Junction locks—were built in the village and then hauled, by horses and later by steam traction engines, across the village and up the lane to the wharf. Once one got loose and blocked the lane for three days. At the wharf the boats were launched sideways into the canal, a violent proceeding which sometimes ended with the vessel wedged across the waterway or stuck halfway up the opposite bank. The whole village turned out to witness a launching, lining the canal and sitting on the brick walls that used to surround the site. Once in the water, the boats had their boilers installed and super-structure added, and were then towed along the cut and down the Grand Junction to the Thames. Hayes & Co gave up the business in 1923 and the workshop became a warehouse again.

After the junction with the cut the Buckingham line passes under A508, turns south west and then under Watling Street immediately north of the traffic lights. Bridge no 2, almost a short tunnel, can be seen beneath the road. On the west side a housing estate soon obliterates the canal, which shortly emerges on the north side of A422. The next bridges have been flattened but the course of the canal is distinct as it traverses the fields and circles through Deanshanger. In the village much of the bed is filled in, but the Wharf house, renovated, stands by bridge no 9.

After Deanshanger the canal crosses to the south side of A422, remaining between the road and the Great Ouse for the rest of its course. Left turns off the main road lead to the canal, one to the site of Thornton Wharf and the next to Leckhampstead Wharf, where there is a pleasant small house and the site of the wharf is occupied by countless hens, while sheep and geese, separated by the canal, exchange noises over it. Having skirted a lake and passed by Old Mill House, the canal is briefly joined by the river.

Disengaged, it follows the river in a northern loop and returns beside A422 on the approach to Buckingham. There are traces of a wharf near the playing fields, but the canal here has been used for tipping. Behind a garage is the site of the basin, an open space with a warehouse-type building beside it. A few yards on and one is in the centre of the compact market town.

Closure of the Buckingham Branch began long before the popular appeal of pleasure cruising was appreciated; hence what might have been a valuable asset to the present network has been lost.

OS sheet 146
The Canals of the East Midlands, by Charles Hadfield
'The Old Stratford and Buckingham Branches of the Grand Junction Canal', by Alan H. Faulkner, *Journal* of the Railway & Canal Historical Society, July 1965

THE NEWPORT PAGNELL CANAL

The Grand Junction Canal (now part of the Grand Union) passed about a mile from the small town of Newport Pagnell. Despite requests from the tradespeople, the company refused to make a branch; so a committee got together, obtained an Act in 1814, appointed Benjamin Bevan, then working for the Grand Junction, to make a survey, and got on with the job themselves. In 1817 the Newport Pagnell Canal was open; 1¼ miles long, it left the Grand Junction at Great Linford and dropped by seven narrow locks to a basin on the west side of the town.

Coal was the main cargo, brought by canal routes from Shipley (on the Nutbrook) and Moira (on the Ashby); there was a variety of other trade as well. Tolls were high and moderate profits were made, annual tonnage at its peak reaching nearly 15,000. Dividends fell, however, with the arrival of the London & Birmingham Railway at nearby Wolverton, although the railway failed to obtain leave to use the canal for a branch line of their own. But in 1862, with little money coming in, the canal company sold out to the Newport Pagnell Railway, notwithstanding opposition from other canal companies and the colliery owners who traded on the waterway. The canal was shut in 1864, the equipment sold off, and the railway took over much of its course.

Now the railway itself has gone. The canal left the Grand Junction by a road bridge, a few yards south of the remains of Great Linford station. The bridge that took the main canal's towpath over the branch has vanished, and a workshop has been built on its site. There is a fine old house, once the Old Wharf inn, on the towpath of the Grand Union; behind this is the lock-keeper's house on the line of the branch. There is no trace of the lock, or of any of the locks on the Newport Pagnell, but the line of the canal can be picked up east of the house and followed across fields until it meets the old railway. The two coincide for about ¾ mile, being crossed by the embankment of the M1.

Approaching Newport Pagnell, the canal deviates north of the railway; allotments now cover its bed and the sites of three locks. The station and goods yard were built over the basin and public wharf; these in turn are now giving way to new industrial building. Only a warehouse by the site of the Old Shipley coal wharf survives, but its future looks uncertain.

Those drinking in 'The Swan Revived' at Newport Pagnell are standing where the committee of the canal first met; those drinking in the 'Black Horse' on the Grand Union are a few hundred yards along the towpath from the junction with the branch. Newport Pagnell is nationally known for the frequent crashes on the nearby stretch of the M1. For anyone with the time and inclination, the line of the Newport Pagnell Canal and Railway still makes a pleasant walk.

OS sheet 146
The Canals of the East Midlands, by Charles Hadfield
'A Forgotten Waterway', by J. S. Faulkner, *Journal* of the Railway & Canal Historical Society, Vol 6 (1)

THE FOXTON INCLINED PLANE

Providing that there is not a queue of boats heading in the same direction, it takes the average pleasure cruiser about an hour and a quarter to ascend or descend the flight of ten locks at Foxton, on the Leicester section of the Grand Union Canal. On the east side of the flight you will see an ivy-clad wall. This is the rear retaining wall of the engine-house of the Foxton inclined plane which, in the early years of this century, would have enabled you to negotiate the 75ft change in levels in twelve minutes.

The story of Foxton is rather a sad one—a story of misjudgements and hopes unfulfilled. Foxton is at one end of the line of the old Grand Union, 23½ miles of canal completed in 1814, linking the Leicestershire & Northamptonshire Union with the Grand Junction Canal at Norton. The line was engineered by Benjamin Bevan; it included 17 locks—the Foxton flight and a further seven at Watford—and two long tunnels, at Husbands Bosworth and Crick. South came coal from the Derby and Nottingham coalfields; north came merchandise from London; the old Grand Union was the summit level of the through route, and had no local traffic of its own. Three reservoirs were necessary to keep the line supplied with water, much of which was lost through lockage to its neighbours at either end. Its financial position weak because of its dependence on other companies, the old Grand Union had to struggle right from the start. And because the Grand Junction wished to discourage barges from using its long tunnel at Blisworth, as their passage prevented two-way traffic, the locks at Foxton and Watford had been built to 7ft width.

As the Victorian era flourished, the fortunes of the old Grand Union declined. The line was expensive to maintain; railway competition increased; tolls were cut and cut, but receipts and dividends fell. However, in 1886 Mr Fellows, of Fellows, Morton & Clayton who had now become the chief carriers on the route, came up with two proposals. The first was that the locks at Foxton and Watford should be widened, so that he could put steamers and wide barges on the route to fend off competition. The second was that the Grand Junction should buy both the old Grand Union and the Leicestershire & Northamptonshire, which was done in 1894, the old Grand Union's selling price being £10,500. Now in control, the Grand Junction could tackle the problem of the narrow locks. The company, worried by the decrease in coal traffic, decided to experiment boldly and sought tenders for the construction of an inclined plane at Foxton to bypass the locks there, postponing the Watford problem until it could be seen how this worked out. For the time being, Fellows agreed to put more narrow boats on the canal.

Work on the incline began in 1898, the designer in charge being G. C. Thomas, the company's own engineer, and the contractors being J. & H. Gwynne & Co, of Hammersmith. It took two years to complete, and cost about £39,000. Four pairs of rails were laid on a slope with a gradient of 1 in 4. On these ran two caissons, which ascended and descended sideways, each with eight pairs of wheels, and counterbalancing each other, being connected with a wire rope. A steam-engine was installed to control the operation and to overcome friction. Each caisson could take two narrow boats or one barge. Boats were floated into the caissons at the top or bottom of the lift, and the gates were closed by hydraulic power. As one caisson went up, the other came down; then at the end of the journey each was rammed, also by hydraulic power, against the exit to the canal, to avoid loss of water, the gates opened and the boats floated out. It took four minutes to get the boats in and out and eight minutes to operate the lift. The incline was operated by three men; a stoker, and one on each set of gates; the cost of operation was not much more than £1 a day.

Unfortunately, unlike the other late Victorian masterpieces of canal engineering, the Anderton lift and the Barton swing aqueduct, the Foxton incline proved a failure. There were faults in construction, as the rails tended to break because of the weight of the caissons, and the cost of maintaining a head of steam all the time was too great for a company whose trade was continuing to fall off. Only the installation of electricity might have helped prolong its life, but there seems to have been no question of that. The company soon decided against constructing a second incline at Watford, proposing instead to widen the locks. Then, having assessed the situation in 1901, the Grand Junction conceded defeat and rebuilt Watford locks to their original narrow dimensions.

The incline continued to be used regularly until 1910. In its last six years it handled a total of about 210,000 tons of traffic, working absurdly below its potential capacity. The Foxton locks were restored in 1909 to deal with what night traffic there was; then in November 1910 the incline was closed and all traffic reverted to the locks. The company also prohibited the use of wide boats north of Stoke Bruerne, because of the delay they caused in the tunnels. The incline was maintained until 1914, being used from time to time when the locks were under repair; after that date it was allowed to fall into decay, and was eventually dismantled in 1927 and the machinery sold for scrap, fetching £250. Thomas the engineer claimed that the incline would have been a success had it not been for the poor state of the northern canals serving the coalfields direct, which led to diminishing enthusiasm on the part of traders and carriers and the falling off of traffic.

The Foxton flight today, on what is now the Grand Union which absorbed the Grand Junction in 1928, presents a busy scene in summer with the crews of pleasure boats manipulating the paddles under the eye of the lock-keeper. As you approach the top of the flight, the old cut to the top of the incline can be discerned on the east side. Dry and overgrown, it can be followed around the ends of the side ponds to the top of the 307ft slope. There is nothing at the top apart from the base of the engine-house. Small trees, brambles and shrubs have forced their way through the slope itself, though it is still possible to scramble down it to the basin at the foot. Here are the remains of the docks into which the caissons were lowered. The basin and the lower cut are watered and used for private moorings. The lower cut emerges into the Market Harborough arm of the old Leicester & Northampton, a few yards from the junction with the main line near the bottom of the flight. During the building of the incline, G. C. Thomas lived in the lock cottage here, to which he added the second storey.

A commercial failure the Foxton inclined plane undoubtedly was. But to anyone, like the writer, who has been stuck for an hour in a drenching rainstorm in a boat at the bottom of one of the Foxton locks while assorted helpers scoured the surroundings to find an implement to raise a broken paddle, an ascending caisson would seem a gift from the gods indeed.

OS sheet 133
The Canals of the East Midlands, by Charles Hadfield
The Canal at Foxton, by M. Matts (from Waterways Museum, Stoke Bruerne)
Engineering, 25 Jan 1900

THE CHARNWOOD FOREST BRANCH

There were two elements to the Leicester Navigation, for which an Act was obtained in 1791. The more important was the so-called River line, a canalisation of the Soar, linking Leicester to the Loughborough Navigation to the north and through this to the Trent and the North-East Midlands. This we know today as

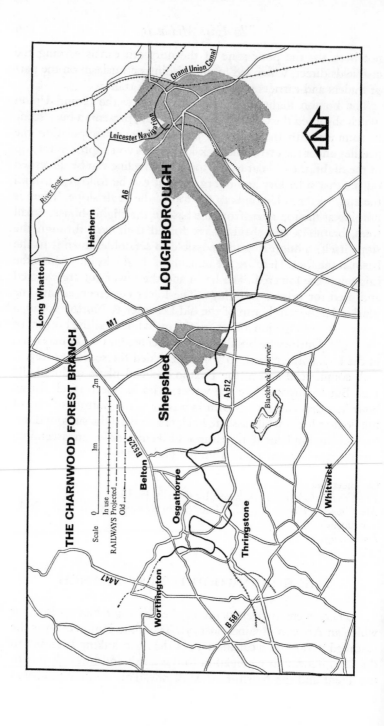

THE CHARNWOOD FOREST BRANCH

Scale

RAILWAYS
In use
Projected
Old

0   1m   2m

Long Whatton

Hathern

A6

Grand Union Canal

Leicester Navigation

River Soar

LOUGHBOROUGH

M1

Shepshed

A512

Blackbrook Reservoir

Belton B5324

A447

Osgathorpe

Worthington

Thringstone

B587

Whitwick

part of the Grand Union Canal, which bought it in 1932. The other was the Forest line, a rail and canal branch heading west from Loughborough through Charnwood Forest to collieries some 8 miles distant. The Forest line was opened in 1794, went out of use in 1799, but was not abandoned officially until 1848.

The rail element of the Forest line comprised a 2½ mile connection from Loughborough Wharf to Nanpantan, rising 170ft, where the level canal began, and shorter lengths at the eastern end of the canal up to the collieries. Fish-bellied rails and wooden sleepers were used. At the eastern end proposed lines to Cloud Hill and Barrow Hill were not constructed, but those to Swannington and Coleorton were in operation for a time.

Traffic was slow to start on the Forest line. The canal committee ran demonstration boats in 1794–5 and went into the coal-selling business themselves, but the canal had insufficient water for regular trading. A reservoir was made at Blackbrook, being completed in 1797; tolls were reduced and boats began to move. Coleorton coal was selling cheaply in Nanpantan in 1798. However, in February 1799 heavy rainfall coincided with a thaw, causing a flood. The reservoir burst; an aqueduct and part of the embankment were destroyed, and that was the end of the active life of the Charnwood Forest canal. Repairs were put promptly in hand and the line was usable again by the end of 1801. But there was no interest; more damage occurred a few years later, and the company admitted defeat and sought to abandon the canal. Not only were they unable to do this; they had to pay £1,900 for the land they had used for the line, as Charnwood Forest was about to be enclosed. The company, who because of their exemption from paying poor rates had made a powerful enemy in Lord Shaftesbury who blocked their bills in Parliament, were not able to abandon the line until 1848 when a landowner introduced a private bill for abandonment, enabling him to buy some of the land along the line.

Most of the Charnwood Forest line is still traceable as it wanders along the contours, although anyone looking for a forest in this immediate area is liable to be disappointed. Nanpantan is 2½ miles south west of Loughborough, on B5350. About 300yd east of the crossroads in the village is a public footpath on the north side of the main road; this is in parts the towpath of the canal, whose bed runs along the foot of gardens, some of which have incorporated it. Snells Nook Lane crosses the canal after ¼ mile, by the entrance to Longcliffe golf club, and the canal can be followed through the golf course until it is stopped by the barrier of M1.

West of the motorway the canal edges northwards to the fringes of Shepshed, where a cemetery and a new housing estate have been deposited on top of it. It then wanders in the direction of Osgathorpe, crossed by a number of minor roads leading north off A512. The bridges have all been levelled but the canal's course is generally obvious except where in a couple of places it has been obliterated by the old branch railway between Loughborough and Coalville. South of Osgathorpe the line divided, near the Junction house where the company had a toll-collector. The northern branch, about ¾ mile, stopped by the foot of Barrow Hill; the shorter southern branch ended on A512, by a stream beside the entrance to Cinder Hill Farm, a few yards from the signpost to Osgathorpe at Thringstone bridge.

OS sheet 121
The Canals of the East Midlands, by Charles Hadfield

THE OAKHAM CANAL

There is enough left of the Oakham Canal to make its existence credible and its pursuit worthwhile. Although abandoned in 1846, nearly the whole of the line can be traced; an expedition not without excitement, taking the explorer through a lion reserve and alongside the walls of a prison. Melton Mowbray and Oakham, the terminals of the canal, are two of the pleasantest towns of the East Midlands, and the countryside between is varied and interesting.

Opened throughout in 1802, the Oakham Canal was very much a local undertaking. Costing nearly £70,000 to make, it was 15¼ miles long, climbing from Melton by 19 locks to Oakham. Of these 19 wide locks there is now almost nothing left, except in some instances an obvious change in levels. At Melton, it joined the Melton Mowbray Navigation, which itself connected with the Leicester Navigation south of Loughborough. Coal and grain were the main traffic, and although the undertaking was not very profitable for its shareholders it increased the prosperity of the towns and countryside it served.

William Jessop made the preliminary survey of the line; the first engineer was Christopher Staveley, a local stonemason, who was succeeded by William Dunn in 1797. Dunn had been involved with cutlery manufacture and colliery management, and he seems also to have proved a competent canal engineer. The line headed eastward from a basin which it shared with the Melton Mowbray Navigation; the Boat Inn, Burton St, marks the spot, though the basin has long been filled in. It passed behind a terrace of cottages called Birmingham Row and headed east out of Melton between B676 and the River Eye. Traces of the cut can be discerned here and there, but the railway, whose construction caused the canal's demise, occupies its bed for some stretches. There are clear indications by the level-crossing at Wyfordby, and on the far side is a large basin, probably once Freeby Wharf, where the only boat-owner on the canal, a Mr Spreckley, used to operate. Saxby Station and Junction, not long ago busy with freight and passengers, obscure the canal and the site of the ninth lock; then the canal swings southward along the edge of Stapleford Park. There are two mileposts in this length, and the canal holds water here-abouts; but the Park is now a lion reserve and exploration may be fraught with more than the usual hazards. By a level-crossing on a minor road between the Park and Teigh the canal emerges as a wide marshy ditch and turns east alongside a cattle-gridded road towards Edmonthorpe. South of Edmonthorpe is the canal's major engineering feature—a large embankment; then the canal swings south again to pass under the road ½ mile west of the attractive Cotswold-type village of Market Overton. On the south side of the road the wharf buildings still exist, inhabited and in good condition; the tree-lined canal holds water and the last evidence of navigation—a rowing-boat. About ½ mile farther south is the site of a large double basin, and a mile on the remains of Cottesmore Wharf, by the Ashwell–Cottesmore road. The marshy course now edges westward, and passes under the Ash-well–Oakham road with the Cottesmore kennels on one side and a prison on the other. The next stretch is maintained by the Oakham Angling Society, and is wide, deep and generally clean. It is culverted under the Burley–Langham road, and then dammed by the anglers to maintain the water level.

On the approach to Oakham, the canal passed behind Spring-field House and the Catmose Vale Hospital, and along the edge of the playing fields of Oakham School. The warehouse by what was Oakham Wharf has been converted into Oakham School Hall.

During its short lifetime, various plans to extend the Oakham Canal were mooted, but none came to anything. The company was much harried in its last years by the 6th Earl of Harborough, through whose estates the central section of the canal passed, and who seems to have been both eccentric and cantankerous. The Earl, however, proved even more hostile towards the Midland Railway, which bought the canal in 1846. By this date, trade was generally poor on the waterway, owing to water shortage, always a problem possibly owing to the failure of the engineers to tap the waters of the River Eye to feed the canal. For another year traffic continued, with some profit, while the railway was building; then the locks were demolished and the materials sold off. Since then, most of the canal has quietly decayed, threading a wilder beauty through the well-kept countryside.

OS sheet 122
The Oakham Canal, by David Tew
The Canals of the East Midlands, by Charles Hadfield

THE GRANTHAM CANAL

Of the abandoned canals in the East Midlands, the Grantham has altered least with the passing of time. A rural waterway, except for the last 2 miles into Nottingham, it resembles a slow-flowing river as it meanders through the Vale of Belvoir for 33 miles—the distance between its terminals is 21 miles as the crow flies. It has run dry near Cropwell Bishop—always a leaky stretch because of the underlying gypsum beds; but otherwise, apart from the absence of boats, it must look much as it did when it bore coal up to Grantham and agricultural produce back down.

The canal was principally a Grantham project; William Jessop was employed to supervise the work, and the line was opened in 1797, at a cost of a little under £120,000. Apart from the Erewash, it was the cheapest per mile of the East Midlands canals to construct; there were 18 broad locks and a cutting at Harlaxton, but no major engineering works. During the first half of the nineteenth century it made fair profits, the company itself trading in coal and coke from time to time, but its tolls were kept relatively high, which encouraged competition from the early railways, land carriage, and alternative waterway routes. The Nottingham to Grantham railway was opened in 1850; the Grantham company was willing to amalgamate with the railway, but it took four years and several lawsuits before the latter (the Ambergate company) fulfilled its agreements, paid up, and took over the canal. As railway companies amalgamated, the canal passed into the keeping of the Great Northern and then the LNER, while traffic on the water gradually dwindled away. After several years of quiescence, the canal was abandoned in 1936.

The basin at Grantham, at Old Wharf Road, has been recently filled in, but it is possible to find the canal along Earl's Field Lane and to walk along the towpath until the canal is culverted to pass under the A1. Hereafter the towpath is walkable for good distances through pleasant rolling countryside, and there are some fine red-brick bridges over the canal. There is an attractive group of buildings by the Rutland Arms, signposted to the east of the minor road north of Woolsthorpe, at the end of a lane. Here is a former maintenance yard with bridge no 61, a lock cottage, two locks, without gates and converted to weirs, some ruined stables and the remains of a short boat. Under the bridge there is an iron marker, stating '28 miles from the Trent'. The canal falls through four more locks northwards; then turns west and south, to pass through the villages of Redmile and Plungar. Here it is narrower and rather more weedy, but it retains water on the southern loop, past the sharp corner known as Devil's Elbow, until it approaches Cropwell Bishop, where it is dry for a length of perhaps 2 miles. It is watered again on the west side of the A46, but on the approach to Nottingham several of the bridges have been replaced by culverts. Passing south of Gamston, it runs into Nottingham on the north side of the A52, and locks into the Trent past the boathouses of the rowing clubs, a few hundred yards north of Trent Bridge at the entrance to the city itself.

Investigation of the Grantham Canal takes one into an unfrequented, undramatic, placid area of country on the Lincolnshire–Nottinghamshire border, easy for both the driver and the walker. The pity is that one can no longer traverse it by boat.

OS sheet 122 (also Grantham end on 113, Nottingham end on 112)
The Canals of the East Midlands, by Charles Hadfield

THE NOTTINGHAM CANAL

The Nottingham Canal was an important link in the waterway pattern of the East Midlands. A local project, it was inspired by the passing of the Act for the Cromford Canal; its purpose was to provide a direct route for coal into Nottingham, which otherwise would have to be carried from the Cromford, when completed, along the Erewash Canal (the senior of the area's waterways, opened in 1779), and then into the city via the Trent, a long haul. The Nottingham promoters employed William Jessop to produce a survey and estimate, and work began in 1792 to cut the line from the Trent, west of Trent Bridge, to join the Cromford at Langley Mill, very close to that canal's own junction with the Erewash. It took four years and £80,000 to complete the Nottingham, which had 19 broad locks rising from the Trent, but no major engineering works apart from embankments. The canal was 14¾ miles long, with a number of short branches, some of them private.

Like most of its neighbours, the Nottingham Canal brought its shareholders reasonably profitable returns for some fifty years. It co-operated with the Cromford company, came to agreement over tolls with the Erewash, and was an important avenue of traffic for the Grantham Canal. Railway competition began to affect trade in the 1840s and, like the Grantham, the Nottingham company was willing to amalgamate with the Ambergate railway. The same process of delays and lawsuits resulted, until the canal was eventually transferred to the railway in 1855.

A better volume of trade was maintained on the Nottingham than on the Grantham, and for longer, but most of it was confined to the few miles nearest the Trent. The stretch from Lenton to Trent lock was transferred to the Trent Navigation, and the canal abandoned in 1937.

Today, nothing of the canal is left between Lenton and a point about halfway up the flight of locks leading to the summit at Wollaton. This can be found on the north of A609, about 3 miles west of the city centre. Here, beside the new East Midlands Electricity Craft Training centre, on Lambourne Drive, are six dilapidated lock chambers—and plenty of rubbish. There is a gap at Wollaton, and then the canal can be found again, in rather better state, passing under the A609 at Trowell, and turning to head north. It runs beside the Trowell–Cossall minor road, a pleasant stretch of water with a good towpath. The junction with a short branch to Robbinetts can be seen at a sharp bend in both road and canal. It passes west of Cossall Marsh on an embankment, and crosses B6007 in a concrete pipe, skirts the west side of Awsworth and the east of Eastwood (the home of D. H. Lawrence) to approach and run parallel to the River Erewash and the Erewash Canal. At New Eastwood, on a road signposted to Shipley Common, there is a good red-brick bridge, and 300yd along the canal to the north west a swing bridge survives (SK 462459).

By the next bridge north, on Tinsley Road, the canal has been filled in and used as a rubbish dump, but water begins again on the north side of the bridge. Bridge Terrace cottages stand on a narrow peninsula between the Nottingham and Erewash canals here. At Bailey Grove a wooden bridge crosses the filled-in Nottingham, now only a few yards from the Erewash, and the two canals join on the north side of A608, opposite Vic Hallam's works and beside the Great Northern Inn. The filled in and levelled off course of the Cromford lies to the north; the toll-house that was shared by the Cromford and Nottingham still stands. There are some canal cottages by the inn. Stop planks are inserted at the end of the Nottingham Canal—though it is not clear what they are supposed to stop.

Up to now, BWB have a statutory obligation to maintain a certain depth of water in both the Nottingham and Grantham canals. If they succeed in dispensing with this obligation, one wonders what will prevent the best surviving parts of the Nottingham Canal from rapidly approaching the condition of the worst; and that condition is very nasty indeed.

OS sheet 112
The Canals of the East Midlands, by Charles Hadfield

THE NUTBROOK CANAL

The 4½ mile Nutbrook Canal is of more interest for its history than for any engineering features. In the early 1790s, a group of mineowners combined to finance the cutting of a canal from the

Shipley estate to a junction with the Erewash Canal: Outram was the engineer, and the canal, descending through 13 locks 14ft 3in wide, to take the Trent barges, was opened throughout in 1796. Reservoirs were constructed near Shipley; they survive today, for the benefit of anglers. But much of the canal itself is now dry; some stretches have disappeared altogether, while others are likely to fall victim to opencast mining operations in the near future.

The Nutbrook cost £22,800 to construct, and for nearly a century proved a moderately profitable undertaking. Coal was the main traffic, but the canal proved an attraction when ironworks were developed in the area—not only because it eased transport problems but also because its water was of great value for feeding boilers and for cooling. Indeed, this ready water supply led the Stanton Ironworks to buy the canal in 1946 and its water, fed in from the Nutbrook itself, is still used for this purpose. Some idea of the usefulness of the water can be gained by comparing the thin trickle that emerges from the culverts into the Erewash Canal with the healthy-looking wide waterway above the ironworks, near Kirk Hallam.

Except for two short stretches, the course of the canal through the Stanton Works has recently been obliterated, although one of the original toll-houses can still be found; 1949 saw the end of Nutbrook traffic at Stanton. In the previous years, slag had become the principal cargo, but during the war the Stanton boats carried a host of miscellaneous items, including wheat, cheese, tinned meat and empty bomb cases. Two early bridges—a footbridge and a railway bridge—cross the canal within the works, but the fine roving bridge by the bottom lock was demolished a few years ago. From the road north of the ironworks the towpath can be followed northwards, an unexpectedly pleasant rural walk. Here is a lock chamber, in good condition, though without gates and converted to a weir. As you head north, the canal dries out; access to the upper reaches can be gained from A609, by a sharp bend a mile south west of Ilkeston. The course can be followed in either direction, with lock remains in various stages of survival. It is hereabouts that opencast mining will soon result in further obliteration.

Shipley Hall has been demolished, and the estate is now owned by the NCB. Potholed lanes cross the area; in a copse on the south side of a reservoir is the outline of the end of the canal (SK 445438), near the arched culvert through which it was supplied. Opencast mining is scheduled for this area too.

Apart from the Stanton length, most of the Nutbrook Canal was closed in 1895, although it seems that it has never been officially abandoned. But the Stanton Works can testify that what is left of it has by no means outlived its usefulness.

OS sheet 112
The Nutbrook Canal, by P. Stevenson
The Canals of the East Midlands, by Charles Hadfield

THE DERBY CANAL

Today, the Derby Canal is more of a linear refuse-tip than anything else. Part of the inter-connecting East Midland canal complex, it was opened in 1796 from a junction with the Erewash Canal at Sandiacre, 8 miles east of Derby, to Swarkestone, 5 miles south of Derby on the Trent & Mersey Canal. There was also a branch northward from Derby to Little Eaton, where it connected with a tramroad bringing coal from Denby and other mines in the area. Through traffic, as well as local trade for Derby, travelled along the canal, stone, corn and cement being important cargoes as well as coal. After a slow start dividends became quite healthy, and in its busiest years the canal carried about 200,000 tons annually. Receipts were affected by railway competition in the mid-nineteenth century, as was common, but despite its attempts the Derby Canal Company failed to sell its waterway to a railway company and retained control of it up to the end. Which came in 1964, though the Company had been trying to close its canal for nearly forty years, and had officially abandoned the Little Eaton branch in 1935. Objections by ICI, who used the canal, helped to postpone the final closure.

And final it was. The proprietors, it seems, saw no future for the canal as an amenity and proceeded to dispose of parts of it for road construction or building land. Hence in Derby itself the canal has been nearly obliterated, and the road traveller will benefit thereby. But there are stretches for which no use has been found other than that of providing a dumping ground for refuse. One such stretch is at Sandiacre, between the junction with the Erewash

M

Derby Canal: broken lock gates at Sandiacre

and the bridge on B6002 (which was reconstructed in 1925 to full navigational standards). Here are the two wide Sandiacre locks, gates rotting and masonry dislodged. The canal runs behind the trim gardens of modern semi-detached houses. It is a stinking, wide, muddy ditch littered with mattresses, bits of cars and bicycles, old cookers—all varieties of household rubbish too cumbersome to put out for the dustman or too much trouble to burn. At least the sometime owners of this rubbish must be grateful to the Derby Canal Co for its provision of this facility for disposal. As there were ten children romping in the filth on my visit in April 1970, presumably the canal is regarded as a useful playground as well.

On the west side of M1, at Breaston, the canal is being filled in and levelled off, but the Navigation Inn survives. North of Draycott it is a muddy ditch; here and there along the line isolated accommodation bridges arch over nothing. On the south side of Borrowash, beside the railway, there is a smashed lock chamber and another rubbish dump. Approaching Derby, the course of the canal disappears under road and other building works. When the southern arm emerges, it does so as another rubbish-filled ditch, the rubbish only diminishing as open country is reached.

An important but little-known item of canal history survived in Derby until 1971. This was the Holmes aqueduct, that lay mostly concealed by a mid-Victorian bridge carrying the road from the bus station to the Cattle Market. Engineered by Outram, it was, as far as is known, the first cast-iron aqueduct to be completed, beating the much larger iron aqueduct at Longdon-upon-Tern on the Shrewsbury Canal by a few weeks. It was 44ft 6in long and took the canal over a stream. In its last years as well as being hidden by the road bridge it was also nearly full with earth and rubbish, but the top of the cast-iron plates forming the sides of the aqueduct could be seen. It is strongly hoped that some part of this historic structure will be preserved.

The only useful water left in the Derby Canal is a few yards at Swarkeston, at the junction with the Trent & Mersey. As far as the first bridge, the Derby is used as the basin of the Swarkestone Boat Club, and a canal cottage is the club's headquarters.

The current OS map of the area shows the Derby Canal as an uninterrupted blue line, so there is no problem in finding out where it is, or was. But unless the cartographers invent a new conventional sign for squalor, there won't be much of it showing on the next edition.

OS sheet 121
The Canals of the East Midlands, by Charles Hadfield

THE CROMFORD CANAL

Two remarkable examples of transport engineering met near the small Derbyshire town of Cromford: the Cromford & High Peak Railway and the Cromford Canal. Opened in 1831, the railway climbed by ferocious gradients over the Derbyshire hills, linking the canal with the Peak Forest Canal at Whaley Bridge; but by this date the Cromford Canal itself was already a flourishing concern. It was 14⅝ miles long, cut from Cromford to a junction with the Erewash and Nottingham canals at Langley Mill, and it quickly established itself as an important part of the East Midlands network. It was opened throughout in 1794, engineered by Jessop and Outram, and cost just under £80,000. The principal traffic was coal and coke; lime, limestone and iron were also carried in large quantities, and after the opening of the railway there was an increased trade in corn and groceries to Manchester. The great cotton millowner, Sir Richard Arkwright of Cromford, was one of the promoters, and the line was planned to serve several mines, as well as quarries, leadworks, and the ironworks at Somercotes and Butterley. Jessop and Outram were two of the founders of the Butterley company. In its busiest years of the 1830s and 1840s, the canal carried well over 300,000 tons a year.

Railway competition and eventual railway ownership contributed towards a steady decline in trade during the second half of the nineteenth century, but the Cromford Canal took a long time to die. Sixty-two years passed between the closure of Butterley tunnel in 1900 and the final abandonment Act of the bottom ½ mile. Nor is it quite dead yet; the stretch between Cromford and Ironville is still watered and many of the major engineering features of the line remain.

Between Langley Mill and Ironville much of the canal has been recently obliterated. How thoroughly this has been done can be seen near the excellent Boat Inn, Stoneyford, where, apart from a lock cottage, there is now scarcely a trace of the existence of the waterway. Two miles north of this point the canal swings west to Ironville—an unattractive but interesting relic of Victorian industrial housing, brooded over by the spirit, if not the visible presence, of the Butterley company. A short branch northeastward to Pinxton left the main line here; most of it is now filled in, but the junction and bridge no 1 of the branch are on the west side of the village. There is some water in the main line here, and the lock chambers are in fair condition.

The canal runs alongside what used to be a company toll road from Ironville to Butterley and enters the Golden Valley on the west side of the first crossroads west of Ironville, by the Newlands Inn. A walk of 200yd along the towpath brings you opposite to the east portal of Butterley tunnel, an insignificant hole in the hillside; 2,966yd long as originally built—later extended by 97yd when a railway was built above the western end—this tunnel is only 9ft wide. The appearance is a little deceptive, as the approach is silted up, but it was always a slow tunnel to navigate, three hours being the maximum time allowed. Whereas the locks below the tunnel were wide, the tunnel itself, and the narrower locks above it, restricted the size of boats and caused delays, as only one-way working was possible. In 1889 subsidence caused the closing of the tunnel for four years; after repairs, greatly reduced trade continued through it until in 1900 more serious subsidence occurred. The Midland Railway, then the owners of the canal, claimed that only complete rebuilding would solve the problems which, they maintained, were caused by mining underneath the tunnel. As they held the expense would be unwarranted, they wanted to close the tunnel entirely. The Erewash Canal Company objected, and managed to get a government inquiry. The commission appointed reported in 1909, endorsing the Midland's decision, and the tunnel, with the navigation above it, was abandoned.

Water now cascades down a stepped weir from the top of the cutting. The line of the tunnel can be followed from the road to Butterley by noting the remains of the shafts on the south side. The west portal can best be found by taking A61 into Ripley and coming out on the minor road to Pentrich. Just past a collection of cottages called Hammersmith is an area of railway dereliction. A lane runs westward beside a playground; it passes under two railway bridges, one built directly on the top of the other, and leads to a sewage farm. A path to the right crosses the top of the west portal and leads down to form the towpath of the canal. The tunnel entrance is at the foot of a massive battered stone wall, the tunnel itself having been extended to this point when the railway was built above.

For the next 3 miles the canal runs one side or the other of A610. By a transport cafe at the junction with B6013 a stretch of canal has been filled in, but a short tunnel remains at the end of the car park. The aqueduct over the Amber at Bullbridge has been removed recently, and another short tunnel is difficult of access owing to gasworks development. At Ambergate the canal swings north west and continues parallel to A6, the railway and the Derwent towards Cromford. From here on, the towpath makes a delightful walk, with Crich Chase to the east and Shining Cliff

Woods opposite; however, although the canal is close to the main road, there are few points of access. On B5035, bridge no 13 is convenient for the towpath. Two miles on from this bridge is the last of the short tunnels—Gregory tunnel, 80yd long with the towpath through it.

In another mile the canal crosses the railway. Then comes the entrance to the short Lea Wood branch, now watered for only a few yards, with a cottage by the junction. A few steps more and you are on Jessop's massive single-arch aqueduct over the Derwent, 30ft high with an 80ft span. This was completed in 1792, but cracked and had to be strengthened. The stonework is in very fine condition, and the date is firmly inscribed over the arch. Beside the aqueduct is the High Peak Pumping Station, which can be viewed by arrangement with BWB. On the opposite side of the canal is the old interchange point for traffic from the Cromford & High Peak Railway; this is an area of great interest for the railway historian.

Cromford Basin is a mile farther on. It is opposite Cromford Parish Church, and forms part of the Midland Storage Transport Service yard. There is a stone warehouse, a covered loading bay, and some rather dirty water.

Butterley tunnel and the Derwent aqueduct are two of the major engineering features of the East Midland canals. Probing into the fascinating Derbyshire countryside, the Cromford Canal must take priority as the most varied and interesting of the abandoned waterways of the East Midlands.

OS sheets 112 (Langley Mill)
    111 (Cromford)
The Canals of the East Midlands, by Charles Hadfield
The Cromford & High Peak Railway, by A. Rimmer

THE CHESTERFIELD CANAL
(Chesterfield to Worksop only)

One of the earlier canals, the Chesterfield was surveyed by James Brindley in 1769. Joining Chesterfield to the Trent, via Worksop and Retford, it was designed to carry principally coal and lead, and to serve the ironworks at Staveley. It was opened throughout in 1777, with 65 locks, many of them double, narrow except for six broad locks on the Retford–Trent section, and a 2,850yd tunnel at Norwood. After Brindley's death in 1772, Hugh Henshall and John Varley were appointed engineers, and the completion of the tunnel in comparatively few years was a credit to their exertions. A few short branches, to pits and quarries, and several tramroads were also constructed.

The canal cost about £150,000, and dividends soon rose to between 6 and 8 per cent. Plans to extend the line, or to connect it with Sheffield, were mooted but dropped, and the canal continued to trade steadily until the advent of railway competition. Then in 1847 the canal company amalgamated with the Manchester & Lincoln Union Railway, with an obligation that the canal be maintained and continue in business. When the Sheffield–Gainsborough railway was built various alterations had to be made in the canal line, and the Norwood tunnel was extended 252yd at its eastern end. For many years the company participated in canal-carrying itself until, now part of the Great Central, it stopped all such carrying in 1892. But trade was greatly diminished, and trouble with the tunnel and subsidence on the upper reaches of the canal frequently impeded navigation. Damage to the tunnel was such that in 1908 it had to be closed for good; this cut off the upper length entirely and also ended all traffic west of Worksop, there being no point in taking boats up thirty locks to get nowhere at the end. Carrying over the rest of the canal ended in 1955, although pleasure traffic has developed promisingly in recent years.

The canal leaves Chesterfield branching off the River Rother on the west side of A619, heading for Staveley. About a mile out of the town, Lockoford Lane (B6050) runs down left off the main road to cross the canal by a modern bridge at the foot of the hill, by the premises of the Chesterfield Scrap Metal Co. There is a lock chamber to the left of the bridge, and the towpath leads alongside the narrow course of the canal, through which a channel of water flows swiftly. A very small, attractive red-brick accommodation bridge comes next, and then the canal meets the river after about ½ mile.

The canal runs beside the great Staveley Ironworks; the lock by the works entrance marks the end of the fall from Chesterfield. From here there is a climb of 14 locks to the summit. A fine view of the heavy industry of the area can be gained from the bridge where the Eckington road crosses the canal; in the distance, over-topping all, is the crooked wooden spire of Chesterfield church. North of the bridge, the canal crawls under the railway line to Sheffield and keeps it company northward. In places the bed is dry, as it is after turning east to skirt Killamarsh, where there is a half-filled-in lock under the road bridge on B6058. Oddly enough, one of the bottom gates of the lock is still intact and on its hinges. These 6ft 11in locks of the Chesterfield are among the narrowest built.

The west end of the Norwood tunnel is reached from A618, about a mile north of Killamarsh, 100yd south of the Angel Inn, opposite a sign to Ellison's Cottages. On the east side of the road the canal is watered; a short distance along is an elegant accommodation bridge with the date 1833 on the keystone. A handsome whitewashed house, which used to be an inn, is at the foot of the flight of locks leading up to the tunnel. The locks are filled in to within a foot or two from the top, serving only to pass water down; the large ponds, however, are in good condition and stocked with fish. The entrance to the tunnel, set in a low stone wall, has recently been bricked in, but one can gain the idea of its comparatively small dimensions. M1 crosses the line of the tunnel, a few hundred yards away.

The east end is near Kiveton Park station, south of the line, along a track the far side of the station yard. The Unbrako factory is on the other side of the canal, which picks up water hereabouts from a stream. The path takes you along the top of a deep, stone-sided cutting, with trees on the banks. At the end is the east portal, also bricked in. This was the end that was extended when the railway was built.

From here the canal keeps close to the railway line, running south east to Worksop. It is not easy of access, and there are only two road bridges in the 5 miles. The channel is dense with weedy growth, and only a little water trickles down the 30 locks. At Turner Wood, however, there is something rather different. This group of cottages on either side of the canal is at the end of a 'No Through' road off the road from Thorpe Salvin to Worksop. Here the pound between two locks has been cleaned out, and flowers planted on the banks. The cottages, apart from one derelict row farther down, are well restored and look clean and gay. The

Chesterfield Canal, rather a doleful sight for much of its length, is a thing of beauty at Turner Wood.

The canal enters Worksop alongside the minor road, emerging in the centre of the town as a living waterway, with boats. Unlike so many derelicts, its disused stretch has not been treated as a rubbish tip; some of it still carries water to serve industry, some of it still holds water to serve fishermen, while, except for Turner Wood, its rural length moulders quietly away in the countryside through which it once carried coal, iron and lead down to the Trent.

OS sheets 112 (Chesterfield)
           103 (Staveley Works–Worksop)
The Canals of the East Midlands, by Charles Hadfield

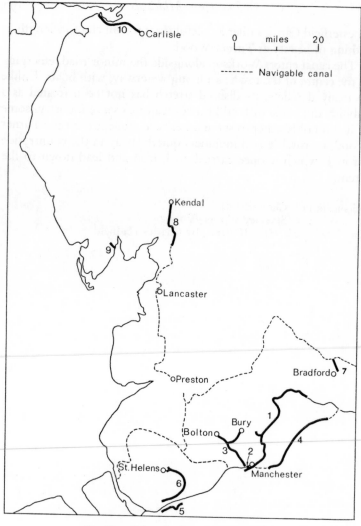

Outline Map 6 The North West

Chapter 6: *The North West*

THE ROCHDALE CANAL

The first of the three trans-Pennine routes to be completed, the Rochdale Canal linked the Calder & Hebble Navigation at Sowerby Bridge to the Bridgewater Canal at Castlefield in Manchester. It opened throughout in 1804, ten years after its Act was obtained, having cost some £600,000. It was 33 miles long, with two short branches, and overcame the Pennines by means of 92 broad locks. The first survey of the line was by Rennie, but the canal was essentially the work of William Jessop. It was a massive undertaking; even today it is impressive as it strides up and over the hills. But the summit level is only ¾ mile long; the Calder & Hebble locks could not take the 70ft barges; and 92 locks make an enormous amount of work.

The Rochdale was, however, an immediate commercial success, and by 1829 it was carrying half a million tons a year, holding off competition from its rivals, the Huddersfield and the Leeds & Liverpool. It provided a valuable connection with Hull for the export of Lancashire merchandise, and carried a heavy trade both in coal and corn. Its success enabled the building of a large wharf and warehouse in Manchester. Ten years later tonnage had risen to over 875,000, though competition from the railways was now beginning to be felt. A rate-cutting war began, until both canal and railway companies had to reach agreement to avoid the suicide of both. There followed years of negotiation, mostly abortive, with railway companies and the Aire & Calder, until in 1855 the Rochdale leased itself to a group of four railways, the Lancashire & Yorkshire being the main shareholder. In the meantime traffic was well maintained, topping 979,000 tons in 1845, and staying at a high level until 1880. But the figures are deceptive; most of the traffic was short-haul between the Bridgewater and Ashton canals in Manchester, and tolls were low because of competitive rate-cutting.

The railway lease ended in 1890, when the canal company began their own carrying business with 68 boats of varying sizes, including some short wide boats for traffic through the Calder &

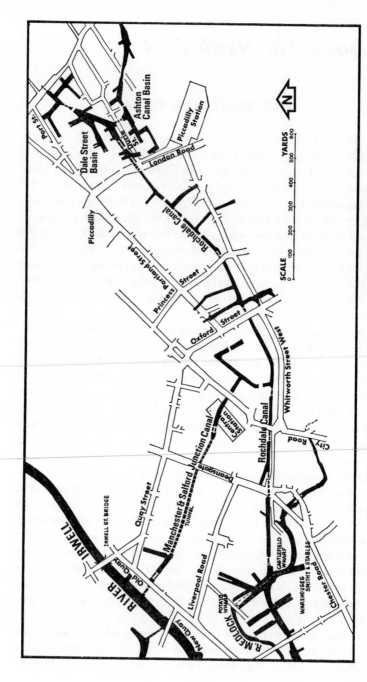

The canals of Central Manchester in the mid-nineteenth century

Hebble's unhelpful locks. This endured until 1921; three years later the company stated that they felt there was no future for canals without governmental aid, a truthful but unheeded observation. Eight reservoirs were transferred to local authorities, which made the company £300,000; indeed, the Rochdale remains a viable concern today, with income from investments, property and water sales, despite the fact that the navigation was abandoned, except for a mile in Manchester, in 1952, the last through journey having been made fifteen years earlier.

It is possible to walk the length of the Rochdale along the towpath, and it keeps close to main roads throughout. The junction with the Calder & Hebble in Sowerby Bridge is opposite the church; there are warehouses, a basin, and plenty of heavyweight mooring rings. It is culverted now under the main road, and climbs through Mytholmroyd to Hebden Bridge, keeping close to the River Roch and A646. At Hebden Bridge, near the Post Office, is a handsome four-arch aqueduct over the river. The canal turns south west, continuing to climb through Todmorden, then heads south to the short summit level near the Summit Inn, on the east side of A6033. There is an old lodging house behind the inn. The descent begins, through Littleborough and to the south east of Rochdale, to which the canal is linked by a short branch by A627. South of Rochdale the main line can be picked up on the west side of A664. Some bridges hereabouts have recently been demolished in the building of a housing estate, but two interesting bridges, Gorrell's and March Barn, are accessible. These are reputed to be the first two canal skew bridges constructed. Gorrell's can be reached through the housing estate (SD 891114), a short walk along the towpath west of the new culvert. Here the stones are large and laid in straight courses. March Barn is the next bridge south-westward; at the back of Arrow Mill, accessible also by a lane through the mill. Winding courses were used here to solve the problem of the angle. These bridges are probably the most significant engineering features on the canal; built about 1797 they were probably the work of Jessop, though as the engineering records were destroyed by fire one cannot be absolutely certain.

The canal is crossed by the main road at Castleton and again at Slattocks; then it winds away to enter Manchester from the north east, joining the Ashton Canal near Piccadilly. Dale Street basin (75 Dale Street) is a car park, but the company's stone gateway still stands. From here, in theory anyway, the canal can be navigated to the junction with the Bridgewater by Castlefield Wharf. There are eight locks and the Knott Mill tunnel, under Deansgate, now 78yd long though originally 335. A journey along this stretch in 1967 took over five hours. Bridge parapets are high in Manchester, and except from the tops of buses the canal is difficult to see, but if the Ashton were reopened and the Rochdale cleaned up there seems no reason why the canals could not make some contribution to the amenities of the city.

The Rochdale locks, made of exceptionally large masonry slabs, are converted to weirs, although some of the top gates are still in position. There are proposals to convert some part of the canal into a 'water park', although this appears to involve reducing the depth to a few inches. There are also proposals to fill in and pipe stretches. Destruction of the Rochdale would be a tragedy; not only does it enhance the countryside and the towns through which it passes, but it is one of the great monuments of civil engineering.

OS sheets 102 (Sowerby Bridge–Mytholmroyd)
            95 (Hebden Bridge–Littleborough)
           101 (Littleborough–Manchester)
The Canals of North West England, by Charles Hadfield & Gordon Biddle
Canals & Waterways (*It Happened round Manchester*), by A. H. Body

THE MANCHESTER & SALFORD JUNCTION CANAL

This canal, 5 furlongs in length, was opened in 1839 to connect the Rochdale Canal with the Irwell, enabling boats off the Rochdale to bypass the Bridgewater. It had four wide locks and a tunnel 499yd long. On the Irwell it was nearly opposite the entrance to the Manchester, Bolton & Bury.

Traffic on the canal was well below expectations, and in 1842 it was taken over by the Mersey & Irwell company. Some trade continued to and from the Manchester, Bolton & Bury Canal, but by 1870 receipts were less than £1,000 pa. The Bridgewater trustees took over the Mersey & Irwell in 1845, thus frustrating any hopes the Rochdale might have had of eluding their clutches, and when the Ship Canal Company took over the Bridgewater the Manchester & Salford Junction went with it.

The 2 furlongs nearest the Rochdale Canal were filled in in 1875 for railway construction, but for a time there were lifts connecting the Great Northern Railway's goods station with the canal in the tunnel below. This remaining section was in use until about 1922, but was not officially abandoned until 1936. The tunnel was used as an air raid shelter during the war, and the entrance to the canal from the navigable portion of the Rochdale can still be seen, as can the entrance from the Irwell, beside Water St, between Quay St and Grape St. The Central Station and the Granada TV Centre now lie on top of the Manchester & Salford Junction Canal.

OS sheet 101
The Canals of North West England, by Charles Hadfield & Gordon Biddle

THE MANCHESTER, BOLTON & BURY CANAL

Originally planned as a narrow canal, the Manchester, Bolton & Bury, which obtained its Act in 1791, was constructed with wide locks in the hope of a connection with the Leeds & Liverpool. However, the line from Bolton via Red Moss to near Wigan that was to provide this link was never built, and a gap remained in the north-western network. But the canal did provide a useful link with Liverpool for Bolton and Bury via the Irwell, which it joined near the head of the Mersey & Irwell navigation.

At first the promoters were chary of using the Irwell at all, proposing an aqueduct over the river to meet the Rochdale Canal direct. In 1808, however, the line was completed, at a cost of £115,500, almost 16 miles long with 17 locks and three aqueducts. It was fed by a reservoir near Bury. Modest dividends began to be paid in 1812, coal, stone, groceries and sundries being the main cargoes. For some years the line made a speciality of passenger carrying, with a return fare of 12½p for the journey. Passengers to and from Manchester changed boats at Prestolee to avoid the flight of locks there; a direct route from Bolton to Bury was also available. Refreshments were served on the journey; in 1818 a party of drunken passengers capsized the boat and some people, including two children, were drowned. About 60,000 passengers a year were carried, but this traffic stopped on the opening of the railway in 1838. This railway, from Manchester to Bolton, was built by the canal company, which turned itself into a railway and canal company in 1831, improving the canal as well as building the railway line. Amalgamation with the Manchester & Leeds Railway came in 1846, and the whole concern became part of the Lancashire & Yorkshire Railway a few years later. For over eighty years the canal continued in business, carrying mainly coal, over 600,000 tons a year were being transported about the turn of the century. Revenue came also from sales of water, and rebuilding in the 1880s, after damage caused by subsidence, reduced maintenance costs.

With the closing of collieries in the 1920s, and further damage due to subsidence, trade fell sharply away. In 1941 the LMS abandoned nearly 7 miles, including the Bolton line, leaving only two detached sections open. The remainder was abandoned in 1961. The MB & B was a long time dying; the moving of coal from a dump to a works in Bury along a few hundred yards of canal continued until 1968.

The canal left the Irwell by Princes Bridge, nearly opposite the point where the Manchester & Salford Junction entered the river. Bits of it can be found lurking behind walls at street ends in Salford, murky and insalubrious. Heading north west it keeps close to the Irwell, which it crosses twice. At Clifton the aqueduct lies behind the Exide factory; here also is Fletcher's Canal (see below). From Clifton to Kearsley the bed is dry and mostly obscured by factory building. By the Horseshoe Hotel at Ringley, on the south of A667, there is a clearly defined stretch which can be walked; there are traces of bridges and a cottage.

At Prestolee the canal becomes unexpectedly interesting. Here it is watered, and walking north-westward from the edge of the village (SD 753060) you find first a bridge in sound condition, then a substantial four-arch stone aqueduct over the Irwell, two massive milestones, economically reading M 7¾ and M 8, and the canal widens to make its turn to the foot of the six locks leading up to the junction for Bury. Near the foot of the flight is a small bridge over what looks to have been a dock; there are masonry remains of four of the locks and the relics of two bridges at the top. The Bury arm, some of it dry, runs eastward on an embankment. For Bolton there is a hairpin left turn and the watered canal continues for nearly a mile, to end abruptly by A6053, east of Little Lever. The aqueduct on this line was demolished a few years ago, and there is scant trace of the canal left in Bolton. By the junction, at Nob End, there is a pleasant group of cottages contemporary with the early days of the canal.

Much of the Bury line is watered, and is stocked with fish. The Bury terminal survives at the foot of Bridge St, by the river bridge, in the factory yard of Rushton & Barlow. The canal runs between factory buildings and into a tunnel under the terminal warehouse. It passes under A58 and emerges in the yard of Joseph Webb's factory, a distance of 141yd. The canal meets the river a few yards farther on. In Rushton & Barlow's yard there is the shell of another warehouse, of grey stone, and two sunk boats lying in an arm of the basin. Two more boats are moored some 200yd along the canal, by another factory. One is an ice-breaker; the other a coal boat, an early vehicle for what is now known as containerisation. Coal used to be carried in boxes, ten to a boat, each holding about 2 tons, loaded and off-loaded by crane. These two boats were those that were the last to operate on the canal, until 1968.

How much longer the boats, and the Bury basin, will survive it is impossible to say; but the boats may soon be waterlogged and part of the basin has already been filled in, while plans exist for its total extinction. Whatever replaces it, though maybe with a gain in efficiency, will never recapture the melancholy atmosphere of what is there now—a nearly unaltered Victorian canal terminal in the heart of an industrial town.

FLETCHER'S CANAL

Joining the MB & B near Clifton aqueduct is Fletcher's Canal, 1½ miles long, made by Matthew Fletcher, a colliery owner. It developed from a scheme by James Brindley to overcome flooding at Wet Earth colliery by digging a channel along which the water could be driven by a paddle wheel. It was used for the carriage of coal on to the MB & B until the colliery closed in 1928; then the Pilkington Tile Co made use of it until it was eventually closed, though not de-watered, in 1935. One can still explore most of it.

OS sheet 101
'The Manchester, Bolton and Bury Canal Navigation', by V. I. Tomlinson, *Transactions* of the Lancashire & Cheshire Antiquarian Society, 1965–6
The Canals of North West England, by Charles Hadfield & Gordon Biddle

THE HUDDERSFIELD NARROW CANAL

'A bold, stupendous and useful undertaking'—so Priestley described the Huddersfield Narrow Canal. Bold and stupendous certainly; its 20 mile line included 73 locks, five aqueducts and three tunnels, one the longest canal tunnel constructed in the British Isles. But it was the least successful of the three trans-Pennine routes, though the most direct.

The Huddersfield's Act was obtained in 1794. The line connects Sir John Ramsden's broad canal in Huddersfield with the Ashton in Manchester and looks straightforward enough on the map until one takes the contours into account. Outram was the engineer, and his solution was to pierce the barrier of Standedge with a tunnel 3 miles 176yd long. The difficulties encountered, mainly due to the large amount of water met with, delayed completion until 1811. Because of flooded shafts and falls, much of the tunnel had to be dug inwards from either end, and demanded more money than the company had available. Millowners along the route were concerned about losing water to the canal; this meant that several reservoirs had to be made, plunging the company further into debt. In all, ten reservoirs were eventually needed to supply the canal. At various times the project looked as if it might never be finished, but John Rooth, appointed superintendent in 1801, brought new energy and organising ability, and saw it through.

The Huddersfield's locks were built to take the conventional narrow boat, but several short narrow boats were made to fit the shorter locks on Ramsden's Canal and the Calder & Hebble, in the hope of through traffic. The rates initially set were reduced to compete with the Rochdale, but the Huddersfield was the loser. Traders complained that the locks were badly constructed, and they had to be repaired. Merchandise was the main cargo carried, followed by coal, but total tonnages were small compared to the Rochdale's—only one-seventh in 1813. The company paid its first dividend in 1824; work on warehouses and reservoirs, however, delayed further profits.

The 1830s were a time of mild prosperity for the Huddersfield, after the company had reached agreements over rates with its neighbours. But dividends ceased when income fell, despite toll reductions to meet competition from the Manchester & Leeds Railway, and in 1844 the canal company gave up the struggle and sold out to the Huddersfield & Manchester Railway for £183,730 —not very much for a canal that had cost £400,000 to construct. Three years later the London & North Western Railway took over and opened their single-track tunnel at Standedge in 1849, very close to the canal tunnel.

Various disasters occurred in the canal tunnel during the next decades, generally due to rock falls or capsizes; trade over the summit was greatly reduced, though quite well maintained at either end. Standedge was closed while the double-track railway tunnel (the one still in use) was cut; at this time the Diggle end of the canal tunnel was extended, to make the length 3 miles 418yd. By 1905 traffic over the summit had ceased, and expenditure on maintenance began to exceed receipts. In 1944 the canal was abandoned, except for a short stretch at the Huddersfield end which lasted till 1963.

The Huddersfield Narrow leaves its junction with the Huddersfield Broad (Ramsden's) in the centre of the town and heads south of west alongside the Colne and on the north of A62, climbing steadily. It is easily accessible from the main road, and is watered throughout. It crosses the Colne several times by single-arch aqueducts; there is a typical example south of Golcar. At Slaithwaite it looks at first as if it has disappeared, but it has been culverted to run under the town centre and a car park and emerges to continue its climb to Marsden.

The north portal of Standedge tunnel (SE 039119) can be found by turning north off A62 to Marsden station and then west to the Junction Inn. There is a lane opposite the inn leading to the BWB maintenance yard, beside which is a bridge over the canal. In front of you is the canal tunnel, with above it the two single-track railway tunnels and the double-track one still in use. The tunnel-keeper's cottage is empty and shabby. The entrance to Standedge is gated and locked, and BWB say it is no longer possible to take visitors through owing to the danger of rock falls. The tunnel was built 9ft wide with 9ft height above water level, although by accounts it has since shrunk to 7ft width in places. It is partly brick-lined, partly cut through gritstone. There is no towpath, and boats were legged through, three and a half hours being allowed for the passage. It opens out into four passing places, but a voyage through it must have been a damp and grisly experience; 656ft above sea level, the Huddersfield here reaches the highest point of any canal in Britain.

From A62 as it rounds the hill you can see several shafts, both railway and canal, the deepest of them reaching about 600ft. The south portal (SE 005079) at Diggle is reached from the next left turn off A62, turning at the foot of the hill towards the railway. The portal is on the right, through a white gate beside a phone box. It carries the date 1893, when it was extended by cut-and-cover from approximately the point where the railway tunnel now emerges.

The canal now locks down through Saddleworth and keeps close to the Tame and the railway. Scout tunnel, 220yd long and cut through solid rock, is a few yards east of A635, just south of Mossley. It has been bricked up above water level at both ends. The canal continues south through Stalybridge and then turns west to join the Ashton Canal at Dukinfield, about 6½ miles from the Ashton's termination at Piccadilly. The Stalybridge tunnel of 198yd is now opened out. The Huddersfield company had a warehouse at the Ashton's basin, only a few yards from the basin of the Rochdale Canal, its more powerful rival.

The masonry of the deep locks of the Huddersfield is still in good condition; the gates have been removed but some of them may be found lying in the grass. As with the Rochdale, the towpath makes an excellent walk, and the anglers fish with equal optimism. There are plenty of Victorian mills, factories and warehouses, set in the valley against the spectacular hills. The Huddersfield's water is valuable to industry, and Standedge tunnel serves to drain the railway tunnel above it. The traveller in the Colne Valley can still appreciate the 'bold and stupendous' design of the Huddersfield Canal.

OS sheets 102 (Huddersfield–Diggle)
       101 (Saddleworth–Dukinfield)
The Canals of North West England, by Charles Hadfield & Gordon Biddle

THE RUNCORN & WESTON CANAL

The Weston Canal was opened in 1810, 4 miles in length,

joining the River Weaver to Weston Point, and a new basin was constructed for it at Weston. Between 1816 and 1866 it was a free navigation, busy with the salt trade. The Weaver trustees were progressive, looked after their employees, and improved the Weston basin over the years. In 1852 they agreed with those of the Bridgewater to a canal linking Weston Point with the Bridgewater at Runcorn, to be built by the Earl of Ellesmere. The Earl died before it was finished and the canal, the Runcorn & Weston, was bought by the Bridgewater trustees, completed, and opened in 1859. It was 1¼ miles long, with two locks 18ft 5in wide.

Runcorn docks were altered and improved as the century passed, but it was the opening of the Manchester Ship Canal, running parallel to the R & W and the Weston around Weston Point, that brought the greatest changes. Runcorn docks declined, and traffic on the canal, never very heavy, diminished. The Bridgewater's flight of ten locks at Runcorn was filled in in 1966, and the R & W was abandoned, though Runcorn docks revived.

What is left of the R & W is a channel of dirty water running through the ICI works into Runcorn docks. For good reasons the Manchester Ship Canal Company is wary of pleasure craft using its waters; hence with the closing of the Runcorn locks access to the Bridgewater Canal from the sea is barred and Runcorn is now a dead end for canal traffic. Those who wish to know what it is like to force a boat through a virtually derelict canal and up a flight of ruined locks should read his account of such a journey in John Seymour's *Voyage into England.*

OS sheet 100
The Canals of North West England, by Charles Hadfield & Gordon Biddle

ST HELENS CANAL

The Sankey Brook Navigation, as the St Helens Canal was first known, obtained its Act in 1755 and was, for the most part, open in 1757, thus antedating the Bridgewater Canal by four years. According to the Act it was not much more than an improvement to the navigation of the Sankey Brook, but as constructed it was as much of a canal as many others always recognised as such. Surveyed by Henry Berry, it was cut from Sankey

Bridges, west of Warrington, to a double lock near Blackbrook, between St Helens and Haydock, just over 8 miles, with three branches, two towards St Helens. There were ten locks, including the double—the first of its kind made—and the cost of construction was £18,600. Supported by a number of Liverpool merchants and local colliery owners, the canal was intended for coal transport; the boats were hauled by men or sailed, and accordingly all the bridges were built as swing bridges.

It was profitable for its shareholders from the beginning, although the expected reductions in coal prices did not take effect until competition from other canals brought a reduction in tolls. The village of St Helens began to expand, and became host to the plate glass industry and copper smelting works. Dividends rose to about 30 per cent, and tonnage carried approached 300,000 pa as the nineteenth century advanced. The company extended the line to Widnes, to obtain access from the Mersey, in 1833, to help meet the increasing demand for coal and to forestall railway competition. The extension, about 3½ miles, cost £30,000, nearly twice as much as the original line. For over ten years the canal was able to keep the local railway—the St Helens & Runcorn Gap—at bay, carrying nearly twice the amount of coal annually, rising to over 440,000 tons in 1845. In that year, the two companies amalgamated as the St Helens Canal & Railway Company, with benefit to both modes of transport. Tonnages continued to rise, and when the railway overtook the canal in 1853, the latter was carrying over half a million a year.

The London & North Western Railway took over the St Helens concern in 1864, undertaking to maintain and improve the canal. Although coal traffic fell away, it was replaced in great part by traffic in various chemicals. Over 300,000 tons were still being carried at the turn of the century, and tonnage did not fall below six figures until the 1930s. By then, various short lengths of the canal had been closed and several of the swing bridges fixed, though the channel throughout was still maintained as a water supply. Business on the canal ended in 1959, with the cessation of sugar traffic to Sankey, and the canal was abandoned in 1963.

The St Helens, with its short branches, is still watered, but the most devoted Lancastrian could hardly claim that it runs through attractive countryside. The scenery is generally flat and featureless, interrupted by the bulks of chemical and heavy industrial works.

Nor is there great architectural quality in towns like Warrington and Newton-le-Willows. But access to the canal is easy, and there is pleasant walking and good fishing on certain stretches.

One such stretch is at Winwick Quay, 2½ miles north of the centre of Warrington. From either of the minor roads east of Burtonwood, which cross the canal, one can walk southwards along the towpath, encountering three of the swing bridges, two broad locks, their chambers in good condition, the old canal cottages and workshops at Winwick, and the crossing of the Sankey Brook. Earlestown, on the western side of Newton-le-Willows, where canal and brook are side by side, is another of the better places from which to see the canal.

OS sheet 100
'The Sankey Navigation', by T. C. Barker, *Transactions* of the Lancashire
 Cheshire Antiq Soc, 1948
The Canals of North West England, by Charles Hadfield & Gordon Biddle

THE BRADFORD CANAL

Opened in 1774, the Bradford Canal was closed in 1867, reopened in 1873 and shut finally in 1922. Today there is very little trace of it left, and what there is is not likely to remain much longer.

Following an Act of 1771, the canal was cut from the unfinished Leeds & Liverpool Canal at Shipley a distance of 3⅜ miles to Bradford. There were ten locks falling from Bradford, the same dimensions as those on the L & L, and John Longbotham, the engineer of the L & L, worked also for the Bradford company. Coal, stone and iron were the main traffic, ironworks in particular developing as a result of the building of the canal. Later, Australian wool also became an important item. In the late 1820s packet boats began daily sailings and within a few years were providing a service, with connections at Leeds, Selby and Goole, to Hull, London, Newcastle and Liverpool.

Bradford grew rapidly. Boats using the canal basin found themselves near the centre of the town instead of on its edge. Mills, dyeworks and factories were built along the canal banks, using it not only for transport but also for water supply. The canal drew its water from Bowling Mill Beck; this proving inadequate, the company, without legal authority, began taking water from Bradford Beck as well. This water was polluted before it reached the canal which, by the 1840s, owing to the discharge into it of domestic sewage and water which industries had used and returned to it hot and even fouler than when it had been drawn off, had become, especially in warm weather, a stinking carrier of diseases. The city council proposed to buy the canal and close it, recompensing themselves by selling off the land. The plan was defeated by the canal company, backed by local industrialists and the companies of the adjacent waterways. The canal committee would have preferred to sell out to a railway company, but their proposal was also defeated. After 1844, the canal revenues began to suffer from the competition of the Leeds & Bradford Railway whose line ran parallel to it along the valley.

Pressure on the Bradford Canal, 'that seething cauldron of all impurity', as it was described by *The Bradford Observer* (quoted by Hadfield & Biddle), continued to be exerted. A court order against the company was obtained in 1866; henceforth no water could be abstracted from Bradford Beck on penalty of a £10,000 fine. The canal company decided to shut off the top ¼ mile, sell off the land, and offer the rest of the canal on lease to the Leeds & Liverpool. As the L & L would now have to provide a water supply as well as new wharves, they refused the offer. Stalemate ensued; then in May 1867 the Bradford company, unable to carry on, closed the canal and drained it.

The canal had been carrying well over 100,000 tons a year and its loss was immediately felt by its users. They began to negotiate with the other interested parties, including the Leeds & Liverpool and the Aire & Calder companies. The Bradford company sold off its property, the top section, now Forster Square, for building. A new company, the majority of whose directors were local stone merchants, was set up, alternative methods of obtaining water, the most important of which was by erecting pumping engines at each lock to pump the water back up from the lower pound, were organised, part of the canal was reopened in 1872 and the whole of the new length of 3 miles in the following year.

The new Bradford company did not last long. It sold out in 1878 to a joint committee of the Leeds & Liverpool and the Aire & Calder, for £27,000, a little more than it had cost to restore the canal. The new committee spent largely on building new warehouses in Bradford, but the canal's trade did not grow in proportion. By 1910 annual tonnage reached 100,000, but it fell thereafter and the expenses of pumping, always high, exceeded the tolls received almost every year. During World War I there was very little traffic. A move to close the canal in 1921 was opposed by the local authorities, but a Bill the next year succeeded and the canal was closed, the land being sold off.

Canal Road, Bradford, is part of A6037. Large decaying warehouses line the east side of the road; cobbled Wharf Street runs on their other side. Very little of the course of the canal is left, though here and there it emerges as scrubby waste ground not yet developed for building. Apart from the bottom lock, the Bradford locks were in staircases; a remnant of Spinkwell locks remains and can be seen from the turning off Canal Road that leads around the gasworks. On the north side of the bridge that crossed the canal part of the lower lock stands isolated in an area of desolation at the foot of a coal tip. The lock is filled with earth and rubble, but the bottom gates are still there, firmly shut. The course of the canal can be followed around the gasworks. One of the next pair, Oliver locks, is on the east side of Canal Road another $\frac{1}{2}$ mile along. The derelict housing of the pumping station stands at its foot; this lock is also filled in and gypsies camp around it. Running parallel to it, the railway line is a useful guide to the course of the canal. A little water can be found in a remnant of canal close to the railway at Frizinghall, beside Oswin Mills on the south side of the road bridge. To the north, the canal is again filled in.

The few hundred yards of the Bradford Canal below the bottom lock, Windhill, are used as moorings for craft off the Leeds & Liverpool.

OS sheet 96
The Canals of North West England, by Charles Hadfield & Gordon Biddle

THE LANCASTER CANAL
(Kendal to Tewitfield)

Most of the Lancaster Canal flourishes today; there are boat clubs and hire firms, and improvements to the waterway are in hand. Boats cruise north from Preston, through Lancaster, across

Rennie's great aqueduct over the Lune, through Carnforth, Capernwray and Borwick. But at Tewitfield navigation stops; the way is barred by the embankment of A76, rising to cross the new motorway. To the north 14½ miles of canal are cut off and abandoned; on the far side of the embankment the Tewitfield locks are rotting away.

The Lancaster Canal obtained its Act in 1792, and five years later the present navigable stretch was open. Not till 1819 was the whole line completed. Shortage of money was the main reason for delay, what there was being needed for the purchase of land for a reservoir; 1813 saw work restarted, with Thomas Fletcher succeeding Rennie as engineer; four years later William Crosley took over from Fletcher to finish the line. Warehouses and wharves were built at Kendal, and a new bridge across the Kent; the town quickly began to develop. Packet boats from Preston and Lancaster began to ply to and from Kendal in 1820, and the first sea-going vessel, carrying Northwich salt, reached Kendal via Glasson in 1827. A few years later a faster packet-boat service began a daily run to Kendal, with refreshments served on board and heating being provided in winter months. In 1842, the canal company took over the sickly Lancaster & Preston Junction Railway, which it ran for profit rather than public service, and began a lengthy squabble with the Lancaster & Carlisle Railway who also claimed the ailing line. They forsook the railway in 1849, but continued running the whole canal themselves for another fifteen years; although making little profit from the waterway, the company remained a powerful and influential force in the area. In 1864, however, the company leased the northern section to the London & North Western, later selling it to them outright; they also leased the southern portion to the Leeds & Liverpool Canal. The coal trade to Kendal, especially to the gasworks which had no railway access, was maintained into the 1930s; then the LMS, now the owners, began to shut down sections near Kendal because of leakages which they thought not worth repairing. Commercial traffic north of Lancaster ended in 1944, and the British Transport Commission closed and drained the canal from Kendal to Stainton in 1955. Hopes for restoration of the watered Stainton–Tewitfield length were shattered by the building of M6 and its approach roads, necessitating the culverting of the canal in five places.

M6 may have killed the northern part of the Lancaster Canal, but only its arrival will save the life of Kendal, suffocating from the traffic which clogs its centre. Canal Head was a mile south of the town, by A65; prefabs have been built along the end of the line. The first canal bridge is on a turning east off Natland road; the course of the filled-in cut is clearly defined and the bridge, like most on the Lancaster, is a confident, substantial structure of stone blocks. All the works on the Lancaster, whether by Rennie, Fletcher or Crosley, give this impression of confidence and solidity; the architectural assurance of the Lune aqueduct is reflected even in the minor accommodation bridges. There are other good examples on the road $\frac{1}{2}$ mile west of Natland, and to north and south of this point on the line of the Lancaster as it runs close and parallel to the Kent. On the west side of Sedgwick is the first of the smaller aqueducts, built on the skew, of substantial stone blocks with a stone-lined trough.

Approaching Hincaster, the canal skirts the steepest part of the hill and runs close beside a minor road. On a stretch of towpath alongside the weed- and scrub-filled bed is a defaced milestone, near another good accommodation bridge. By some cottages on the otherwise empty road the canal turns sharply east to enter Hincaster tunnel (SD 509851), 378yd long, completed in 1817. This tunnel is stone-lined at each end and along the water line, but the rest of it is brick—at that time an innovation in the north west and only consented to after widespread investigations by the canal committee in the Midlands. There is no towpath through, but from either end the tunnel looks to be in remarkably fine condition—another tribute to the craftsmen of the Lancaster. The horse path over the hill to the east portal is beside the cottages; it passes under two small footbridges, also in this canal's recognisable style, and the railway, and leads down to a cutting by the tunnel entrance. There is water in the tunnel and approaches.

In another $\frac{1}{2}$ mile the watered section begins; here the canal is on a low embankment by the junction of four roads south west of Stainton. There are stop planks under a bridge to the west, with weeds one side and water the other. A short walk eastwards, the canal crosses St Sunday's Beck by a small skew aqueduct, of the usual good stonework. Under the aqueduct, the beck itself has been floored with stone, with a path beside it. Two more aqueducts, over minor roads, and a great number of bridges—there are eight within a mile at Holme—can be found on the canal as it makes south for Tewitfield; but this is also the country of the M6 and the mean-looking concrete culverts. The eight 14½ft wide Tewitfield locks—the only locks on the canal apart from the seven on the still-used Glasson Dock branch—are parallel to the motorway and close to it. They have been converted to weirs, the gates removed and mouldering beside them. As it supplies a chemical works, the water still flows and is fished by local anglers; but it is dirty, and the Lancaster hereabouts is a melancholy sight. South of the locks the end of the navigable section is being developed, but the proximity of the motorway makes it unlikely that it will provide the pleasantest of moorings, despite the nearby pub.

OS sheet 89
The Canals of North West England, by Charles Hadfield & Gordon Biddle
'Canal Head, Kendal', *Trans* Cumberland & Westmoreland Antiq &
     Arch Soc, LXVIII (NS) 1968, by P. N. Wilson
(Information on Hincaster tunnel from G. Biddle)

THE ULVERSTON CANAL

Still looking much as it did in the peak years of the early 1840s, the Ulverston Canal links the small town of Ulverston, 9 miles from Barrow-in-Furness, with the polluted waters of Morecambe Bay. A straight and level 1½ miles, it turned Ulverston into a port, exporting mainly ore and slate, and was used by 944 vessels in its busiest year, 1846.

The canal was opened in 1796, at a cost of something over £9,000. Its early organisation, like the movements of the Ulverston Channel which enabled larger ships to enter the canal, was somewhat haphazard; trade was slow to grow and profits took long to accumulate. Matters improved slowly during the 1820s, and regular sailings began to London, Liverpool and Scotland, followed in 1835 by passenger service by steam packet to Liverpool, for which the canal company demanded the extortionate rate of £10 a year for every passenger landed—and the poor fellows were only allowed 5lb of luggage at that.

After 1846, trade fell off as the Furness Railway extended its lines through the area; in 1849 canal receipts were less than half of what they had been three years earlier. In that year a new breakwater to keep the Channel flowing to the foot of the canal was completed, but it made no difference to the decline in traffic. The Furness Railway bought the canal in 1862, for £22,000, and it continued to be used by a few thousand tons of shipping a year until 1916. In 1945 the canal was officially abandoned; it is now owned by Ulverston UDC, and provides a water supply to a large chemical works on its southern bank.

The basin is behind the Canal Tavern, ¼ mile east of the centre of Ulverston—a pleasant enough town convenient for touring the Lake District. A road runs along the northern bank of the canal, although there is a gate at the far end of it which is permanently locked. There was no towpath, as the canal was designed for use by sailing vessels; the entrance lock could take coasters of up to 120 tons burden, 27ft beam. There are remains of paddle gear in the upper gates, which are gradually decaying; the lower gates are fixed, and a concrete dam has replaced most of the woodwork. The lifting footbridge above the lock has gone, and a railway swing bridge to the chemical works no longer swings. There is substantial stone walling along parts of the canal, and some derelict works on the southern bank.

Conveniently, the Ulverston leads from pub to pub; the attractive-looking Bay Horse is to the south of the entrance lock, and there are a few old cottages thereabouts. A short stone pier extends into the bay at Canal Foot; to the north, the Leven viaduct crosses the Cartmel Sands; to the south, Chapel Island looms like a stranded, tree-topped whale. A boy sleeps on top of a lock gate; another fishes pessimistically in the canal. Two old women talk quietly on a green iron seat, and the dirty water of Morecambe Bay covers and uncovers the apparently endless sand. It is a peaceful, rather melancholy scene; wholly Ulverston, unique.

OS sheet 89
The Canals of North West England, by Charles Hadfield & Gordon Biddle

THE CARLISLE CANAL

The life-span of the Carlisle Canal was a mere thirty years. Serious discussion of a waterway to improve communication between Carlisle and the sea, the River Eden being a shallow and difficult navigation, began towards the end of the eighteenth century. Associated with this scheme were ideas for connecting Carlisle with Newcastle by canal. In 1807 a committee was appointed to take action and William Chapman produced a report. It was ten years before a decision to proceed was reached; then money was raised and an Act sought, being obtained in 1819. Work began the next year, after the Forth & Clyde and Lancaster canals had been inspected to see what lessons might be learned from them. Disagreement with the committee led to Chapman being sacked as consulting engineer before the canal was opened in 1823.

The canal was 11¼ miles long, from a basin in Carlisle to Fisher's Cross, renamed Port Carlisle, on the Solway Firth. The eight locks were 18ft 3in wide, to take coastal vessels, and drawbridges similar to those on the Forth & Clyde were constructed. The cost of construction was a little over £80,000. Timber, coal and bricks were important traffic, and a packet boat service was begun in 1826, the company building a special passenger jetty at Port Carlisle, and an hotel for passengers in transit to Liverpool. The dream of a Newcastle–Carlisle canal ended in 1825 when it was decided to build a railway, which would cost much less. The canal committee supported the railway, as it would increase their own trade. As parts of the line were opened canal tolls began to increase; when Newcastle was reached in 1839, tolls topped £6,000 and dividends improved to 4 per cent. An improved packet boat service had already commenced and a new waterwheel and pumps installed in view of the prospects of extra traffic.

Then in the mid-1840s came difficult years for the canal. Competition loomed from railways building in the north west, in particular the Lancaster & Carlisle which, when completed, would provide a rail link with Liverpool and Manchester, and from other coal-exporting ports with improving facilities. Canal tolls were reduced; profits fell, as this failed to attract more trade. The committee began to contemplate turning the canal into a railway. In 1850 passenger traffic declined owing to the availability of cheaper alternative routes; further toll reductions proved fruitless, and in 1852 the company decided to convert. The canal was closed in 1853 and the railway opened a year later, the line being laid in the canal bed. This Port Carlisle branch railway itself closed in 1932.

The course of the canal/railway is close to Hadrian's Wall and also to the minor road from Carlisle to Bowness. Taking A595 out of Carlisle and forking on to B5307 you come to the canal basin on the right. A large three-storey brick warehouse with stone quoins stands at the top of the slope. It bears the date 1821 on a cartouche. On its right is a two-storey building that used to be the canal office. The basin was on the far side. To the right is a long low sandstone building. This is the top of the lime and coal vaults, built on a split level. Loads could be tipped into the stores from the basin and loaded thence into waggons from the lower level which can be found down a lane to the right.

On the track to Port Carlisle a canal warehouse and lockhouse can be seen. Several of the old canal bridges cross the line, though they have been raised to give railway headroom.

Just before Port Carlisle, railway and canal diverge. There are the remains of two locks, one the sea-lock of large stone blocks, mostly filled in but with the coping visible. To the left of the sea-lock, looking out to the Solway Firth, are the remains of the timber jetty; to its right the isolated wharf, built about 1839. The railway used to run out to this across a viaduct supported by wooden trestles. Solway House is the old Solway Hotel, where packet-boat passengers waited for the steamers, and the last house along the sea-front was once the Steam Packet Inn.

OS sheets 76 (Carlisle)
         75 (Port Carlisle–Burghby Sands)
The Canals of North West England, by Charles Hadfield & Gordon Biddle

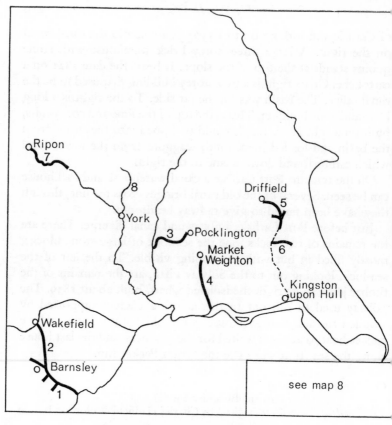

Outline Map 7   The North East

1 The Dearne & Dove Canal
2 The Barnsley Canal
3 The Pocklington Canal
4 The Market Weighton Canal
5 The Driffield Canal
6 The Leven Canal
7 The Ripon Canal (& Ure Navigation)
8 The Yorkshire Foss Navigation

Chapter 7: *The North East*

THE DEARNE & DOVE CANAL

The pattern of inland waterway transport in industrial York-shire was largely determined by the river navigations. The various canals—the Selby, Knottingley & Goole, Barnsley, Stainforth & Keadby, Dearne & Dove—all connected with river navigations running through the Yorkshire coalfields. Together, the Barnsley Canal and the Dearne & Dove joined the Aire & Calder to the Don Navigation.

The Dearne & Dove Canal, so-called because it follows the valley of these rivers, was an offshoot of the proprietors of the Don Navigation. Both the Don and the Aire & Calder companies wanted to extend into the south Yorkshire coalfield; as it hap-pened, neither obtained a monopoly and the canals promoted by each joined each other at Barnsley. The Act for the Dearne & Dove was obtained in 1793; Robert Whitworth was appointed engineer, and the canal, $9\frac{5}{8}$ miles long with 19 broad locks on the main line and two short branches, was opened in 1804, having cost just under £100,000. It left the Don on the east side of Swinton and headed north-westward past Wath-on-Dearne and Wombwell, joining the Barnsley Canal on the south-east side of Barnsley. It was mainly a coal-carrying canal, both its branches also serving collieries at Elsecar and Worsborough where there were reservoirs for the canal's water supply. Until the arrival of the railways it traded well, carrying over 200,000 tons a year in the early 1830s.

Faced with railway competition the Don company first leased the canal themselves, in 1846, and then amalgamated with the South Yorkshire, Doncaster & Goole Railway, in 1850. This new company, known as the South Yorkshire & River Dun Company, bought the Dearne & Dove for £210,000 in 1857, adding it to the Sheffield Canal and the Stainforth & Keadby, which the company already owned. A few years later the South Yorkshire & River Dun Company itself was leased, this time to the Manchester, Sheffield & Lincolnshire Railway Company, who began to draw off the waterborne trade. The Dearne & Dove, with the other canals in its group, changed ownership again in 1894 when the Sheffield & South Yorkshire Navigation Company bought it as part of a scheme to improve communication between Sheffield and the Humber; however, the railway retained some financial control and the condition of the canal itself, expensive to maintain and subject, in this mining area, to subsidence, was deteriorating. Traffic declined; the Worsborough branch closed in 1906 (except as a feeder). Continued decline brought the closing of the Elsecar branch in 1928 and the last through boat reached Barnsley in 1934. Having first decided to close the canal the company kept it open for short-haul traffic, which ended in 1952. Apart from ½ mile at the Swinton end, the canal was abandoned by the British Transport Commission in 1961.

This ½ mile stretch, by the Canal Tavern on the Swinton–Mexborough road near Swinton station, looks deceptively busy. Barges, motorised and dumb, cram the pounds of the lower of the five locks; but the barges are in poor condition and do not look as if they are often used. After this ½ mile the canal is filled in, as it is for most of its length. Near Adwick, about a mile along and the far side of the railway, the 472yd tunnel was bypassed when the railway was built in the late 1830s. It can be found in the rough ground to the left of the railway. From Adwick the canal kept on the south side of the railway line to Barnsley; minor roads leading north off A633 cross its course. There is a good stone bridge along Wetmoor Lane over the filled-in canal; many of the other bridges have been removed, or soon will be. The Elsecar branch has retained its water; it leaves the main line near the junction of B6089 with A633 and heads south west past Hemingfield to end in Elsecar by the Elsecar Main Colliery. There were six locks on the branch, now converted to weirs. The upper part of the branch runs beside B6097. It is a miserable stretch of water, overlooked by massive coal-tips. The reservoir is a few hundred yards beyond the end of the branch.

Most of the rest of the main line runs through an area now devoted to a West Riding land reclamation scheme. Apart from a short stretch between Wombwell and Barnsley where the canal crosses to the south of A633 (there used to be seven locks here and the junction with the Worsborough branch, which can still be detected), where the canal survives as a weed-filled ditch, it will not be many months before the Dearne & Dove Canal has been virtually obliterated. But the basin at the end of the Worsborough branch, water-filled and with the Wharf Inn beside it, is quite pleasant.

OS sheet 103

THE BARNSLEY CANAL

Obtaining its Act on the same day in 1793 as the Dearne & Dove, the Barnsley Canal was opened from Wakefield to Barnsley in 1799 and completed to Barnby Basin in 1802. As the Dearne & Dove was a product of the Don Navigation, so the Barnsley was engendered by the Aire & Calder company, desirous of improving their share of the coal trade. William Jessop was the consulting engineer and John Pinkerton the main contractor; the canal was made for about £95,000, rather more than the estimate. It was a broad canal, for Yorkshire keels, with 19 locks. Water was pumped from a reservoir at Cold Hiendley; later another reservoir was built next to this, at Wintersett.

Coal was the main traffic, but lime, limestone, agricultural produce, ancillary goods for linen manufacture and, for a time, iron were also carried. For the first few years, however, things were difficult. Trade was below expectations, mainly due to the failure of Barnby colliery; money was short and the company in debt. In 1808 the company obtained another Act to raise more money, to increase tolls and to obtain leave to build certain railways. In 1810 a horse-drawn plateway from Barnby Basin to Silkstone was opened. The high-quality coal from this pit, together with coal from other mines connecting to this railway by short branches and from the reopened Barnby colliery, made its way to the canal and established the company's prosperity. Coal carriage rose to well over 100,000 tons a year in the 1820s.

The Don and Aire & Calder companies both tried to buy the canal to safeguard their coal trade when threatened by railway competition. They failed to do so. The Manchester & Leeds Railway was likewise unsuccessful, but the Barnsley company could not retain their independence indefinitely in the face of price-cutting and powerful railway competition. In 1854 they leased the canal to the Aire & Calder, for far less than they could have got had they accepted the first offer. Trade improved under

Aire & Calder managment. In 1871 they bought the canal, retaining it until 1948. The top section of 1 mile from Barnby to Barugh locks was abandoned in 1893, by which time the coal traffic on this length had all gone to the railway whose line, now long abandoned, runs alongside the course of the canal. Trade on the rest of the line continued, though much diminished, until the canal was closed for six months after a burst in 1946. Abandonment by the British Transport Commission came in 1953.

The site of Barnby Basin is on the north side of A635, 3 miles west of Barnsley, west of the embankment of the motorway. The canal course passes under A637 and B6428 at Barugh and then follows the River Dearne on its south side around the north of Barnsley, an area now of both dereliction and development. There are large warehouses at the former Barnsley basin. It turned sharply north east to cross the river by a five-arched masonry aqueduct, demolished after abandonment; the position of the aqueduct is marked by the 'N' of 'Barnsley' on the OS map. Immediately south of the aqueduct was the junction with the Dearne & Dove Canal. The canal turned to follow the north bank of the river for ½ mile and then swung north into an area heavily intersected today by railway lines. It can be seen as a ditch from minor roads 1 mile east of Monk Bretton and again ½ mile east of Carlton; the bridges have been flattened. The canal is well defined as it approaches and bisects the small town of Royston. There is an interesting bridge on B6428, west of Royston and Notton station. It has two pairs of gates to shut off the road, and the roadway of the bridge could then be lifted by machinery housed in four brick columns, and electric powered. It was built by the West Riding County Council, and opened in 1934.

Parts of the canal are watered here and there, used as reservoirs by the National Coal Board, whose tips, like black ziggurats, dominate the countryside of the southern half of the Barnsley Canal. By Cold Hiendley, however, it merges into rural tranquillity, healthy looking and preserved for fishing. The great Cold Hiendley cutting, much of which had to be blasted out by gunpowder, can be approached from the minor road leading east from Notton (SE 367133). The sides of the cutting are wooded; we are in pleasant rolling country. Northwards the canal passes its reservoirs, skirts Haw Park, and comes to resemble an aristocratic ornamental water as it runs alongside the wall of the estate of

Walton Hall, 'the seat', as Priestley says, 'of the ancient family of the Watertons'. But the lock on the north side of the drive to the Hall is filled in, and after it the canal is dry.

The junction with the Aire & Calder was at Heath, on the south-east side of Wakefield. A638 crosses the line of the canal near 'The Jolly Sailor'. The Wakefield Power Station now sits on the Barnsley Canal, although its acquired aristocratic connections, as represented by the fine mid-Georgian houses of Heath, are not far away. Appropriately too for a canal, however derelict, whose first proprietors included 'the Duke of Leeds, Lord Hawke, the Countess Dowager of Bute, the Earl of Wigtoun, seven baronets, and almost all the landholders in its immediate vicinity'.

OS sheet 102
'The Barnsley Canal; its First Twenty Years', by W. N. Slatcher, in *Transport History*, March 1968

THE POCKLINGTON CANAL

The Pocklington Canal has various distinctions. It was constructed, with George Leather as engineer, for less than the original estimate of £32,000; its bridges are of exceptional design; although the last traffic passed in the early 1930s, it was never officially abandoned; and it seems virtually certain that in a few years time it will be back in full working order. The canal runs from the pleasant town of Pocklington, at the foot of the Yorkshire wolds, in a south-westerly direction to a junction with the Derwent, 9½ miles distant. It was a local project; an Act was obtained in 1815 and it was opened three years later with an extraordinarily detailed schedule of tonnage rates dividing the canal into twenty sections and listing no fewer than 126 different items. Mainly, however, it conveyed agricultural produce to the West Riding and brought back coal, lime, fertilisers, building materials and the products of industry.

The canal traded quietly until, in 1847, it was bought by the York & North Midland Railway, which later became part of the LNER. Tolls were increased and maintenance deteriorated; de Salis wrote in 1904 that there was very little trade and the upper section was practically derelict. The Yorkshire keels were unable to navigate above Melbourne Basin, without off-loading some of their cargo on to flats to lessen their draught. The last commercial boat, Mr J. W. Brown's keel *Ebenezer*, struggled through to the terminal basin at Canal Head in 1932; two years later, the last pleasure boats reached Melbourne. Navigation ended, and the canal was left to the anglers.

Following nationalisation, the future of the Pocklington remained in suspense for several years. A proposal to sell the canal to Sheffield Council who wanted somewhere to dump their surplus chalk from a water extraction plant was defeated by local opposition; so also were proposals to reopen the navigation. BWB were in two minds, not convinced that it should be abandoned but not feeling there was sufficient reason to put money into its restoration. So the 1968 Transport Act classified it as a 'remainder' waterway, whose future would be considered in a few years time.

Very recently the prospect has brightened. Many canals have their local preservation or amenity societies, which raise money and organise working parties to improve or restore their waterway. Not all of them, however, may be as thorough or hardworking as the Amenity Society of the Pocklington Canal. Formed in 1969, this group obtained a costed report on restoring the navigation from an eminent civil engineer, Dr Cyril Boucher, drew up a detailed plan, obtained the co-operation of BWB and began their own voluntary clearing and repair work. Signs of this are evident to anybody who walks the towpath. Financial help from local and regional authorities, together with the likely improvement of the Derwent, could make the Pocklington Canal a centre of inland waterway activity by the end of the 1970s.

The canal begins at Canal Head, on A1079 a mile south of Pocklington, opposite the 'Wellington Oak'. The basin itself is small, and there are no terminal buildings except for a warehouse, now a barn, on the southern side. A good wide towpath accompanies the canal throughout. There are five locks before the first road bridge; this is scenically the most beautiful part of the canal and can stand comparison with far better known stretches elsewhere in the country. The larks sing most clearly under these wide skies. Some of the channel has been cleared and the lock chambers are in reasonably good condition, although all need new gates. The fifth, sixth and seventh locks down, Coats, Walbut and Thornton, are by three of the canal's four remarkable bridges. These, of brick, combine strength and utility with elegance; the parapets seem to flow, rather than curve, to widen the road approaches. The sharply humped Church Bridge at Thornton has especially accentuated lines. Each bridge has four semicircular buttresses, about 8ft high, one on each outer facing of the arch.

At Bielby, halfway between Coats and Walbut bridges, the canal makes a right-angled turn; here there is a short arm towards the village. There is a similar arm at Melbourne, with the remains of a wharf. West of Melbourne, several fixed accommodation bridges have replaced the original swing bridges. Two miles west of Melbourne, Hagg Bridge takes the York road, B1228, over the canal; the parapet has been replaced by fencing, presumably to widen the road. The canal turns southwards to join the Derwent at Cottingwith lock, near the village of East Cottingwith. A track past the village's small cemetery leads to the towpath, within sight of the lock. Cottingwith lock has all its gates and paddle gear. On this lock, as at several of the others, the beams at some time were replaced by lengths of railway line, bolted together. The gear on the bottom gates is worth examining. The sluices were operated by turning a large wheel, of dimensions appropriate to an elderly motor-car. Similar machinery was used on the Stroudwater Navigation in Gloucestershire.

The canal properly ends at the main channel of the Derwent, another 400yd along, with an inn on the far side of the river. The Derwent is tidal, but a barrage may be built at the river mouth. Should this happen, the river navigation may be restored as far as Malton, making about 47 miles of cruising water available from Pocklington.

Another, much longer, canal through beautiful countryside, the Brecon & Abergavenny, has recently been restored to navigation by the combined efforts of the two County Councils concerned and BWB. This benefits not only boat-owners and hirers but also walkers, anglers and naturalists. If a canal is left to rot, eventually it becomes of value to no one. The Pocklington, drawing its water from the adjacent beck, has no problem of water supply, nor is it customarily used as a rubbish dump; so two of the difficulties which sometimes face the restorers are not present. All that seems to be needed is the money.

OS sheet 98
The Pocklington Canal (Pocklington Canal Amenity Society)

THE MARKET WEIGHTON CANAL

At the foot of the Yorkshire Wolds is Market Weighton, with a large expanse of flat farming land stretching away to the Humber, 9 miles south. Drainage of these lands was always a problem; and drainage was the first consideration of the promoters of the Market Weighton Canal. The Act of 1772 authorising its construction said as much in its preamble, and now that the canal is closed to boats drainage remains its sole purpose. Initially John Smith was appointed consulting engineer, being replaced by Grundy in 1773; the Pinkertons, who worked on the Driffield and Barnsley canals, were the contractors and part of the canal was opened by 1776, though more money had to be raised to bring it to completion. Market Weighton itself was never reached; instead the canal terminated at a small basin some 2 miles from the town, at River Head. About 1834 a short private canal was built by Sir Edward Vavasour from Canal Head on the Market Weighton–Holme road, connecting with the main line by Lock Farm, ¾ mile away.

The history of the Market Weighton was relatively uneventful. Modest dividends, rising to 7 per cent in the late 1840s, were paid, and for several decades the trustees had little to concern them save trivia about footloose cows and aberrant behaviour at the locks.

Towards 1850 negotiations began with the York & North Midland Railway, which eventually bought the canal, including Vavasour's branch, for £14,405. Under the agreement the trustees continued to manage the waterway, which for a time thereafter benefited from the purchase as the railway's progress beyond Market Weighton was for several years delayed. Receipts were well maintained until the 1880s. The years 1881–4 were for some reason particularly good ones, but then a rapid decline began. The tolls on coal were reduced in the hope of increasing this small percentage of the traffic; however, the only result was a further reduction in takings. By 1888 the company had only £35 in hand. Moreover, the top 3¼ miles of the canal, above Sod House Lock, were becoming impassable, owing to silting up. This stretch was not essential for drainage and in little demand for navigation; it had caused difficulty since 1865 and by 1894 was unusable. In 1900 this part of the canal was abandoned.

Page 229 (above) *Rochdale Canal: March Barn bridge. Note the winding courses of what was probably the first true skew bridge over a canal;* (below) *Manchester, Bolton & Bury Canal: a coal boat and an ice-breaker near the Bury terminal*

Page 230 (above) *Lancaster Canal: one of the fine stone bridges south of Kendal;* (below) *Barnsley Canal: the electrically-powered lifting bridge at Royston, opened 1934*

(above) *Pocklington Canal: paddle gear at Cottingwith lock;* (below) *Pocklington Canal: Church Bridge, one of the four strong and elegant road bridges*

Page 232   (above) *Driffield Canal: the basin at Driffield;* (below) *Louth Canal: Alvingham lock, a four-bay brick lock chamber*

The trustees appealed to the North Eastern Railway, successors to the York & N Midland, for money for dredging and repairs, to no avail. When they received a bill for repairs to the sea-lock, the railway declined to pay and formally withdrew their support. A firm of local brickmakers, Williamson & Co, the main users of the canal, agreed to pay up to £175 pa for twenty years to keep the navigation in being. The Aire & Calder Company also agreed to contribute up to two-thirds of the Market Weighton's expenses, but trade continued to decline despite dredging operations. The canal at Newport was used for aquatic sports and some pleasure boating before World War I, though this brought little revenue. When Williamson's guarantee expired in 1917 the canal was closed to navigation. It reopened in 1920, after the Ministry of Agriculture made the company a grant for dredging. Tolls, however, now produced well under £100 pa; as the years passed, only the occasional boat used the canal, the last entering the sea-lock in 1958.

The two arms, to River Head and Canal Head, are now insignificant drainage channels; the terminal building at River Head, on a by-road across Weighton Common, is incorporated in a farm. The road to North Cliffe, leading off the south side of A163, passes Dick Nest and turns sharply east. In a few yards it crosses the canal. The bridge has been flattened, but a lock chamber survives some 250yd to the north, made of large stone blocks. It is full of rubbish and chopped down trees. The canal is filled in on the upper level; there is a little water below the lock, draining off the fields. The canal is generally dry from here down to Sod House lock, 2 miles south. This is on the east side of an airfield accessible from a track to Wholsea Grange, in an area of landing lights. Now converted to a weir, the lock marked the head of navigation in the canal's last sixty years. The canal takes up water from a drain and remains watered to the junction with the Humber. A mile south it takes up the water of the River Foulness. It passes Sandholme Landing, an old tileworks, the piers of the viaduct of the old Hull & Beverley Railway, which the trustees had agreed to making the canal crossing in 1850, the village of Newport on A63, and heads across Walling Fen for another 3¼ miles to Weighton lock on the Humber, nearly opposite the mouth of the Trent. This sea-lock has two pairs of sea-gates and two pairs of navigation gates, so that it could work either way depending on the state of the tide in the river. There is an interesting inscription on the outer face of the sluice wall beside the lock: 'Mr Grundy Engineer Mr Allen Surveyor Mr Smith Carpenter Mr Jefferson Mason Anno Domino 1773 Repaired 1826 By Joseph Whitehead.' Owing to Whitton Sand, entry to the lock from the west was impractical, and was usually only advisable from the east when the tide was high. The restoring of navigation on the Market Weighton Canal is not a serious consideration, despite the fact that both North America and the Land of Nod can be found on its banks.

OS sheet 98

THE DRIFFIELD CANAL

The top 5 miles of the Driffield Navigation is the Driffield Canal. The Navigation also includes part of the Frodingham Beck and of the River Hull to the mouth of the Aike Beck, ½ mile above the junction of the river with the Leven Canal. It was made following an Act of 1767; John Grundy, who worked on the Louth Canal, was the engineer. An enormous body of commissioners, totalling ninety-five, was appointed to administer the navigation, which took five years to complete, and cost something over £15,000. Like the other East Riding navigations, the Driffield took agricultural produce down to the industrial towns and brought back coal, building materials, fertilisers and groceries.

The river portion of the navigation gave trouble and caused expense; improvements to this and the necessity of rebuilding Hull Bridge caused the commissioners to run into debt. Additional tolls were levied, but an Act of 1817 stipulated that tolls were to be reduced when all debts were paid off and thenceforth the undertaking was to be financed only to cover expenses and not to make a profit. By 1906 all debts had been paid except for the last £200.

The concern seems to have traded quietly until the Hull & Bridlington Railway, whose line passed through Driffield, opened in 1847. Corn tolls were cut right down to compete, but two more railways entered the area in the following years, the Driffield & Malton and the line to Market Weighton. Despite improvements to the Hull, trade inexorably declined. Both powered and sailing keels navigated to Driffield until the beginning of World War II, but no trade took place after 1949. The locks became derelict and the fishermen took over. However, the actual channel is now well maintained as, since 1960, it has provided several million gallons of drinking water a day for Hull.

The canal basin and wharves at Driffield make up perhaps the most attractive feature of the small town. The group of buildings are south of the railway, at River Head. The stream that feeds the canal is culverted under the road; the basin is on the south side of the road with large grain warehouses beside it, that on the west side being 22 windows long. By the roadside at the head of the basin is a hand-operated crane, and a larger crane, made by Gray Waddington & Co of New Dock Works, Leeds, repainted and in fine condition, stands on a well-kept grassed area near the public wharf a short distance along. Driffield lock is some 600yd down the canal. The whole composes one of the pleasantest canal scenes in the country; a live scene, moreover, as the warehouses, belonging to E. B. Bradshaw & Sons, are still in use, though served by lorries instead of boats.

From Driffield lock the canal turns eastward to meet and accompany B1249 to Wansford. Whin Hill and Wansford locks are solidly built and the walls stand firm. Big trees line the canal as it passes through the village. The top gates of the lock survive; below the lock a sunken boat recalls that the canal once had other uses than supplying drinking water. South of Wansford the road swings away from the canal, but the towpath can be followed past Snakeholme lock to Brigham, a small village at the end of a No Through road. At Brigham the canal is crossed by a swing bridge bearing Driffield Navigation notices warning traction engine drivers to keep off. From here southwards the waterway is navigable and is used by sailing clubs and an occasional motor-cruiser.

Under a mile from Brigham is the junction with the Frodingham Beck. The beck is navigable for about a mile north-eastwards from the junction, to the swing bridge by Frodingham Wharf. A short branch to Foston Mill left the beck near the wharf. A stone set in the tower of Frodingham Church records the height at which the water was to be kept at the bridge. Another branch, to Corps Landing, left the beck about a mile below the junction with the canal, but this has been derelict for many years.

The Driffield is a healthy-looking canal. It has not been abandoned, and there seems no reason why it ever should be. As it is used for land drainage, the River Authority keep it clear and maintain the banks. The works, however—the locks and bridges —are a different matter. For the commissioners are still the legal authority for the canal itself—if there are any commissioners left. So for bridges to be repaired and—who knows?—the navigation perhaps one day reopened to Driffield, new commissioners will need to be appointed or a new authority constituted. Until the lawyers can solve the puzzles set by the Parliamentary Acts, it seems that nothing can be done.

OS sheet 99
Railway & Canal Historical Society, 'Tour Notes', Sept 1969, by J. Hogwood
'The Driffield Navigation', by A. D. Biggin; IWA *Bulletin*, May 1970

THE LEVEN CANAL

Mrs Charlotta Bethell, a widow, was the begetter of the Leven Canal. Owning much land in the East Riding around Leven, she wanted a direct link with the River Hull, and so with the Humber estuary, for the export of agricultural produce and the import of coal, lime and building materials. Her canal, 3¼ miles long, was, except for the first few hundred yards, cut in a straight line due west to the river, where there was a lock big enough to take the Yorkshire keels and with doubled pairs of gates as the tidal river was sometimes higher, sometimes lower, than the canal. Jessop made the estimate; his figure of £4,041, however, proved too low and tolls soon had to be increased. The canal was open before 1805 and lasted as a navigation until 1936, remaining in the ownership of the family throughout. It seems to have served its purpose well enough and was returning moderate profits into the early years of this century.

Apart from the deterioration of the buildings at Leven Wharf, and the replacement of the lock by a sluice, the Leven Canal probably looks much as it ever did. Access to the wharf, the only one on the canal, is by a footpath on the south side of the substantial New Inn, on A165 south of the crossroads in the centre of the village. The basin is small and damply muddy; it is cut off from the canal by a bank of turf. There is a warehouse on each side; the southern one at some time was lowered by one storey and re-roofed; the other, built according to the wall ties in 1825, is now being treated in the same way. Between the basin and the road is an elegant house in Regency style, with a good pillared portico. The rear windows overlook the basin. It is possible that the house, now occupied by a firm of solicitors, was built for the canal manager. The towpath can be followed as far as Leven lock. The bridge near Little Leven now permits the passage of nothing larger than a rowing-boat, but the canal is well watered and is used for fishing.

OS sheet 99

THE RIPON CANAL

The Ripon Canal makes up the northern length of the Ure Navigation. The Ure joins the Swale to form the Yorkshire Ouse, and the navigation was 10¾ miles long, of which the canal comprised 2¾ miles. Following an Act of 1767, the line was opened in 1772. The man in charge was William Jessop, then at the start of his career and a pupil of John Smeaton; the resident engineer was John Smith.

Coal was the main cargo to Ripon, being distributed thence to towns in the North Riding; agricultural produce and lead were carried southwards. After a good start conditions deteriorated; the commissioners appointed under the Act to manage the navigation had done their job well but had also run into debt. The time came when there were no commissioners left who were qualified to act as such, for by some legal quirk no provision was made for appointing new ones. In 1820 a new Act enabled some of the creditors to take over and to raise money for putting the navigation back into good order. Competition from the Great North of England Railway, which opened a line from Darlington to York in 1841, affected the waterborne trade. Six years later the Leeds & Thirsk Railway bought the navigation for just over £35,000. In 1854 it passed to the North Eastern Railway; tonnage carried fell to generally less than 10,000 tons a year, little of that entering the canal section to Ripon. By 1904 practically nothing was being carried higher than Boroughbridge and the canal became derelict, though it was not abandoned until 1935.

The Ripon Canal is now the home water of the active Ripon Motor Boat Club, whose formidable headquarters float by the bridge at Littlethorpe. Ripon Basin is, not surprisingly, by Canal Road, near the Navigation Inn. Along one side of the basin there were several coal wharves, each walled off from its neighbours, and with its own gates to the street and little office alongside. This particular arrangement seems to be unique. Canal Sawmills now occupy the site; there is a number of buildings, but the basin itself is only a muddy patch. Above looms the cathedral, which contains the crypt of a monastery founded in 669, one of England's oldest Christian buildings. The canal itself is watered and runs out of Ripon alongside the Boroughbridge road, B6265. There is no navigation here; the canal is culverted under a road bridge and the two top locks are derelict. Shortly after this bridge, on the road to Littlethorpe, the canal turns southwards, leaving the road. It lies on the east side of Littlethorpe, a track and a narrow road leading to two well-proportioned red-brick bridges. South of the second bridge, where the canal looks now in particularly good condition, a few hundred yards along is Ox Close lock, where the canal joins the Ure. The lock has been smartly renovated and the modern paddle gear is enclosed. Now that Linton lock on the Ouse has been repaired (by no means for the first time) the prospects for cruising to within a mile of Ripon seem set fair.

OS sheet 91

THE YORKSHIRE FOSS NAVIGATION

Although the Foss Navigation was a river improvement scheme rather than a canal, it is of interest because the scheme developed at the time of the canal mania of the early 1790s, and because two of the greatest of canal engineers, Jessop and Rennie, were to some degree concerned with it.

The intention of the promoters was to make the Foss, a small river which joins the Ouse in York, properly navigable, at the same time solving the problems of flooding to the north of the city. Jessop made a survey of the river from York to Sheriff Hutton bridge, which involved eight locks. He later surveyed farther north west to Stillington, recommending a canal to by-pass a bend in the river. An Act was obtained in 1793, and the work entrusted to John Moon, as superintendent. When, two years later, Rennie was called in to inspect the works he discovered that Jessop's survey had been disregarded and none of the locks built in the places recommended for them. Moreover, the construction had been badly done. Moon was sacked, William Scruton finished the line to Strensall, and soon afterwards the committee abandoned the idea of extending the navigation to Stillington. Later, a new engineer, William Pontey, was appointed, and in 1804 the navigation was completed as far as a basin on the south side of Sheriff Hutton bridge. The two top miles were in fact a canal, leaving the river by a staircase pair a mile north-east of Strensall but not quite rejoining it at the bridge.

The Foss was moderately used until the opening of the York to Scarborough railway in 1845. In 1851 York Corporation bought the navigation for £4,000, abandoning it above Yearsley Bridge eight years later. Towards the end of the century some improvements were made at the southern end and a little trade revived for a few years, only to die away for good.

The Foss joins the Ouse south of the centre of York near Skeldergate Bridge; Blue Bridge Lane, off Fisher Gate, leads to the junction. Castle Mills lock and lockhouse are about 400 yards up river. It winds northwards through the city; Foss bridge, Foss Islands Road and Foss Bank indicate its course. The road north through New Earswick, Huntington, Towthorpe and Strensall, runs parallel to the river, keeping on its east side. There is a lockhouse between New Earswick and Huntington, and another at Haxby Landing (SE 616579). About a mile north east of Strensall the cut leaves the river, with a lockhouse and the remains of the locks (SE 644618). The site of the terminal basin is on the south side of the bridge over the river half way between Strensall and Sheriff Hutton, near the junction with the road to Stillington.

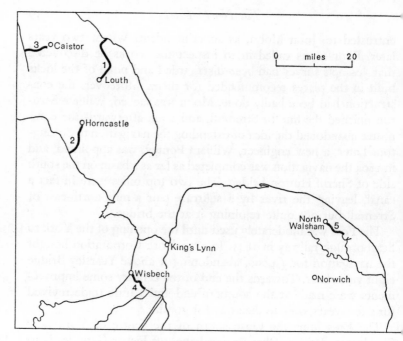

Outline Map 8   The East

Chapter 8: *The East*

THE LOUTH CANAL

Had the gentlemen of Louth been quicker off the mark, the honour of opening the age of canals might have been theirs; or at least they could have disputed it with the proprietors of the Sankey Brook and the Bridgewater. For John Grundy surveyed a line for a navigation from Louth to the Humber in 1756. The Act, however, was not obtained until 1763, and the line was opened throughout within the next four years. Some of the delay was due to the elusiveness of John Smeaton, called in as consultant, whose business left him little time for expeditions into the north-east corner of remote Lincolnshire. Eventually Smeaton suggested some revisions and the canal was constructed, nearly 12 miles in length with eight locks, the last a sea-lock at Tetney, falling over 5oft to the Humber. Some use was made of the River Lud, but most of the Louth is orthodox canal.

The canal was not particularly well made, and more than the £28,000 originally raised was needed to improve the works. One of the Commissioners, as the controlling committee was called, a Mr Charles Chaplin, lent the necessary money in return for a ninety-year lease on the tolls. Between 1777 and 1828 Mr Chaplin virtually ran the concern, but there were doubts as to the legality of the agreement. The terms were altered, and the tolls reduced, by a second Act in 1828, although the Chaplin family retained the lease for some years. Possibly as a result of this arrangement the Commissioners were not very busy. In 1789 complaints began about the poor condition of the canal, said to be far too shallow; two horses were needed to pull a boat through the mud, and the price of coal rose because of delays and the impossibility of fully loading the boats. Moreover, salt water was getting into the canal. Whereas boatmen complained that the canal was too shallow, landowners protested that the water level was too high. The Commissioners blamed the lock-keeper at Tetney for negligence, but it was not until 1811 that the canal was cleaned and improved. A report was made on the canal in 1828, in which it was stated that several of the locks were in poor repair, and some further improvements were made.

Although the canal was not very busy, Louth became a small port, exporting mainly corn and wool and importing coal. There was a battle with the Customs, who sought to impose duty on the coal as being brought in by sea. But it proved to be one of the few battles the Customs lost, as Tetney was adjudged to be within the Humber estuary. Disagreements over the weight of coal being shipped led to the institution of 'Coal Meters'—men appointed 'for the true and faithful admeasurement of coals navigated on the Canal'.

The canal's life in the Victorian age was relatively untroubled, although trade was affected by the building of the railway between Grimsby and Louth. Towards the end of the century angling became an important activity; the canal was stocked with fish and some revenue accrued. By 1915 the navigation was no longer used, and five years later the company applied to the Ministry of Transport for leave to close the waterway, which was granted in 1924. The canal is still watered and used for drainage of the surrounding lands, which had been a subsidiary purpose since its inception.

Louth is a pleasant town, much of it eighteenth century, with a fine church, and boasts Tennyson as an old boy of its Grammar School. The basin is on the north-east side, at River Head by the Woolpack Inn. There are large warehouses and an air of spaciousness and some dignity. Top, or Louth, lock has been converted into a weir. The canal heads north east past Keddington and Alvingham and is accessible from minor roads on both sides. There were five locks on this stretch, all of the same construction which appears to be unique to this canal. One was called Ticklepenny's; this family had long connection with the canal. A good example is Alvingham lock, where the road running south east from the village crosses the canal (TF 365909). The chamber is of brick, but instead of being straight each side consists of four elliptical bays, with wooden posts inserted where the bays meet. Presumably the object of this type of construction was to provide additional strength. Grundy, who was appointed engineer in 1765, probably designed them; they were certainly all so constructed when the 1828 report was made. The locks were of slightly different dimensions but all could take vessels 72ft long and 15ft wide. The canal has a towpath, but in its later years it was used mainly by Yorkshire keels and billy-boys.

Out Fen lock, 1½ miles on from Alvingham and the last before
Tetney, was conventionally built with straight sides. The canal
now heads north west across flat land. There is a derelict warehouse by the bridge at Austen Fen; at Fire Beacon, 2 miles farther,
there used to be two wharves. Tetney lock is 2 miles east of Tetney
by the minor road to North Coates. It is now a sluice, but was
originally built with two pairs of sea doors and two pairs of
navigation doors, and a sea sluice beside it. The lock-keeper was
instructed to regulate the level of water in the canal according to
the degree of immersion of a beam in the lock chamber. From the
lock there is another mile to the end of the canal at Tetney Haven,
on the mouth of the Humber opposite Spurn Head. Despite the
proximity of Grimsby this is empty countryside; the villages are
small, the skies are wide, and the wind is keen by the Louth Canal.

OS sheet 105
(historical information from the Canal Minute Books in Lincolnshire
  Archives)

THE HORNCASTLE CANAL

The Horncastle Canal was very much a local undertaking. In
part a canalisation of the River Bain, it linked Horncastle with the
Witham and hence with Lincoln and the Sleaford Navigation. It
incorporated part of the line of the older Tattershall Canal, bought
by the proprietors. Jessop was consulted on the survey, and an
Act was obtained in 1792.

The committee had its troubles. The first engineer lasted only a
year; he was succeeded by two engineers, John Dyson and Thomas
Hudson. There were difficulties with incompetent brickmakers,
and with a miller who ran floodwater into the uncompleted works.
Cash ran out and a second Act to raise more funds was necessary;
the committee accused Jessop of recommending an unskilful surveyor who was responsible for their losses. Lawsuits were threatened over damage to adjacent lands, and floods delayed the completion of the canal to Horncastle. The committee was diligent and
inspected the line frequently, both by water (as far as possible) and
on horseback, but it was 1798 before the line was opened as far as
Dalderby, still over 2 miles from Horncastle. There it rested while
Rennie's advice was taken; he recommended continuing, so work
restarted.

Then began the canal committee's battle with the Champion. The then holder of this hereditary office, the purpose of which is to provide a challenger for the King's enemies at his coronation, was the Hon Lewis Dymoke, a member of the canal committee. In 1801 the canal started to make its way across his estate between Dalderby and Horncastle. The Champion's loyalties were not divided. He demanded £600 for his rights in a stream; the committee offered £200. He asked the penurious company for payment in advance before the canal encroached on his land, and maintained that the company were deviating from the original line. The company said that there was no original line other than the one they were following. In 1802, unsurprisingly, the Champion's name disappeared from the list of committee-members. The following year there was a further barrage of claims and complaints, and in 1804 a demand for £403 12s 9½d for lands cut and covered, a new bridge, and £240 for damage to a mill. Conciliation having failed them, the company 'prepared themselves to meet the attack'. It does not seem to have been pressed home, however; nevertheless, in 1806 the Champion is requiring culverts to be made immediately, and in 1807 he complains about the dykes and drains which the company cut to relieve his land from flooding. Then he writes to the company claiming expenses for all his actions, including those he withdrew. The company thank him for his 'gentlemanly language', but cannot see their way to complying. In 1810 there are disagreements over compensation for a haling-path, and in 1813 the largest claim of all—over £1,000 for damage alleged to be caused by leakage from the canal. One quarrel at least was settled the next year, when the Champion accepted £4 compensation for the haling-path but, lest the company think the war was over, he attacked again with a demand for the repair of an unsafe bridge. It seems to have been the last shot, however; in 1820 a new Champion, the Hon and Rev Champion Dymoke, is appointed chairman of the canal committee. Amity now abounds; two years later we find the chairman getting a load of old sandstone from the company for nothing!

Other things had happened in the meantime. The canal had been opened to Horncastle, although the superintendent, William Walker, had been asked to resign on grounds of ill-health. His successor, George Douthwaite, was not an unqualified success; 'the superintendent', say the minutes for January 1809, 'has for some time past spent a great deal of his time in public houses in the town instead of attending to the Interests of the Company'. Douthwaite died in 1810, and the company gave his widow five guineas to enable her to get back to her friends.

There was some financial progress. A first dividend was paid in 1813, and dividends averaging 5 per cent were paid in succeeding years, reaching a peak of 8 per cent in 1841. Coal, lime, timber and agricultural produce were the chief cargoes; the canal was kept in good repair and the shareholders seemed satisfied. In 1846 the Great Northern Railway proposed a line from Tattershall to Horncastle; the company began negotiating with a view to selling out to the railway, but the line was altered, and the canal was bridged at right angles near Tattershall instead. Carriage of material for the railway helped to maintain the dividends, which did not drop below 5 per cent until after 1855. In the previous year the connection with the Dymokes ended, when Sir Henry Dymoke resigned after twenty-five years as president of the company. Even in this there was a reminder of the love-hate relationship of the Champions and the canal, as the reason for Sir Henry's resignation was his support for a railway between Horncastle and Kirkstead, on the Witham, which the company was opposing. The construction of this railway caused a drop in receipts, despite a raising of tolls by agreement with the railway company. Trouble occurred with the commissioners of the Witham, who stopped navigation on the river for several months in 1866 and 1869 for repairs. An expensive lawsuit over a wharf did not help, although the company won the case; dividends fell to between 1 and 2 per cent, then to nothing in 1875. Essential repairs were expensive, and more were needed; in 1877 the committee felt that it was 'hopeless to continue the undertaking without further capital'. Nevertheless, a proposal for abandonment did not secure a seconder, and the committee sought an estimate for putting the canal in good order. This quoted a figure of £3,562; the company thought it could be done for less and borrowed £400 from a bank. Repairs were started, but were inefficiently carried out; then a new threat arose from the proposed Witham Drainage Bill, which provided for lowering the level of the river and hence would render the canal useless. The committee struggled on for a few more years but, owing money and with no hope of recovering trade, gave up and closed the navigation in 1885.

Horncastle is an attractive market town, which used to be the site of one of the largest annual horse-fairs in the world. There are monuments to the Dymoke family in the church, and the house of the naturalist Sir Joseph Banks, first chairman of the company, is in West Street. There were two canal basins, at present divided by a swimming pool. The south basin has been reconstructed as a river channel, but the north basin survives, lined by warehouses with mooring rings in their walls. The canal lies on the west side of A153 between Horncastle and Coningsby; it is healthy-looking and used for fishing. The locks have been converted to weirs, but the original brickwork can be seen in places. At Tattershall, a village dominated by the massive brick-built keep of its medieval castle, the water is led off along the course of the Bain. The straight cut to the Witham is mostly dry, and the entrance lock has been replaced by a turf bank. The Witham is busy with fishermen and boats, while the Horncastle Canal, all battles done, sleeps in peace.

OS sheets 114 and 113 (junction with Witham only)
Historical information from the Canal Company's Minute Books in the Lincolnshire Archives

THE CAISTOR CANAL

Information on the Caistor Canal is lacking. It was made as the result of an Act of 1793, with the purpose of exporting agricultural produce of North Lincolnshire through the River Ancholme and of bringing to the Caistor area coal, lime and general merchandise. However, it got no nearer to Caistor than $3\frac{1}{2}$ miles, terminating by the crossroads at Moortown, a small village on B1434. From Moortown it ran almost due west to the Ancholme, descending by six locks, according to Priestley, although I can only find reference to five: Moor, Hill, Willow, Ings and Beck End on the river. It seems to have been abandoned in 1855 but, so far as is known, the records of the company have not yet come to light.

Caistor is a small town of Roman origin set on a hill, some 11 miles from Grimsby on A46. It has a good church, a flamboyant memorial to Queen Victoria's Diamond Jubilee in the shape of a black and gold lion which serves as a pump, and some pleasant, if shabby, buildings. It also has a Navigation Lane heading in the direction of Moortown. Although the 50ft contour curves round the east of Moortown, there seems no reason on the ground why the canal could not have locked up and approached nearer to the town it was intended to serve. Had it done so it would have terminated in the vicinity of the present sewage works, but neither maps nor investigations on the ground suggest that this happened.

Signs of the canal can be found behind the telephone box at Moortown crossroads; there is no trace of it on the east side of B1434. For a short distance it has been obliterated by cottage gardens; then it can be seen again on the north side of B1205. When the road swings south, the canal keeps straight on, now taking up some water from a stream. It is crossed by the road on the north side of South Kelsey and thence heads due west for the Ancholme as a deep, and sometimes damp, ditch. The entrance lock to the Ancholme, lacking its gates, is close to a point where the old river loops across the new.

OS sheet 104

THE WISBECH CANAL

A 500 page *History of Wisbech and Neighbourhood* was published in 1898. Of this considerable work, fewer than 200 words are devoted to the Wisbech Canal. And of those words the most significant are: 'the undertaking has not proved a remunerative one, and the shares have been recently sold at a low price'.

The canal was constructed under an Act of 1794. It was cut from the Nene at Wisbech to a junction with the Old River Nene and Well Creek at Outwell, a distance of 5¼ miles utilising part of an old river course. Well Creek connected with the Ouse, and hence it was thought that the trade of Wisbech would be widely extended. So possibly it might have been, had the canal been differently constructed. But it depended upon the Nene at Wisbech for its water supply, and as it was built above the level of the river it could only be filled up at spring tides. 'Putting the tide in', as it was called, could take place only for a few days every fortnight, and in the days before the operation was due the water level in the canal often ran very low.

The Wisbech Canal traded throughout the nineteenth century, but it does not seem to have been much of a success. In 1882 tolls of £157 were taken at Wisbech, and £175 at Outwell. A passenger service was in operation; known as Whybrow's Packet, it charged 2d for a single journey. In 1884 a light railway, the Wisbech & Upwell Steam Tramway, was constructed alongside the canal, charging the same fare for passenger journeys. Tolls received at the Wisbech end of the canal fell immediately, but there was an increase at Outwell where goods were shipped through from the river for transfer to the railway. The canal, with its irregular service, soon proved the weaker of the two rivals; the improved figures at Outwell did not last long. The canal company sought to obtain Parliamentary powers to abandon the canal about the turn of the century, but failed. Tolls fell to £35 at Wisbech and £21 at Outwell in 1914. Soon after, trade stopped altogether. The canal was eventually abandoned in 1926. The little railway, however, managed to chug along until 1966.

In recent years most of the course of the Wisbech Canal has been filled in. The entrance lock from the Nene was just below the new bridge over the river by the town's police station. A roundabout has been constructed over the bed of the canal, which left the town centre along the direction of the new Downham Market road, A1101. The cut keeps on the east side of the road, being crossed shortly by the derelict track of the railway branch line to March. The road passes over the canal by the 'Royal Standard'; parts of the next length have been used for rubbish tipping. Farther south, beneath a bridge opposite the 'Prince of Wales' there is a section of damp canal bed not (so far) filled up.

Accompanied by the line of the steam railway, the canal keeps on the west side or A1101 into the village of Outwell. The scene here in the last century must have been attractive; the canal entered the village with a road on either side of it lined with well-built houses facing each other across the waterway. On a smaller scale it resembles the splendid eighteenth-century architectural triumph of the Brinks at Wisbech, where two rows of especially fine houses face each other across the Nene. Behind a bus stop just to the north of Outwell Church was the canal's junction with Well Creek and the old course of the Nene. Here again the canal is filled in, and gardens of houses planted on top of it. The Outwell lock was 97ft long, but vessels approaching that length could only enter the canal at Wisbech when the river and canal made a level, as the Wisbech lock was only 50ft.

OS sheet 124
A Roadside Steam Tramway, by E. J. S. Gadsden & others, 1966

THE NORTH WALSHAM & DILHAM CANAL

North Walsham, 7 miles south east of Cromer, was originally a wool town, but much of it was destroyed by fire in 1600. Its present prosperous appearance is in part the result of the canal, which linked it via the River Ant to Yarmouth and so to London. For two years Nelson was at school in North Walsham, until at the end of 1770 he left to become a midshipman on the *Raisonnable*. The canal came later, the Act for its construction being granted in 1812. Because of the opposition of certain local interests construction was delayed for some years; it was not until 1825 that work began, with J. Millington as engineer. The canal was completed in a year; it left the Ant upstream of Wayford Bridge, 2 miles west of Stalham on A149, and curled its way roughly north-westward to Antingham Ponds, about 8½ miles distant. There were six locks, rising from the junction, 50ft long and 12ft 4in wide to take the Norfolk wherries, which had to be bowhauled by the wherrymen when the wind was unsuitable for sailing. The surplus water from the four lower locks provided power for mills built beside them. Grain and flour were carried to Yarmouth and coal and building materials brought back; the tonnage rates also allowed for passengers at a 1d a mile, and Wines and Spiritous Liquors at 5d a mile per ton, among a comprehensive list of less glamorous and far cheaper items of merchandise.

The canal traded with modest prosperity until the mid-1840s, when rail competition and the improvement in local roads made the cost of canal carriage appear expensive. By 1886 there was little trade, and the canal company sold the waterway for £600 to a miller from North Walsham, Edward Press. He believed that the future of the canal lay in pleasure boating, and he and others began to build pleasure craft for hire. However, there was little money to spare for maintenance, and the top portion of the canal from Antingham Ponds to Swafield Bridge, including two locks, became disused by 1893.

In 1907 the canal was put up for auction, its income being estimated at £400 pa. It fetched £2,550; but the new owners, the General Estates Co Ltd, of London, did little to keep it in good condition. Its banks, 10ft high in places, needed careful attention, as was seen when a breach occurred following floods in 1912. The North Walsham & Dilham changed hands again in 1921 and an attempt was made to improve conditions by dredging. But trade was now virtually over, and with little revenue from other sources navigation through the canal ended in 1935. Since then the local river and drainage boards have shown little enthusiasm for maintaining the canal, although the bottom 2 miles to Honing lock and part of the cut to Dilham are still usable by light craft. The canal still holds water up to Swafield Bridge, near North Walsham; its restoration would not be an impossibility and would add a beautiful 7½ miles to the cruising waters of Broadland. The Ant junction is accessible only by water or along the towpath, but the canal can be picked up by road on the south side of Honing, on the road to Dilham. Dilham itself is connected to the Ant, and hence to the canal, by a navigable cut. There is a brick bridge over the canal south of Honing; but of more interest is the lock at Briggate, about a mile west of Honing, by a mill and warehouse. The lock has a brick chamber; there are iron balance beams on the decaying gates, with small platforms by the lower gates. Most of the paddle gear survives; 200yd to the north are the piers of the viaduct which used to carry the railway from Stalham to North Walsham.

The canal heads northward, skirting Meeting House Hill and White Horse Common. South east of North Walsham it is crossed by a minor road at a point only 4 miles from the coast. Here is another mill and warehouse, but the bridge has been recently rebuilt and lowered. The lower gates of the lock have gone, but the upper pair still remain in decay. All roads heading west from North Walsham cross the canal, which becomes progressively narrower. At Spa Common there is a small old warehouse on one side of the canal and a pretty flint cottage on the other; on B1150 the bridge has been turned into a culvert, but the warehouse has again survived the years, as has the one by Swafield Bridge on B1145. From here on, what was the canal is now a stream or water channel, leading off from Antingham Ponds, a tree-fringed stretch of water 2 miles north west of North Walsham.

More than 2,500 hired craft use the Broads and rivers of East Anglia each week during the summer, as well as several hundred privately owned boats. Boats are even being hired at Christmas-time for a Yuletide afloat. Every mile that could be added to the system would help to relieve the pressure and bring benefit to all concerned. Seven and a half of these miles could be contributed by the North Walsham & Dilham Canal.

OS sheet 126
'The Ancient Navigations of Broadland', by James Forsythe; IWA *Bulletin* No 86, Jan 1969
'The North Walsham and Dilham Canal', by Geoffrey Goreham; *East Anglian* magazine, March 1964

OTHER ABANDONED AND DERELICT CANALS

Ashby-de-la-Zouch Canal. Top 6 miles, Measham to Moira, abandoned 1944. (*The Canals of the East Midlands*, by Charles Hadfield)

The Arbury Canals. A group of short private canals off the Coventry Canal. (Articles by Philip Weaver, *Journal* of the Railway & Canal Historical Society, Jan & April 1970)

Basingstoke Canal. Odiham to Basingstoke, including Greywell tunnel. (*London's Lost Route to Basingstoke*, by P. A. L. Vine; *The Canals of South & South East England*, by Charles Hadfield)

Calder & Hebble Navigation: Halifax Branch Canal. 1¼ miles long, abandoned 1942. (*The Canals of Yorkshire and the North East*, by Charles Hadfield) (in preparation)

Cann Quarry Canal. A converted mill leat, near Plymouth. Became disused during 1830s. (*Cann Quarry Canal & Railway*, by Edwin Welch; reprinted from the Transactions of the Devonshire Association for the Advancement of Science, Literature & Art)

Doctor's Canal. Joined Glamorganshire Canal near Treforest. 1 mile long. Closed 1914. (*The Canals of South Wales & the Border*, by Charles Hadfield)

Isle of Dogs Canal. Became part of West India Dock, 1829. (*The Canals of the East Midlands*, by Charles Hadfield)

Par Canal. From Par Harbour, 1¼ miles long. Disused about 1855. (*The Canals of South West England*, by Charles Hadfield)

London. The Grosvenor, Kensington and the Cumberland Branch of the Regent's Canal have been abandoned and mostly have now disappeared. (*The Canals of the East Midlands*, by Charles Hadfield)

South Wales. There are several short abandoned canals between Neath and Tenby. These include: the Earl of Ashburnham's, General Warde's canals, Glan-y-wern, Hopkin's, Lansamlet, Mackworth's, Morris's, Pembrey, Pen-clawdd, Penrhiwtyn, Red Jacket, Trewyddfa, Wern, and the uncompleted Kilgetty Canal. See *The Canals of South Wales & the Border*, by Charles Hadfield.

Elsewhere in England there are several short branches, many of them originally privately owned, which are disused or officially abandoned.

GENERAL BIBLIOGRAPHY

(Excluding books referred to in the bibliographies at the end of each section)

W. T. Jackman: *The Development of Transportation in Modern England* (1916, reprinted Frank Cass & Co, 1966)

Joseph Priestley: *Historical Account of the Navigable Rivers, Canals and Railways throughout Great Britain* (1831, reprinted David & Charles, 1969)

H. R. de Salis: *Bradshaw's Canals & Navigable Rivers* (1904, reprinted David & Charles, 1969)

L. A. Edwards: *Inland Waterways of Gt Britain & Ireland* (1962)

Charles Hadfield: *British Canals* (1950; 4th ed 1969. This contains a very useful bibliography)
    The Canal Age (1969)

L. T. C. Rolt: *The Inland Waterways of England* (1950)
    Navigable Waterways (1969)

Journal of the Railway & Canal Historical Society

Transport History (3 issues a year)

D. Gladwin & J. M. White: *English Canals* (1967)

ACKNOWLEDGEMENTS

There are many people whom I must thank for their assistance.

The Section on the BCN owes much to the notes of Mr Philip Weaver, whose book on the engineering history of the system is greatly looked forward to. Also to the help of Mr Harkness of the Birmingham City Architect's Dept.

I am very grateful to Mr Frank Gregson (Grand Western), Mr W. Howard Williams (Shropshire inclines), Mr F. C. Dredge, clerk to the Bude–Stratton UDC (Bude), and Mr Clive Thomas (Glamorganshire and Cyfarthfa), all of whom devoted time and trouble to helping me. And to Mr Peter Stevenson, Librarian of the Railway & Canal Historical Society and the expert on the Nutbrook Canal, Mr P. G. Rattenbury, who made sense of the Kidwelly & Llanelly for me, and Mr B. A. A. Knight, who brought me up to date on the Chard Canal. Many thanks also to the following, who allowed me to make use of their own researches: Mr Robin Atthill, Mr G. Biddle, Mr J. H. Boyes, Dr A. M. Boyd, Mr J. R. Cooper, Mr & Mrs Dodd, Mr F. Hawtin, Mr J. Hogwood, Mr C. E. Lee, Mr Ian Morley, Mrs S. M. Nix and Mr C. J. Solomon, of the Pocklington Canal Amenity Society, Mr Frank Smith, Mr R. K. Stainton, Mr V. I. Tomlinson and Dr E. Welch. Mr G. L. Robinson, Borough Surveyor of Droitwich, gave me much useful material; Lord Clifford and the Estates Surveyor, BR Western Region, allowed me to tramp over the Hackney and Stover canals. Mr T. R. Whitney, of Merthyr Tydfil, was one of several very helpful librarians; I am also indebted to the staffs of various Record Offices and Archives Depts, especially those of Lincoln and Gloucester. Mr C. R. Hussey and Mr D. Young helped with some of the fieldwork in the West and Wales.

All the photographs are my own; Forest of Dean Studios, Coleford, were very co-operative with these. The maps of single canals are the work of Mr Graham Turner, and the area maps were drawn by Mr Michael Young. The line drawings are by Mr Peter Major.

The map on the Birmingham canals on p 171 is reproduced by courtesy of the Waterways Museum.

I have acknowledged my debt to Mr Charles Hadfield, but must here express further gratitude for the promptness with which he answered so many questions.

Finally, my thanks to my wife, for suffering so many abandoned canals about the house, and to my son Adrian, who accompanied me on most of my explorations with a keen eye for an embankment or a change in level and a remarkable flair for reading a map.

Index

(The principal entry for each canal is in **bold type***)*